MINA P. SHAUGHNESSY
HER ✦ LIFE ✦ AND ✦ WORK

MINA P. SHAUGHNESSY

HER ✦ LIFE ✦ AND ✦ WORK

JANE MAHER

Nassau Community College

National Council of Teachers of English
1111 W. Kenyon Road, Urbana, Illinois 61801-1096

Grateful acknowledgment is made to Paul Hosefros/NYT Pictures for permission to reprint the photo of Mina Shaughnessy on the cover.

MANUSCRIPT EDITOR: Sheila A. Ryan
PRODUCTION EDITOR: Peter Feely
INTERIOR AND COVER DESIGN: Jenny Jensen Greenleaf

NCTE Stock Number 50292-3050

It is the policy of NCTE in its journals and other publications to provide a forum for the open discussion of ideas concerning the content and the teaching of English and the language arts. Publicity accorded to any particular point of view does not imply endorsement by the Executive Committee, the Board of Directors, or the membership at large, except in announcements of policy, where such endorsement is clearly specified.

Library of Congress Cataloging-in-Publication Data

Maher, Jane, 1947–
    Mina P. Shaughnessy : her life and work / Jane Maher.
        p.   cm.
    Includes bibliographical references (p.   ) and index.
    ISBN 0-8141-5029-2
    1. Scholar, Mina Shaughnessy—Biography. 2. English teachers—
United States—Biography. 3. Women college teachers—United
States—Biography. 4. Universities and colleges—Open admission—
United States. I. Title.
PE64.S36M34 1997
820'.71'173—dc21
    [B]   96-37306
                                                                                      CIP

For my children
Laurie, Tricia, and Paul

Open Admissions is forcing the real question—not how many people society is willing to salvage, but how much society is willing to pay to salvage itself.

—Mina P. Shaughnessy
"Open Admissions and the Disadvantaged Teacher"

CONTENTS

ACKNOWLEDGMENTS ix

— ONE —
A Full and Good World 1

— TWO —
A Necessary Prelude 29

— THREE —
Experience and Dedication 70

— FOUR —
The House That Mina Built 91

— FIVE —
Toward a More Democratic Educational System 124

— SIX —
Errors and Expectations 147

— SEVEN —
A Grand Experiment 197

APPENDIX A *Open Admissions and the Disadvantaged Teacher* 249
APPENDIX B *Diving In: An Introduction to Basic Writing* 255
APPENDIX C *The Miserable Truth* 263
APPENDIX D *Speaking and Doublespeaking about Standards* 270
APPENDIX E *Statement on Criteria for Writing Proficiency* 279
APPENDIX F *Some Needed Research on Writing* 284
APPENDIX G *The English Professor's Malady* 291
APPENDIX H *Basic Writing* 299

WORKS CITED 311
INDEX 315
AUTHOR 331

ACKNOWLEDGMENTS

I first began teaching basic writing in Brooklyn, New York, in 1978, the same year that Mina Pendo Shaughnessy died. After less than a week in my classroom—a room very similar to "the worn urban classroom" that Mina described in the preface to *Errors and Expectations*—I went to the man who had hired me and begged for help. He, too, was struggling to find ways to help the underprepared students who were entering college in larger and larger numbers as a result of Open Admissions, and he suggested that I read *Errors and Expectations*. I have been reading it ever since—for information, for confirmation, for inspiration.

Mina Shaughnessy's dedication to and confidence in Open Admissions students was particularly gratifying to me for another reason as well: I attended the College of Staten Island, a division of the City University of New York, as an Open Admissions, part-time, evening student. It took me seven years to earn my undergraduate degree. During those same seven years, Mina was working tirelessly to improve the quality of college education available to students like me, students who, for any number of reasons, were not expected even to attend—much less succeed—in college.

Under the best of circumstances, teaching is a difficult profession, but Mina was often forced to teach, and later to direct and guide other teachers, under terrible conditions. As Adrienne Rich recalls, "We all worked hard in those days. It was a small embattled program and we felt, teachers and counselors alike, that we bore a peculiar burden of proof against those—academics, administrators, politicians—who had prejudged and precondemned Open Admissions students as unworthy of college education."

We can be inspired by Mina Shaughnessy, of course; that is one of the purposes of biography. But more than that, we can see our best selves in her: when we put our students' needs before all else; when we refuse to accept the opinion of others about our students' abilities and worth; when we help our students to recognize and employ the power of language; when we acknowledge, as Mina did, "that we cannot isolate the phenomenon of disadvantage from the society that caused it."

In writing this biography, I requested information from Mina Shaughnessy's family, friends, and colleagues, all of whom responded with great patience and with great enthusiasm for the project. My gratitude to the following people for communicating with me, either through interviews or correspondence, about the life and work of a most extraordinary woman: Leslie Berger, Alison Bernstein, Bob Boynton, Kenneth Bruffee, Jean Campbell, Edward P. J. Corbett, K. Patricia Cross, Benjamin DeMott, Richard Donovan, Janet Emig, Tom Farrell, Betty Fosdick, Marilyn French, Barbara Quint Gray, Theodore Gross, E. D. Hirsch, Georgia Jensen, Leonard Kriegel, Patricia Laurence, Robert Lyons, Dorethea McGill, Patricia Neal, Kathleen O'Hare, Ann Petrie, Edward Quinn, Ann Raimes, Donald Shaughnessy, Blanche Skurnick, Virginia Smith, Richard Sterling, Alice Trillin, Margo Viscusi, Edmond Volpe, Barry Wallenstein, Lottie Wilkins, Gerald Willin, and John Wright. I am also grateful to Barbara Dunlop, the City College archivist, and to the staff of Oxford University Press for granting me access to files and documents.

Mina's brother, George Pendo, of Spearfish, South Dakota, spent many hours with me describing their childhood, and he gave me complete access to the letters, photographs, and notebooks in his possession. In February 1996, I sent him a copy of the manuscript; less than a month later, he called to tell me how pleased he was—assuring me that I had "done justice" to Mina. George died in May 1996; I hope he knew how grateful and indebted I am to him. George's wife, Norma, has also provided much information and encouragement, answering my many questions with great thoughtfulness and insight.

Mina met Priscilla Weaver Brandt on the first day of classes as an undergraduate at Northwestern University; it was the beginning of a lifelong friendship that soon included Alan Brandt, Priscilla's husband.

Alan and Priscilla spent many hours helping me to locate letters and photographs, but more important, they spent many more hours talking with me and later reviewing the manuscript, helping me to understand the full, rich, complex life Mina led outside of academia.

In the preface to *Errors and Expectations,* Mina Shaughnessy thanked Marilyn Maiz, her assistant, first at City College and later at the Instructional Resource Center, for having been "her companion" from "start to finish," and for giving "honest and informed criticism of each chapter" (viii). I, too, must thank Marilyn for providing information and guidance throughout this project—for providing the same honest and informed criticism of this biography as she provided for *Errors and Expectations.* It is impossible to express adequately the debt I owe to her; this biography could not have been written without her help.

Bill Baskin read the chapters of the manuscript as I wrote them. His suggestions and comments—made with great tact and kindness—were invaluable to me. I am grateful to the trustees of Nassau Community College for a six-month sabbatical, during which I completed much of the research for this biography. Thank you to Stephen North, Marlo Welshons, Sheila Ryan, and Pete Feely for their sound advice and constant support.

I am most grateful to Adrienne Rich for the time she took from her extraordinarily busy schedule to answer scores of questions about Mina, her close friend and colleague. But I am even more grateful for the words of encouragement she provided on the day we met at City College, the place where Mina first began the research that would result in *Errors and Expectations.* I was concerned that I would not be able to present her life completely and accurately, that I would not get it right: she had accomplished so much, known so many people, had an impact on so many lives. "Don't let that stop you," Adrienne Rich advised. "Of course you can't get a life entirely right, but you can get it righter." I hope I have succeeded in doing so.

My husband, Pat Maher, my closest friend and ally, will not have to read this biography. He has been living with it for three years.

CHAPTER ONE

A Full and Good World

*M*ina Pendo Shaughnessy seemed to be the quintessential New Yorker: tall and beautiful, sophisticated, well spoken, well read, well dressed, interested in literature, art, music, and politics. One of Mina's colleagues at City College remembers thinking when he first met her in 1967 that she must have been teaching writing to disadvantaged students "out of a sense of *noblesse oblige*. She was a typical Upper East Sider, well dressed, stately, very well bred. One imagined that she left campus and went off to a dinner party with the most influential people, or to a theater opening. I was just flabbergasted when she told me she had been born and raised somewhere in the Midwest; I can't remember precisely where."

In fact, Mina Pendo Shaughnessy was born in Lead, South Dakota, to Ruby Alma Johnson Pendo and Albert Pendo on March 13, 1924. Her brother, George, her best friend throughout her childhood, had been born a year and five days earlier. Lead (rhymes with *deed*) was, at the time of Mina's birth (and still is), a gold mining town with a population of eight thousand, located about fifty miles west of Rapid City, less than three miles from its twin city, Deadwood, where Wild Bill Hickok was shot in a saloon in 1876, and less than ten miles from Spearfish, a town named by the Lakota Sioux Indians long before they were herded onto reservations. *Dances With Wolves* was filmed in the Black Hills that surround and rise majestically above these towns, and Native Americans live on the Pine Ridge Indian Reservation, the site of the Wounded Knee Massacre, located approximately sixty miles southeast of Lead. However, Mina's brother, George, recalls that while they were growing up, "we hadn't yet come to terms with the fact that we had taken away the Native Americans' lands, and we had little or no contact with them."

Lead is a classic mining town. The Homestake Mine, founded by William Randolph Hearst, employed more than one thousand miners at the time Mina was born, and it dominated every aspect of the townspeople's lives: they attended the Hearst Free Public School; borrowed books at the Hearst Free Library; shopped at the Hearst Mercantile Company, referred to by everyone as the company store. There were no labor unions in Lead; George Pendo recalls that the mere mention of the word could "cost a man his job." He recalls hearing, as a young child, of the time early in the century when the Homestake owners brought in strikebreakers from Missouri to quash an attempt to form a union—several men died, and there was a general animosity toward Missourians for many years after the incident.

Although one can see the magnificent Black Hills from anywhere in Lead, the town itself is an exquisite example of man-made ugliness. When the mine first began operation in 1876, it was not the practice to backfill mined out areas. As a result, large tracts of land began to cave in. By the late 1920s, the brick and stone buildings of Lead's commercial area, sitting on ground that was sinking as much as thirty-five feet, began to crack and heave. The situation became so serious that residences and commercial buildings had to be moved, leaving an enormous area that came to be known as the "subsidence zone." It was eventually converted into a public park that is known locally as the "Sinking Gardens." In addition, one of the mountains in the center of Lead proved to contain a particularly rich lode. In this case, surface-mining methods were used to extract more than forty million tons of gold from the mountain, leaving a deep oval-shaped open cut in the top of the mountain, as if a giant had taken a huge bite out of it. Brochures advertising tours of the mines try to make the best of this situation by noting that in 1916 a tightrope walker crossed the 4,500-foot wide, 960-foot deep gouge, but the fact remains that gold mining, at least as it has always been practiced in Lead, South Dakota, wreaks havoc with the environment. The citizens of Lead were not concerned with the appearance of their surroundings, however. Without the mines, there would be no work. In Lead, everyone either worked in the mines or provided services to those who did.

Albert Pendo, Mina's father, was a miner. He was born in Lead in 1900, the third of eight children, two of whom died shortly after birth.

His father, Rado Pendo, had emigrated to Lead from a town called Mocici in Croatia in 1887. Soon after he arrived, he established the Mule Deer Saloon, a particularly propitious choice of occupation, given the number of men who were "mucking" for gold in the mines more than a mile below ground all day. He met and fell in love with Elin Peyron, who had emigrated from Sweden with her family, but she refused to marry him unless he sold the saloon. He did as she wished but probably regretted it for the rest of his life as one job or enterprise after another failed: he worked in the mines, then in a mill, started a butcher shop, and later started a construction business building roads. (After his children were grown, he moved to Wyoming to raise his own cattle.) Rado Pendo was a devout Catholic, but his wife was an even more devout Lutheran, so the children (except for the oldest, Ralph, who remained a Catholic all of his life) were raised as Lutherans. Mina's father, Albert, completed the eighth grade, as required by law, but he had no further education when he began to work in the Homestake Mine at the age of seventeen.

Mina's mother, Ruby Johnson, was born in San Francisco in 1896. She was one of seven children born to Peter and Susanna Jane Peterson Johnson, both of whom had emigrated to the United States from Sweden and settled in California. The Johnsons moved from San Francisco, California to Douglas, Alaska in 1890 when gold was first discovered there, and Peter Johnson quickly rose to the position of foreman in the Treadwell Mine. However, the ocean broke through the mine, causing it to collapse (an event that made headlines throughout Alaska because of the loss of lives and the irreversible damage to the mine). As a result, Peter and Susanna Johnson and three of their children, including Ruby, moved to South Dakota in 1919, along with many other Treadwell mine families. Jobs were plentiful in the Homestake mine, so these men were able to find work immediately. Ruby had already completed a two-year teaching certificate program at the State Normal School in Bellingham, Washington in 1917 and had begun to teach grade school in Alaska before the move. Ruby's older brother, Charles, her favorite, had graduated from the University of Washington in Seattle with a degree in mining. Soon after the Johnson family arrived in Alaska, he met and married a woman named Mina (pronounced with a long *i*), a shortening of the name Wilhelmina, after Queen Wilhelmina of the Netherlands. When Charles contracted pneumonia and died, Ruby was devastated. After Charles's death, Ruby maintained close contact with her sister-in-law, even after she relocated to California and remarried. Thus, when Ruby's second child and first daughter was born in 1924, she named her Mina.

When the Johnsons arrived in Lead, South Dakota, they moved into the Swedish section of town. Lead was a town whose neighborhoods were determined by nationality and religion. Mina's brother, George, remembers that there was a Finnish Lutheran section of town, a Swedish Lutheran section of town that included Norwegians, an Italian Catholic section, a Yugoslavian section, and a Serbian section; there was even an area that was referred to by everyone as Slavonian Alley. The largest group of residents was comprised of the English Episcopalians. Many of these groups had their own clubs and churches. George remembers that as a child he overheard two women talking about a man who had recently died. When one of the women said she would have a Catholic mass said for the man, the other woman responded that she "might just as well pray for an old, dead cow." George also remembers that Albert Pendo thought it was important to describe himself as Austrian to further distinguish himself from the Yugoslavians, and he showed some annoyance when people assumed that his name was Italian. However, these distinctions did not prevent the children of Lead from mixing and socializing with each other, particularly in school.

Although the Johnsons adapted quickly to life in Lead, having come from another mining town and already knowing many of the miners and their families who had also traveled to South Dakota from Alaska, the "Treadwell miners" who took jobs at the Homestake were never fully accepted. Peter Johnson had been a foreman in the Alaskan mine, but because he was a latecomer, he was never able to rise above the position of shift boss at the Homestake. In fact, in 1929, after ten years of working at the Homestake, at the age of sixty, he decided to give up mining and start a chicken farm in Oregon. (Despite the Depression, he was able to eke out a living and at least be free of the brutal conditions in the mines. He was lucky to have escaped the fate of so many miners: silicosis, or miners' consumption, caused by silica dust constantly coating the lungs. Many miners did not live past the age of fifty.)

Albert Pendo and Peter Johnson, Ruby's father, worked side by side in the Homestake Mine as shift bosses. Ruby first became interested in Albert Pendo when her father came home from work one day and talked about "an awfully nice young man at the mine." They were married two years later, on June 21, 1922. While there were the inevitable strains of finances, raising children, differences in temperament (Albert was brusque, impatient, and hot tempered; George remembers that he would often utter the phrase, "Jesus suffering Christ," while Ruby was gentle and patient), it was a marriage that endured for more than fifty years until Ruby's death in 1975. The first strain may well have been the quick and close arrival of their two children: George was born in March 1923 and Mina was born in March 1924, but there were many other family members living close by to provide help and support.

A month before Mina was born, Albert Pendo wrote a note to his wife. It belies his eighth-grade education; despite the grammatical and spelling errors, it is clever and humorous, probably an intentional parody of the sermons he and Ruby heard every Sunday morning at the Augustana Lutheran Church. In addition, it reflects the playfulness and intimacy of the household where Mina and her brother George grew up.

> Lead, S.D.
> Feb. 7th, 1924

My Dear Little Wife:

Since eating my supper last nite the thought come's back to me that two years ago, lacking a few months, we pledged ourselves to be as one always considerate of each other, it occurred to me that as time goes on we may become lax in certain of our duties which so far you have so nobly performed. Far be it from my intensions to reflect in any way upon your past performance of these duties but it behooves us all to be constantly on the lookout for little tasks which if neglected work discord while if willingly performed create & maintain harmony which is issential to happiness. Not wishing in any way to impose upon you and making allowance for past favors there still remains one thing. Please when you put a hamburger sandwich in my lunch put an onion in it. Trusting you will take this in the right spirit. I remain your devoted husband.

Ruby Pendo so valued this note, printed in pencil in small, crowded letters on the back of a Homestake Mining Company time sheet the size of an index card, that she saved it with the family's birth and baptismal certificates.

Albert Pendo's letter to his wife, Ruby, asking her to put an onion in his hamburger sandwich, 1924. Courtesy of George Pendo.

Ruby also saved Mina's baby book recording "baby's first days" in which she made sporadic entries relating to Mina's first year. Both this book and her birth certificate indicate that Mina was actually named Ruby Mina Pendo. No one knows precisely when the transposition took place, but no one can recall her ever being referred to by any other name but Mina, and when she was enrolled in the Hearst Free Kindergarten in 1929, she was registered as Mina Ruby Pendo. The book contains a lock of Mina's blond hair, and in the entry for her first Christmas, Ruby wrote: "Part of the day was spent with Grandma and Granddad Johnson. Went to Grandma Pendo for dinner and received many useful gifts." The book provides a space to indicate the date on which baby began to crawl, but Ruby wrote above the space that Mina never crept, "she just slid around." Her first pair of shoes was purchased in November 1924 "at the Hearst," and Mina's behavior at her christening "was very good." One of Albert Pendo's sisters and one of Ruby Pendo's brothers were her godparents. Ruby Pendo also recorded Mina's first prayer, recited when she was two years old, along with a notation: "God bless Daddy, God bless Mamma, God bless Goggie (George), God bless everybody, make me good boy (as she always insisted on saying)." George recalls that Mina imitated everything he said and did, thus the male noun.

Mina and George Pendo, 1927. Courtesy of George Pendo.

The Pendos bought a very small house at 308 Bleeker Street, a steep road near the center of town. (All of the roads were steep; Janet Emig once described Lead as "that astonishing perpendicular mining town.") While the house was modest by most standards—a narrow, wooden-framed two-story structure with a small porch and a tiny front yard—it was much like the other houses in town. Although Albert and Ruby were extremely thrifty by necessity, the children never felt deprived. George remembers that, even during the Depression, neither they nor the other townspeople suffered economically because the Homestake mine continued to operate. During Mina's childhood, the Pendos remodeled the second floor of their house and rented it to two English teachers from the Lead elementary school, Miss Amelia Perman and Miss Edith Johnson. The two women lived with the Pendos for fifteen years. They used the Pendo kitchen and joined them for most meals, and they would look after George and Mina when their parents were out. George remembers that they often played word games at the dinner table and corrected everyone's grammar. He and Mina were extremely fond of the two women. "They were almost like aunts to us," George recalls. "They loved us very much and we loved them."

Many years later, Mina would describe her childhood as one that was "filled with teachers whom I admired." She was referring not only to her mother and to these two women, but to two of her aunts as well. Two of Albert Pendo's sisters were teachers. Florence had completed her teacher training in South Dakota and taught in Rapid City. In 1940, she moved to California, and she would often write letters to

Ruby Pendo's schoolhouse and students, Alaska, 1917. Courtesy of George Pendo.

Albert and his family, describing her favorite students. Esther taught in a one-room schoolhouse in the town of Belle Fourche, north of Spearfish. Although Ruby did not return to teaching until Mina and George were much older, she talked about her students in Alaska, and George and Mina often looked at a snapshot she had brought with her. She and her eleven students are standing outside a small schoolhouse in a fishing village called Chichagof on the coast of Alaska. The students ranged in age from five to eleven or twelve.

One of Mina's closest childhood friends, Georgia Jensen, remembers that "everybody knew everybody" in Lead, and because Lead was a town where people were generally aware of what others did for a living and what they earned, wealth and social status were simply not factors that were considered or discussed very often. The Pendos, Georgia Jensen recalls, were regarded as warm and friendly people, particularly Ruby. "She was a beautiful person, very giving, generous, and extremely intelligent. She was college educated; this was relatively rare in those days. Mina adored her and was proud of her. It was evident that they were best friends." Georgia recalls that before World War II, Ruby could not have taught even if she wanted to. Married women were simply not hired as teachers; they were expected to stay at home.

Mina and George grew up with their grandparents, aunts, uncles, and cousins nearby, and there were visits throughout their childhood to relatives in California and Alaska. During the late 1930s, their maternal grandparents moved to Oregon to raise chickens and their paternal grandparents moved to Wyoming to raise cattle. Neither enterprise was particularly successful, but the unspoiled, sparsely populated areas in which they settled were a welcome contrast to the many years spent in a dusty mining town. Mina and George would often spend several weeks during their summer vacations visiting their grandparents and, as George recalls, "being spoiled."

There were frequent visits from family members and neighbors, and George remembers that evenings were always spent reading and listening to the radio. Although Albert Pendo could read and write proficiently, he never read aloud to the children. When Ruby read to them each evening, however, he would sit and listen. George remembers that there seemed to be hundreds of books in the house, particularly books and magazines for children. Mina loved school, and she was an excellent student. Records from kindergarten through eighth grade indicate that she earned grades of *A* and *B* in every subject, with the exception of gym, in which she earned mostly *C*s. George remembers that, although Mina received a plaque from the Girls' Athletic Association, "there were no athletic activities for girls in those days." He also remembers that Mina would read under the covers long after her parents had told them to turn the lights off. Among the papers that Ruby saved is a certificate of merit that Mina received from the World Book Look-it-up-Club. "We never say 'I don't know,'" it reads, "we never guess; we look it up." George remembers that Mina started to take piano and cello lessons at the age of eleven, and she practiced regularly, without having to be told. (Although she played the cello in her high school orchestra, her love for the piano stayed with her for her entire life.)

George worked hard as well, but although he was a grade ahead of his sister, his teachers inevitably compared him with Mina and accused him of being lazy. Mina took great pity on George, and during the tenth grade she wrote many of his essays for him. "I got good grades that year," George recalls. George also remembers copying all of Mina's answers out of a workbook they were both assigned, but while she would receive *A*s for her answers, he would get *C*s.

Although George was a year older than Mina, she quickly surpassed him in height. By the time Mina was in the eighth grade, she was already as tall as her father, who was five feet eleven inches. As a result, she was terribly self conscious and often walked around with her knees bent. Mina was thin; she had large blue eyes; long, thick blond hair;

The Pendo family: Mina, Ruby, Albert, and George. Courtesy of George Pendo.

and a radiant smile. She wore her hair parted on the side, falling in a silky pageboy around her shoulders. In her high school yearbook photograph, despite the eight-line description of activities that appears under her name, she seems out of place—she looks so much more mature and sophisticated than her peers. Although she was strikingly beautiful, however, her friends recall that she seemed utterly unaware of the effect her appearance had on others. Many years later, Mina told a friend that she used to hound her mother with the question, "Am I pretty?" Invariably, her mother would answer, "Now don't you worry, you're a fine looking girl." Mina was always more serious and mature than most girls her age, Georgia Jensen recalls. They talked about books a great deal and always knew that they would go to college. Although Mina was, according to Georgia, "perfectly comfortable with boys and loved to listen to music and dance," it was her brother and best friend, George, who took her to her junior prom.

Mina's high school course load was rigorous; in addition to the core subjects, she took vocal music, instrumental music, declamation, drama, dancing, French, Latin, Spanish, and economics. She graduated fourth in her class of 124 and was given the "Goldenlode" award for character and personality, an honor just below that of valedictorian. George remembers that although Mina seemed to learn quickly and effortlessly, she always worked very hard and never fully appreciated or understood how impressive her accomplishments seemed to others.

However, it was outside of school, particularly during the summers, when George and Mina were happiest. In 1933, when George was ten and Mina was nine, the family drove for three days to visit the Chicago World's Fair. In 1935, Albert Pendo took a month-long vacation and traveled with Ruby and the children as far as San Diego to attend the exposition there, stopping at Denver and Las Vegas. At the end of the month, Albert returned home by train while Ruby and the children continued up the coast to Oregon, Washington, and Alaska to visit her brothers and sisters. Ruby saved a letter that she wrote to Albert, describing their route through Portland and Billings. The children were a little restless and cross, she noted, and they told all the other adults on the train that they missed their daddy "because he had to take another train." George remembers that he, Mina, and his mother were away from Albert for almost three months during that trip, a separation that was based as much on Ruby's need for some "peace and quiet and a respite from Albert's temper" as a desire to see her relatives. Despite these occasions, George recalls, his parents worked at their marriage and loved each other deeply. Divorce in the 1930s, particularly in South Dakota, simply was not an option that anyone considered. In fact, George cannot recall even hearing of a divorce in Lead during his childhood.

In 1939, the family drove to California and Seattle and then took a boat to Alaska to visit Ruby's relatives. George still remembers that he and Mina went panning with their Uncle John, but they found no gold that day. The family referred to these adventures for years afterward, recalling specific events, people they met, places they saw; George has saved scores of pictures from these trips. More than thirty years later, Mina recalled one of those trips in a Father's Day note she wrote to Albert from California, where she was attending a conference. "Being in California has somehow reminded me of our family trips to California, especially the year we went to Sawyer's Bar. Those days come back to me now so clearly. The world seemed to me then so secure. And you and Mom made it such a full and good world." And in a journal that Mina was required to keep for a college acting course, she wrote an account of one of the few times she had been on the ocean to satisfy an assignment describing an event when she could "see sound":

My contacts with the ocean have been rare, and since my ancestors have been rather earthy people, I have no instinct to aid me. I do remember one special time, however, where there was a good fog and all the trimmings. It was in Juneau, Alaska. We had been up on the damp, wooded parts of the island hunting for two days, and on our way back had run into a bad storm. We were all wet, hungry, and tired. By the time we reached Juneau, the weather had settled into its usual slow, penetrating rain, but by the time we had unloaded a heavy fog had settled. It reminded me of a blotter. When the fog horns would blow, it seemed that if you could watch the sound waves, they would travel like the ink when it touches a blotter. The lantern that one of the men held kept swinging, and I watched the weak light travel back and forth. When we bumped against the side of the tug, it sounded soft because the wood was soft from being soaked in water.

Religion played an important role in the family's life, and George believes that Mina was strongly influenced and affected by the religious training they received as children. They attended Lutheran services every Sunday. When they were in grade school, they attended classes before Sunday services, and when they were in high school, they attended mandatory confirmation classes every Saturday. George recalls that as a result of these classes they were "very familiar with and convinced of the value of the Bible and the Ten Commandments." Both Mina and George were confirmed, and many of the social events that the family attended were sponsored by the Lutheran Church. Mina loved to sing hymns and had, Georgia Jensen recalls, "a lovely contralto voice." Mina was deeply religious at this time, according to her brother, George, and at various periods throughout her life she would exhibit such a deep spirituality that it confounded her friends.

Stronger than religion, however, was the influence of their parents' values and behavior. Mina and George grew up in the house of a miner, in a mining town. As a result, they had a deeply ingrained consciousness of the earth and its formation. Along with the books and encyclopedias that Ruby provided for them, they were surrounded by geological maps and surveys. They knew that they lived near the center of the continent. Albert and his friends talked about lodes and veins and formations and shale. Each evening, he would tell his family how much muck had been "carried up" that day out of the Homestake. They understood the damage that water could do to an underground shaft, having heard the stories and seen the pictures of the destruction of the Treadwell Mine in Alaska.

Mina and George knew how hard the men worked, and under what conditions. They knew that their livelihood and the livelihood of most of their friends depended upon the amount of gold that was extracted from the Homestake Mine. They knew that, when they were infants, their father worked the night shift and that he would have to "muck his sixteen" in order to get paid. This expression, made famous by the song "Sixteen Tons," meant that each man had to fill sixteen one-ton ore cars by shoveling with a scoop, at depths of 2,400 feet, the material that had been loosened by blasting and drilling during the previous shift. They celebrated in 1929 when their father was promoted to mine foreman and would no longer be required to "muck" underground. They knew that during the winter months, while working the day shift, their father entered the mine when it was cold and dark and left when it was cold and dark.

As a result of this deep sense of the way the mine operated and its relationship to their well being, Mina and George were instilled with what George describes as an "appreciation of and respect for the resources nature gives us, along with the knowledge that you work for everything you have." More than anything else, George recalls, "we came to understand that the quality of the work we performed would most likely determine our future and our happiness. As a result, hard work was very important to us, possibly more important than our relationships. It was something we didn't mind doing. In fact, we enjoyed it."

On January 8, 1938, when Mina was fourteen, she wrote a letter to her parents, who had traveled to New Orleans for a (rare) vacation without the children. It reflects the activities she and George enjoyed, the habits of thrift and hard work that her parents were imbuing in her and her brother, and most important, the affection and security that Albert and Ruby provided for their children.

Dear Mother and Daddy,

I got my permanent today and like it very much. The girls sure like it.

I got that dress you sent away for today and it is a very nice one.

I decided to take Algebra, English, Science, and Occupation for High School. Miss Knowlton thought that would be best.

Aunt Helen asked me to go skating with her and Bob out at our cabin but then we decided not to go because it would be to [*sic*] far to walk.

I bet you are having a nice time.

Tomorrow we are going out with Gosses to the cabin to skate or maybe to some lake. They are very good to us.

We let Queen up tonight and I can hear her chewing a bone.

I took a bath last night. I am sleeping in your bedroom and it doesn't seem as skarry [*sic*].

We have to get up tomorrow to go to Sunday School so I guess I better close.

Lots of love,
Mina

P.S. George took the washing up.

After writing a row of Xs and Os, Mina wrote on the third side of the four-sided stationery, "Too bad I couldn't fill this page because I'm wasting some good paper." (Although Mina's mention of the arrival of her new dress seems to be an attempt to fill her letter with news of home, it is also an indication of a passion for beautiful clothes that re-mained with her for her entire life.)

The cabin to which Mina referred in her letter was a one-room, unheated shack with no indoor plumbing, located in Hannah (about ten miles from Lead), a town so small that it is not listed on maps of South Dakota. According to South Dakota law at the time, if an indi-vidual staked out and maintained a mining claim at least four feet deep, ten feet wide, and twelve feet long on federally owned land for five years, he or she could take possession of two acres of land surrounding the dig by paying five hundred dollars. More and more people, recog-nizing a loophole when they saw one, began to "mine" the area in and around Hannah, and hundreds of South Dakotans were able to build summer cabins on these plots of land. Albert always referred to the family's mining claim as "the Ruby Load." With the help of friends, he constructed a one-room cabin and eventually added indoor plumbing. There was no electricity, however, so the Pendos relied on kerosene lamps, used a coal and wood stove, and heated their water by running it through pipes connected to the stove and then channelling it into the water tank.

Ruby and Albert would take the children to the cabin as soon as school ended for the summer, and Albert would commute back and forth by car on weekends. George recalls that the "two aunt teachers," Edith Johnson and Amelia Perman, would often spend weekends at the cabin. It became a family tradition for Albert to set off a stick of dynamite early in the morning on the Fourth of July. Occasionally, Mina and George would invite friends from town (Georgia Jensen remembers "wonderful weekend visits when we spent the evenings playing big-band music on a wind-up phonograph"), but for the most part, they spent their summers together swimming, fishing, hiking in the hills, and horseback riding. The Pendos kept and cared for several horses, and George remembers that Mina practically "grew up on a horse. She was a fine and graceful rider. We rode horses more than we walked during the summers at the cabin."

The surroundings in which Mina and George spent their summers were magnificent. The Black Hills form a dome rising 4,000 to 7,000 feet above the surrounding northern Great Plains. The highest point has an elevation of 7,242 feet. Often the snow in the mountains did not melt until June, and Mina and George would "pile on sweaters" in the early mornings. George remembers that he and Mina could identify all of the trees that grew near the cabin: quaking aspen, ponderosa pine, lodgepole pine, white spruce, and mountain ash. They watched the flowering plants and bushes bloom in sequence as the summer progressed and would often pick flowers for their mother. They would pack a lunch and hike for hours, reaching elevations of 5,000 or 6,000 feet before heading back home. More than forty species of birds nested in the hills during the summer. Despite her familiarity with nature, however, Mina never overcame her aversion to snakes, particularly the garter snakes that inhabit the rocky soil.

The cabin was so isolated that there was no mail delivery, and George remembers that there was no official address. They simply told people they were located on Ward's Draw near Cyclone Hill and Horseshoe Curve. At the cabin, as at home, Mina and George were required to do chores and help with expenses. They earned money by locating and capturing lambs that had strayed from a nearby sheep camp. They earned five dollars per head, but it could often take an entire day to run down one lamb, and George remembers that on many occasions Ruby had to spend an entire evening removing wood ticks from Mina's thick, long hair.

The last two pages of three-page letter Mina wrote to her parents in 1939, exclaiming, "but oh how I do want to win!" Courtesy of George Pendo.

Both at the cabin and at home, the Pendos had frequent visitors, some of them quite eccentric. Mina's favorite character was Old Johnny Perrit. He was very short, had an English accent, and wore a beard down to his waist. He was billed in local festivals and rodeos as the man who had found the biggest gold nugget in the South Dakota Hills. He often came to Sunday dinner and told fantastic tales about the Black Hills. In an attempt to reciprocate, he invited Mina and George to his cabin for breakfast. They went occasionally, but George remembers that Mina was never comfortable eating the food, because her father had once mentioned that Johnny would spit on the grill to determine if it was hot enough to make the pancakes.

In December of 1939, when Mina was a high school sophomore, she was chosen to represent her class at a regional "declamation contest" being held in Philip, South Dakota. She wrote a letter to her parents on Senechal Hotel stationery explaining how she felt about the contest. Despite her best efforts to mask her strong sense of competition, her desire to do well and to succeed—a desire that grew stronger throughout her life—is evident. It is almost painful to see her try to contain, or at least control, the struggle she was enduring. The first page of the three-page letter is missing, but one suspects that Ruby, who wrote Mina's name and the date on one of the surviving pages, kept only these pages because she was so moved by the determination reflected in the letter.

I am writing this before the Declamatory contest. I have just said my piece over and feel more self assured.

If only I can keep calm through the piece I am sure I can do fairly well.

I do want to win terribly bad.

I hope I can get a definite mood and hold the audience through that mood.

It is such a beautiful story, I hope the audience sees it the way I want them to. I will be so happy if I can go home victorious and if I don't I must remember I am only 15 years old and a sophomore. I still have time to do more. There have been others before me who have not won in these contests and as Miss Braum says it is not a life or death matter, but oh how I do want to win!

Perhaps Mina's conflicting emotions can be explained by the influences of the Midwest and of her Lutheran upbringing. In fact, there is even a Norwegian word for this ambivalence, *janteloven:* individuals are not supposed to think they are special or act as if they are more capable or more talented than anyone else. Mina carried this belief with her throughout her life, this sense that her accomplishments should not reflect on *her* talents or on *her* abilities, and it was most evident when she communicated with her parents, masking her ambition with a desire to please them and to repay them for all the things they had done for her. In one of the letters she wrote to them several years after graduating from college, she closed with the following paragraph: "You both have done so much for me—more than most parents it seems—and it makes me want to please you and to work hard. I hope I never disappoint you too much." And in a letter written to her parents in 1954, after quoting a glowing recommendation she had received from a professor for whom she had done research, she wrote: "I'm just bragging to you. Don't tell any others about this, but I know you like to hear things like this and I always feel you are more responsible for whatever I have accomplished than I am."

No one can remember if Mina won that declamation contest in 1939, but during her high school career, it was becoming evident to everyone that, in addition to her fine academic ability, she possessed great acting, speaking, and singing talent. Even as a sophomore, she was given the lead roles in the high school plays. Although they were school productions, drama was emphasized so strongly in Lead High School during this period that many people described the plays as the equivalent of regional theater productions. It was Mina's performances in them that would later earn her admission to Northwestern's prestigious and competitive theater and speech department.

According to an entry in her high school yearbook in 1942, Mina earned first ranking in the poetry division of the Kiwanis Speech Derby while her friend Vivian Brown won for humorous prose. The yearbook entry continues, "Mina and Vivian earned the rank of superior, entitling them to go on to the divisional contest. At the divisional, Mina Pendo again was ranked superior, and represented this division at the state tournament." In addition, Georgia Jensen remembers that her mother drove Mina and her to a declamation competition in Chadron, Nebraska, during their senior year. Although Georgia Jensen no longer remembers precise details, she does recall that Mina had overcome any trace of nervousness by this time. "Mina never exhibited any competitiveness, but by then she knew what she was doing, she was self-assured, and she liked doing it."

Mina also earned the lead dramatic role in the high school senior play, a production of *Three-Cornered Moon,* and the choral lead in *The Pirates of Penzance.* It was almost unheard of for the same student to earn the lead roles in both senior productions. George remembers these productions as wonderful opportunities for the family, including aunts, uncles, and cousins, to get together. They were well attended, and they were an enormous source of pride and enjoyment for Ruby and Albert Pendo. People complimented them on Mina's performance for months afterward. Georgia Jensen remembers that Ruby "was as proud of Mina as modesty permitted." Mina is also pictured in the yearbook as a member of the yearbook staff and the camera club. (In both cases, she is in the back row—she was still one of the tallest students in the school.)

Although Mina graduated from Lead High School six months after the United States entered World War II, the war did not affect her college plans. Georgia Jensen remembers that there was never any question about whether she and Mina would attend college. Their mothers had attended college; they were both excellent students, and although neither family was wealthy, "they would find the money." It was common for those Lead High School graduates who planned to attend college to enroll in local schools: the girls attended Spearfish Normal (now Black Hills State University), and the boys (those who did not enlist) attended either the South Dakota School of Mines and Technology in Rapid City or the University of South Dakota in Vermillion. (George enrolled in the University of Nevada and later attended Washington University School of Dentistry in St. Louis, Missouri.) Most students who left the state usually attended the University of Minnesota or the University of Nebraska. Mina considered both of these schools because they had good drama and English departments. However, her acting talent was so extraordinary that Miss Braum, her drama teacher, encouraged her to "go east," and provided her with glowing recommendations. Mina applied to the School of Speech at Northwestern University in Evanston, Illinois. At the time, Alvina Krause was an assistant professor in the department, and she was famous not only for her rigorous training methods but for her valuable contacts with writers, directors, and producers. (Other graduates of this program include Charlton Heston, Cloris Leachman, and Patricia Neal.)

Mina's two-page application contains the usual information; however, in the space provided for parents' education, she indicated that her father, who had not attended school beyond the eighth grade, had completed four years of high school. In the spaces provided for "vocational preference," Mina indicated "stage" as her first choice; "radio" as her second choice, and "teaching" as her third choice.

Tuition at Northwestern for the 1942–43 academic year was three hundred dollars, a relatively huge sum for Albert Pendo, who at the time was earning two thousand dollars a year. Fortunately, there was no tuition at the University of Nevada, where George was completing his undergraduate work, so Albert and Ruby had to pay only one tuition. George remembers that his mother would manage from time to time "to scrape together a very few dollars and send them to Mina for pocket money." Very few letters from this period have survived, but one indication of the financial strain the Pendos were under is evident in a note that Mina sent home in March 1943. "I've written three letters tonight," she explained to her parents, "and now I have to use another stamp."

Mina enclosed in the letter a package of tiny picture postcards representing the various buildings of the campus, noting that she purchased them because they had cost only twenty-five cents. She made notations on the back of some of them, indicating, for example, that her

Mina while attending Northwest-ern University, Evanston, Illinois. Courtesy of George Pendo.

English class was held in University Hall. In addition, she enclosed a snapshot of herself. In the photograph, she is walking toward the (un-known) photographer, smiling confidently, cradling newspapers and gloves in her arms, a purse slung over her shoulder. Her demeanor is relaxed; she is looking directly at the camera—still utterly unaware, it seems, of her remarkable beauty. These pictures were Ruby and Albert's only exposure to Northwestern until Mina's graduation. The train ride from Rapid City to Chicago took two days, and it was expensive.

During the first week of classes at Northwestern, each speech major was required to choose a sonnet and read it in front of an assembly of students and faculty. Shortly after the readings, Mina approached an-other first-year student, Priscilla Weaver, and told her that she had liked her reading very much. This meeting was the beginning of a lifelong friendship. Priscilla, and later her husband Alan Brandt, would become Mina's closest friends: when Mina got married, they held the wedding dinner in their home; when they had children, Mina was named their guardian; and when Mina died, Priscilla and Alan were with her.

Priscilla cannot even remember the name of the poem that she recited, much less the name of Mina's poem, but she does remember how unusual it was for someone to take the time to approach another student and pay her a compliment. Most speech and theater majors already knew, even on the first day of classes, that they would be competing with each other for roles and later for auditions in professional productions. And of course, Priscilla noticed Mina's appearance, "an unaffected Midwestern beauty that simply took you by surprise—a movie star with no make-up."

Priscilla had come to Northwestern from California, drawn as Mina had been by Alvina Krause's reputation. Mina and Priscilla roomed in the same dorm during their first two years at Northwestern. During their junior and senior years, tired of dorm life, they rented a room together in a private home, where Mina took piano lessons with the children who lived there. Mina pledged and was accepted into a sorority during her first year, but within weeks the workload in the School of Speech became so heavy that she dropped out.

The friendship between Mina and Priscilla continued to flourish; Priscilla remembers that she and Mina earned desperately needed spending money by performing for women's clubs. "We got a lot of bookings," Priscilla recalls. "We went as far as Peoria, doing scenes from *I Remember Mama*. Alvina Krause admired our ambition and reminded us often of the value of performing in public—no matter how small the audience."

Mina's academic career at Northwestern was as successful as her high school career had been. She maintained a grade-point average of 3.7 or above during all four years, and for each of her last three years, she was awarded partial scholarships, including a particularly prestigious one known as the Edgar Bergen scholarship, based on merit. Many years later, when she was being asked to address larger and larger audiences on the issues of Open Admissions and basic writing, people were mesmerized by Mina's bearing and beauty, her voice, her diction, her carriage, her conviction. E. D. Hirsch described it as "that electrifying effect that Mina always had on those who heard her speak" (1). Some suspected that it was the result of her dedication to her students and to the cause of Open Admissions. Although it most certainly was, it was also the result of four years of rigorous training in articulation and projection at one of the most prestigious schools of speech in the country.

Most of Mina's required courses reflect her speech major and theater minor: in addition to more than thirty credits in literature (including a course that introduced her to Henry James, one of her lifelong literary passions), she took Training of Speaking Voice, Introduction to Theater, Public Speaking, Introduction to Radio, Acting, Interpretation of Drama, Theater Backgrounds, Creative Oral Interpretation,

English Phonetics, and Persuasion. During her sophomore year, she was required to take one semester of physical education, and just as she had in high school, she received the lowest grade of her college career, a *C*.

Priscilla Brandt remembers the long hours that she and Mina spent in the library doing research; she remembers in particular a history course they took—they enjoyed reading and discussing (for hours) the works of Jonathan Edwards. Priscilla remembers that Mina would attend religious services "occasionally" while she was at Northwestern, but was put off by the "Evanston religious scene": she described it to Priscilla as a congregation of people who "practice religion with their fur coats on."

Among the documents that Ruby Pendo saved, there is a folder that Mina had labeled "Acting Notebook" for her course with Alvina Krause. Although it contains only forty handwritten pages, it provides a record of the thorough immersion in acting, speech, and theater that Mina received. There are "enunciation" exercises containing columns of words containing, for example, the "A as in palm" sound, definitions, passages from plays and poems, illustrations of "tactile" representation of the senses (for olfactory, Mina pasted into her notebook a picture of onions).

Mina was becoming aware of regional speech patterns—and how to avoid them. In a section entitled "Midwest Menace," she wrote the letter *R* and listed the habits to avoid: The Midwest *R* is "made in front of the mouth with the tip of the tongue"; one should "avoid a tense tongue and retracted tongue." Instead, one should "begin with 'ah' then make it 'dra.'" One could practice by reciting the following verse:

> Hark, hark, the merry hearted lark,
> Singing the song of the holy seven
> Aping the angels' harmonies
> On the golden harps of heaven.

One of the assignments was to visit a museum and observe carefully one exhibit. Mina chose the statue of an African female dancer and wrote a four-page description. The essay is highly descriptive and analytical, thus making the concluding paragraph seem inappropriate, even out of place. "I walked out feeling large and clumsy, but by the time I stood by those huge pillars at the entrance, I had dwindled considerably." Professor Krause gave the entire exercise a grade of *A*- and then wrote: "There is no need for you to feel large and clumsy! Improve your carriage and posture, stop slumping and you are the ideal figure."

One suspects that this folder was valuable to Mina because of the positive comments made by Professor Krause, whose reputation as a difficult and demanding teacher and coach was well known. "Good observations and appreciation," she wrote at the end of one of Mina's descriptions. "Good thinking" she wrote on another. And on a piece entitled "Art," a piece that Mina had revised, she wrote "Superior." The descriptions and memories of home and family that Mina recorded in this journal, however, provide an account of events and incidents that would otherwise remain unknown. In trying to justify her claim that art is not possible without three basic essentials, the artist, the medium, and the audience, Mina offered the following example. "Throughout my childhood, I listened to the simple melodies of Slavic songs sung by old 'Slavs' who usually congregated in some kitchen to sing songs and drink wine. I never thought of these songs as art until I heard a concert pianist play some of Mozart, whose themes are built around these melodies."

Mina drew on her summers at the cabin at Hannah and her visits to her grandparents in Oregon for an exercise she was required to write on "Tactual Response":

I guess I can only tell you of my tactual response by describing some of the things I remember.

I think first of animals—the nose of a horse, soft and rather moist. I usually rub the palm of my hand against it although the tip of the fingers gives the most accurate account; chickens feel smooth and slippery, and there's something about a new, warm egg that makes you touch it lightly; the rough scaly skin of a pig's back covered with coarse stiff hairs makes even your fingers feel dry; a cow has a lovely skin if she's healthy—something like a horse only more mellow, and you can wrinkle it in your fingers; sheep have a soft but firm feeling like a thick mattress; squirrels have fine thin hairs that are almost too fine to feel. Then I remember the smoothly uneven rows of corn and the slight resistence [*sic*] when your finger presses a kernel; the gritty, flouncy feeling of chard right after it has been picked; the firm stiff head on cabbage as compared with the softer, leafier head on lettuce. I'm thinking now of a tactual response I get through my feet—when we irrigate, I feel the ground get soft and gradually give to my weight and creamy wet soil oozes around my feet and between my toes.

The typewriter keys are getting hard and slippery so I guess I'll stop.

One other reference to Lead in the journal described the night of Mina's high school graduation—a rite of passage that seems not to have changed very much since 1942. "On the night of my high school graduation," she wrote in a "Visual-Auditory response" to Strinberg's character, Anna Christie,

about four of the college kids decided to give us a party. Since they were much more informed upon the ways of the world, the entertainment was left to their discretion, and it took the form of alcohol in varying concentrations. I unfortunately got enough to make me act like a fool and still know it. I couldn't sleep much that night, and finally at 5:30 in the morning I got up, dressed, and started for a walk. By 6:30 I had gone outside the town, past the graveyard and stood on the edge of a road that looked down on rows and rows of hills. It was cool with just a slight breeze; the hills were a dark greenish black. Several pines close by were just barely wisping from the breeze. Then I felt something of what Anna must have felt. I felt healthy and clean.

During summer and holiday breaks, Mina usually returned home to Lead. George remembers that she did not seem to change very much from one visit to the next, or if she did, "she kept it from us. She was devoted to Mother and Father and never wanted to worry or displease them in any way." It was at about this time that Albert and Ruby Pendo purchased five acres of land in Spearfish, a tiny town surrounded by ranches approximately ten miles from Lead. Albert would not retire from the mine for another fourteen years, but he was beginning to plan for the time when he would no longer have to live in town. Although the family continued to live in Lead, in the house on Bleeker Street, they visited what came to be called "the five acres" as often as they could. They hiked, hunted, and fished. They cleared the land and grew vegetables that Ruby would later preserve.

George had met a young woman named Norma, whom he married in 1945, and they purchased a home in Rapid City, where he had

Alvina Krause's theater company at Northwestern University, 1946. Priscilla Weaver Brandt is second from the left; Mina is fourth from the left; Alvina Krause is seated on the couch. Courtesy of Priscilla and Alan Brandt.

started a dental practice. Mina and Norma quickly established such a good relationship that George and Norma named their first daughter Mina.

During the summer between her junior and senior years, however, Mina did not return home. She had been invited by Alvina Krause to join an acting company that would travel to Eagles Mere, Pennsylvania. The actress Patricia Neal, who was a sophomore at the time, was also invited to join the troupe, along with Mina and Priscilla, and she wrote about that summer in her autobiography, *As I Am*. The tall "crazy" girl who did not want to go to New York to whom Neal refers is Mina.

> For years Alvina Krause had nurtured a dream of starting a theater of her own. She found an old building standing empty near the mountain resort of Eagles Mere, Pennsylvania. The opening season's company would be limited. I was last in rank, but I knew Alvina liked my work. I was elated to see my name on the list.
>
> That summer was fun. I spent a lot of time running around town getting furniture for props and making tuna casserole as a member of the kitchen team, but those duties did not keep me from acting. I worked like a dog to lose my southern accent for Noel Coward's *Blithe Spirit*.
>
> Talent scouts found their way to Eagles Mere and flashed temptations of Hollywood, but I wanted only the real thing, the theater. I was more interested in an offer made to a girl in the company who

Mina in the role of Regina in The Little Foxes, *performed at Eagles Mere, Pennsylvania, summer 1945. Courtesy of George Pendo.*

was even taller than I was. She must have been about six feet. One of the scouts said he would suggest her name to the Theater Guild for Eugene O'Neill's *A Moon for the Misbegotten.* The main character was just her size, and there would be auditions soon. I couldn't believe it when she said she didn't want to go to New York. She had to be crazy. Wouldn't I love to show up for that audition in her place! (55)

Ultimately, Patricia Neal did get to try out for the part in O'Neill's play; Mina had decided that it was more important that she return to Northwestern to get her degree. During the summer season at Eagles Mere, however, she earned the lead role in Lillian Hellman's *The Little Foxes,* and her performance was spectacular. During the closing scene in which Regina withholds her husband's life-saving medication, Mina appeared on stage wearing a floor-length, low-cut black velvet gown and opera-length black gloves, her long blond hair pulled up on the back and top of her head in loose waves. Her carriage and beauty were so striking that members of the audience sensed that they were witnessing something very special. Mina had turned down an opportunity to perform on Broadway; instead, Priscilla recalls, she brought Broadway to Pennsylvania.

Although Mina had indicated on her college application that her first choice of a vocation was the theater, and although she and Priscilla decided to move to New York directly after graduation to pursue acting careers, Priscilla remembers that Mina remained surprisingly "unstage struck." Perhaps her professors had also sensed this; in the letters of recommendation that Alvina Krause and James McBurney, the dean of the School of Speech, wrote, there is mention not only of Mina's acting ability but her scholastic achievements as well. "We think of her as one of our best products," McBurney noted. Krause, who perhaps knew her better than any other professor wrote:

I have known Mina Pendo for five years. In my own courses, she consistently ranked first in scholarship. As for general academic standing in the university, she was throughout her career here, the regular recipient of honor scholarship awards on the basis of outstanding scholarship and achievement. While her academic record here is superior, it does not indicate her creative ability, her wide range of interests, her unlimited capacity for work, her maturity and understanding. As a scholar and as an individual, she is held in high esteem by all who know her here at Northwestern.

Priscilla Brandt remembers that Mina had "other dimensions." Although she loved to laugh and have fun, and although she dated several men during college, she was also scholarly and serious. "While most aspiring actresses headed for New York determined to succeed on the Broadway stage no matter what it took," Priscilla recalled, "Mina seemed to already know that many other things could make her happy."

CHAPTER TWO

A Necessary Prelude

Mina Pendo was twenty-two years old when she graduated from Northwestern in 1946 and drove with her best friend, Priscilla Weaver, to New York. They had very little money between them, but a friend agreed to give them a ride as long as they helped with the driving. "We drove all night while Steve, the owner of the car, slept in the back seat bouncing around among our luggage," Priscilla recalls. "It was dark, we didn't know the way, and neither Mina nor I could drive very well. But we didn't care, we were going to New York, and that's all that mattered." (In fact, neither Mina nor Priscilla had valid driver's licenses.)

When they arrived, Mina and Priscilla shared a bedroom in a rooming house at 139 West 75th Street. The rent was nine dollars a week, Priscilla recalls, far more than they could afford. To save money, they moved to a room in Queens, and Priscilla can still remember the sound of the refrigerator fan next to her ear as she tried to sleep. She found a job as a tour guide at Rockefeller Center, a welcome source of regular income, and the evening hours enabled her to go to auditions and callbacks during the day. Initially, Mina tried out for parts whenever there was an audition, but she soon grew tired of the competitiveness and uncertainty. Priscilla remembers that within months of their arrival in New York, Mina "started looking for alternatives to a career in the theater." Mina held a series of jobs during this period; the one she most liked to describe and laugh about in later years was that of cigarette and coat check girl at the Versailles, a New York nightclub, very much like the Copacabana. Friends recall that Mina would describe, in great detail, the black net stockings she had to wear as part of her "uniform."

During the day, she would perform for ladies' clubs, doing poetry readings and monologues. "Mina would do these proper little performances of 'literary works' during the day and then knock 'em dead at night in her tight little costume," Priscilla recalls. "We laughed about the incongruity of it, but believe it or not, we were having fun. We loved New York and could never imagine returning home to live." George Pendo recalls the time Mina described a man she had met in New York who wanted to furnish her apartment for her. "I may be from South Dakota," she told George, "but I'm learning fast about New Yorkers."

Mina and Priscilla often invited friends to their one-room apartment and served their specialty: a casserole made of a layer of tuna, a layer of potato chips, and a layer of canned mushroom soup. As soon as the guests left, Mina and Priscilla would gobble up the leftovers, even though they knew it would be more prudent to save the remainders for their breakfast.

Priscilla and Mina both loved clothes, and they would often go without food in order to save enough money to buy a new outfit. Priscilla remembers that, soon after they arrived in New York, they went shopping and bought identical shirtwaist dresses, reasoning that they simply would not wear the dresses when they were together. However, a few weeks later, as they walked toward each other on Fifth Avenue, having planned that morning to meet for lunch, they realized that they had worn "the dress." "We were a sight," Priscilla recalls. "Mina was almost six feet tall and thin; I was five feet seven inches and heavier. She had blond hair; I had brown hair—we simply could not stop laughing at ourselves. We were best friends, and things like that happened all the time."

Less than a year after she arrived in New York to pursue a career in acting, Mina realized that she was not happy: the lack of money, her diminishing interest in acting as a profession, the sense that she was at a standstill intellectually, all contributed to her decision to attend graduate school. No one was surprised; she had always been an excellent student. Her choice of school surprised everyone, however. She decided to take courses in Bible study at Wheaton College in Wheaton, Illinois. Although the school offered degrees in several disciplines, it described itself in its brochure as "a Christian liberal arts college," and at the time Mina attended Wheaton, all of the institution's correspondence and communications prominently displayed the motto "For Christ and His Kingdom."

George Pendo recalls that Mina did not consider returning home during this period in her life. "Perhaps she didn't know what she wanted," he notes, "but she did know what she didn't want. Mina's need to be successful, to make her mark, and her strong competitive nature led her away from South Dakota. What were her options here? To teach at Spearfish Normal? She simply didn't see any opportunities that she wanted to pursue at home." Many years later, Mina would tell Janet Emig that although she loved her childhood in South Dakota, even as a young girl she always had a feeling that it would be nice to be else-where. "When the gypsies used to pass through town on their way to wherever they were going," Mina said, "I used to wish that they would take me with them." This need to be somewhere else does not explain entirely her decision to enroll in a graduate program in Bible study, however. She had always loved school and had been a good student. In addition, given her decision that an acting career in New York was not for her, perhaps the idea of returning to the West—but not too far west, led her to consider returning to Illinois, where she had been so happy as an undergraduate. Perhaps these factors, combined with her interest in religion—an interest that was not simply intellectual but based on the faith that had been imbued in her throughout her childhood—led her to Wheaton College.

Mina traveled from New York to Illinois by train, using money her mother had given her combined with what she had been able to save. Taking money from her parents at this time was particularly painful for Mina. Her father had been working ten-hour shifts in the mines for more than twenty-five years, and in anticipation of his retirement, he and Ruby were trying to save enough money to purchase more land. Like his father before him, Albert Pendo wanted to raise cattle, be his own boss, and enjoy the outdoors. George had earned a degree in dentistry and had completed training in orthodontics, so he was financially independent. Although Ruby and Albert could not afford to help Mina in any substantial way, George remembers that his mother "always sent a little something to Mina, although I don't know how she managed to do it." Mina felt guilty taking the money. In a letter dated September 6, 1949, one of the few letters surviving from this period, she wrote: "I was all set to save every nickel on my trip, but wouldn't you know I would get hungry. I've eaten both my lunch and dinner on the train ($1.25 lunch, $1.50 dinner). It makes me sick to spend so much but evidently not sick enough!"

Very little is known about Mina's life during the year she spent at Wheaton. Transcripts indicate that she took three upper-level undergraduate courses during the fall and spring semesters: Bible: Christian Theology; Bible: Methods of Bible Study; and Bible: Advanced Bible Survey. She received two *A*s and a *B*. Friends and family remember that her behavior and appearance changed drastically while she attended Wheaton. "She became almost monastic," Priscilla recalls. "She gave up smoking, stopped wearing make-up, and began to attend church regularly again. I think Mina actually considered joining some sort of religious order at this time." George can recall very little about this time in Mina's life: "Only that she started attending church services regularly again, and that she told me she couldn't believe how far she could stretch her money by eating Jello three times a day."

Although her grades were excellent and although she was offered a scholarship to continue her studies at Wheaton, Mina decided to return to New York. She had begun to think about a teaching career in English. As a result, she applied to and was accepted as a "special" (part-time) student in Columbia University's master's program in literature for the fall 1948 semester. Mina moved into a seventh-floor apartment (where the elevator broke down with great regularity) on Riverside Drive, near Columbia University. During her first semester, she enrolled in two courses: World Perspectives in Modern Literature and The History of Philosophy. The literature course was taught jointly by Mary and Padraic Colum (both of whom had been close friends of James and Nora Joyce). It is hard to understand why Mina received a *C* for this course, given the fact that her permanent file in the Columbia University Placement Bureau contains a letter written by the Colums, dated February 1949, indicating that she "has been an exceptionally good student and has written several brilliant papers." Mina earned an *A* for the other course she took that semester, and she earned *A*s in both of the courses she took during the spring 1949 semester: The Foundations of Modern Europe 1500–1815 and English Literature from 1830 until the End of the Century.

Money was still a problem. Mina worked at several jobs during this period, including a part-time clerical position at Columbia, to defray expenses, but as a part-time student she was ineligible for scholarship money. Although she enjoyed her courses and her professors, she explained the frustration she was feeling over both money and employment opportunities in a letter she wrote to her parents during the spring

1949 semester. The reference to her new suit, however, is evidence that her passion for beautiful clothes had returned; the "monastic" period to which Priscilla had referred was definitely over.

Dear Folks:

No excuse for the delay except for unexpected time takers.

Sunday, as you know, I went to my history professor's for the afternoon. She and her husband live outside New York and drive to work (both teach at Columbia). They have a small place but a huge living room—rustic and very comfortable—the afternoon was very pleasant.

I wore my new [underlined twice] suit. Yes I finally got the long awaited brown gaberdine suit and a pair of brown shoes—practically liquidated me but I look wonderful in it—will send a picture—in fact, took two pictures Sunday. Putting everything on my back, like the cousin Jacks—Dad says. This will be my spring outfit. I got it this weekend mainly because I had arranged for two interviews for teaching—one on Tuesday afternoon for a job in Plainfield New Jersey High School. Then another one Monday evening for a job at Hunter College High School in New York. They are both pending because of the one lack—my master's degree. They were both impressed with me as a person, I know, and want to have me but the boards of education around here require masters degrees. I'm discouraged today. If I don't get a fellowship I don't see how I will get the master's, and if I don't get the master's I won't be able to teach in the kind of place I would like to teach—it seems like a riddle. Even if I do get some kind of scholarship, I'll have to borrow money—it doesn't seem wise to work for years and go to school during the summer; it takes so many summers and meanwhile you make no advancement—furthermore I don't want to teach in high schools. We have calls for teachers from every part of the U.S.—even South Dakota, and even South Dakota (Yankton) demands at least a masters. Well perhaps something will solve the problem—I'll hope. Maybe I should have stayed at Wheaton where those people would have paid for the education. I still think I did the right thing in coming here.

Love, Mina

Mina soon found a part-time teaching job at The National Bible Institute, a college affiliate of the Bible Presbyterian Church, an institution that published a weekly newspaper called the *Christian Beacon* and made radio broadcasts to more than four hundred stations, identifying itself as the "Twentieth Century Reformation Association." At the time, the school was located on West 55th Street in Manhattan. In 1950, it changed its name to Shelton College, but it was still licensed by the state to grant degrees only in the areas of religion and theology. (In 1953 it relocated to Cape May, where its license was revoked by the New Jersey Board of Higher Education.) Mina did not accept the position at The National Bible Institute because of its religious affiliation; as Priscilla Brandt recalls, Mina's interest in religion had by this time diminished. Her decision was based on expediency. Priscilla remembers that had Mina not found that job when she did, she would have been forced to withdraw from Columbia.

Mina requested a letter of recommendation from the chair of the English department of Shelton College and had it placed in her permanent file at Columbia. The letter clearly indicates that she was a superb teacher, but the description of her course load also indicates that as an adjunct she was probably overworked, even overwhelmed, trying to prepare for teaching at Shelton while taking courses at Columbia. The letter, signed by Marian J. Downey, is the first of many such letters attesting to Mina's talent and dedication. In teaching, as in acting, she was a natural.

Miss Mina Pendo . . . taught in Shelton College during the past two years courses in speech, writing, and literature for freshmen and sophomores, with an additional class in great books for juniors and seniors.

Miss Pendo's work was satisfactory far beyond that of the usual beginning teacher. Her teaching was so effective that she was able to secure the enthusiastic cooperation of her students. We should gladly have retained her services and should welcome her back should she choose to return. It is a pleasure to recommend her as a highly successful teacher.

Mina spent the summer of 1949 in South Dakota with her parents. By this time, they had purchased the small parcel of land in Spearfish, so she had an opportunity to live in the country and to observe her parents' new lives as ranchers and farmers. (It was at this time that Albert began the tradition of hanging the picture of the current president of the United States in his toolshed, using an old toilet seat as a frame. "He didn't put JFK's picture, there, however," George recalls. "Dad was a staunch Democrat.")

It was during this visit that Mina told her parents about a man named Dan, whom she had met at Columbia University, a brilliant Latvian student of Russian. George recalls that although she was relatively reticent on the topic, her parents assumed that the relationship was a serious one.

Mina finally had an opportunity to spend time with her niece, Mina Jeanne, George and Norma's daughter. During this summer, an injured fawn strayed onto the property. Its front left leg had been broken, probably by a trap, and Mina's father quickly determined that the animal should be put out of its misery. However, George remembers that "both Minas" made such an uproar that Albert finally relented and permitted them to take the fawn to a vet. The leg was set and healed quickly, and the deer soon became as tame as the Pendo's dog. The two Minas watched the fawn, whom they named Helene, approach the salt lick every morning. More than fifteen years later, Mina published a children's story entitled "Helene" in *The Golden Magazine,* in which she described Helene's departure at the end of the summer: "I was standing next to her, rubbing her head and saying all sorts of things she didn't understand. She stayed only a short time and didn't bother with much of a good-bye; she just turned and loped up the hill after the others without a backward glance" (67).

It was a wonderful summer for Mina; in a letter to her parents, written during her train trip back to New York, she wrote: "Last night for dinner we had, among other things, corn on the cob and tomatoes—it made me lonesome for Spearfish, and I started on a bragging spree about how we ate off the land all summer. By this time they are, of course, acquainted with my white-haired Mina." However, the time that Mina spent with her parents that summer gave her an indication of the effect the change in their lifestyle would have on her mother. Ruby's workload had increased tremendously. Many of Albert's friends from the mine would come to the ranch on the weekends to help make repairs, install plumbing, or dig wells. As a result, Ruby would have to prepare huge meals for these men. In addition, the Pendos had taken on a $25,000 mortgage for an 820-acre ranch near Spearfish, and Ruby decided to return to teaching in the fall to help with the added expenses. "Pretty soon your first week of teaching will be over, Mom," Mina wrote to her mother, "and I'll be anxious to know how you fared. I hope you were not too lonesome." She was referring to the fact that her mother would have only two students in her new position as a first-grade teacher in Sponge, a town near Spearfish.

Ironically, one of Ruby's students turned out to be Kathy Jensen, the daughter of Georgia Jensen, with whom Mina had had such a close relationship throughout her school years in Lead. (Kathy recalls that it was a wonderful experience: Ruby spent an enormous amount of time holding the girls in her lap and reading to them.) In another letter from this period, Mina asked if her parents had "been able to make the payment." Clearly, she was worried about them, and George recalls that she would often call him at his office to make sure that their parents were okay. "You'll tell me if there's a problem, won't you?" she would ask him, knowing that her mother would never give her any news that would worry her.

By this time, George and Norma Pendo had installed a telephone in their house in Rapid City. However, Ruby and Albert Pendo did not install a phone for several more years. From time to time, Mina and her mother would make arrangements in advance for Mina to call her at George's house. Ruby never quite adjusted to communicating by telephone, however. George remembers that after all the arrangements had been made to compensate for the different time zones and to find a time convenient for both of them, when his mother and Mina finally managed to hear each other's voices, they could not think of anything to say. Mina began one of her letters to her mother by saying: "Just now hung up from our talk together. Such a wonderful connection and we even thought of something to say, didn't we Mom? I'm afraid if you had a telephone I would weaken often."

When Mina returned to New York from her parents' home at the end of the summer, she resumed her teaching at (the renamed) Shelton College while she completed her course work for the master's degree: English Literature in the Seventeenth Century, English Literature in the Eighteenth Century, Shakespeare, Introduction to Literary Research, and Milton. Her course in Milton was the beginning of a passion for his work that lasted throughout her lifetime (an additional passion— she retained her original devotion to Henry James). When Mina's first work was published in 1967, it was a poem entitled "Milton." (Her second publication was an essay about James's *Washington Square*.) It is difficult to determine which professors Mina had for specific courses at Columbia, but it is known that Mark Van Doren and Maximilian Walten, her adviser, were two of her favorites.

Mina's choice of a topic for her master's thesis was a pragmatic one; she was still teaching at Shelton, leaving her little time for the creativity (and painstaking attention to detail) that would make her later writing so important in its field and so pleasurable to read. She never listed "An Annotated Bibliography of Masters' Theses Written at Columbia University: 1930 through 1939 on Seventeenth-Century English Literature" on her resumé or in applications for grants or sabbaticals. The topic was probably suggested to her by Maximilian Walten, with whom she took a seminar in 17th Century English Literature. (One suspects that the results of her thesis would be useful to his research.) Mina completed her course work in June 1951 and received the master's degree in December of the same year. Clearly, she wanted to complete the requirements as quickly as possible so that she could teach full time.

The idea of pursuing a Ph.D. degree was out of the question at the time, both financially and emotionally. Furthermore, Mina had no reason to believe that the lack of a Ph.D. would hinder her teaching career. Obviously, Walten, her master's thesis adviser, agreed; he wrote a glowing recommendation for her placement file:

Miss Mina Pendo was a member of my Pro-Seminar in 17th Century English Literature during the school year 1949–1950, and she completed her M.A. thesis under my direction. I thus had an opportunity to observe her as a student in a class and also as a student in intimate personal conferences with her mentor.

I found her to be conscientious and thorough in all her graduate work, to show great promise as a scholar, to possess remarkable qualifications as a teacher, and to be a fine person in every way.

It gives me great pleasure to recommend her strongly for any kind of teaching position in the field of English. She is very attractive in appearance [remember, this was written in 1950] and has a charming personality; she has an excellent voice and delivery; she is sympathetic and understanding; she is intelligent and profound; she has a splendid knowledge of English literature and the ability to transfer this knowledge to students in an enthusiastic, interesting, and otherwise effective way.

Athough Mina was consumed with her work at this time, she and Priscilla maintained their close friendship. Priscilla had begun to date Alan Brandt, an intelligent, funny, and charming New Yorker. She remembers that Mina's friendship was particularly important to both of them at that time; Alan's mother was unhappy because Priscilla was not Jewish, and Mina encouraged them to "follow their hearts." Mina said that if Priscilla did not marry Alan, she would. In terms of Mina's relationship with Dan, however, Priscilla did everything she could to convince her to end the relationship. Jealous and possessive, Dan began to follow Mina and to question Priscilla about Mina's whereabouts. His actions became so impulsive that Priscilla feared for Mina's safety.

Even though Mina now had a master's degree and excellent references, she still could not find a full-time teaching job at the college level. Rather than apply to high schools, she decided instead to accept a position, offered to her through Columbia's placement bureau, as a research assistant to Raymond B. Fosdick, a prominent New York attorney whose primary responsibilities involved handling the affairs of many of the Rockefeller foundations. His legal career had been extraordinarily successful, even before he became associated with the Rockefellers. In 1919, President Woodrow Wilson had appointed him as Under Secretary General of the League of Nations. After the United States Senate voted against joining the league, Fosdick maintained his friendship with the then ailing President Wilson. In addition, he was often asked for advice and counsel from members of the league. He was a brilliant lawyer who had contacts with some of the most influential politicians and businessmen in the country. Although he earned both a bachelor's and a master's degree from Princeton University, he could not afford to attend law school full time, so he attended New York Law School in the evening and taught at the Henry Street Settlement during the day. (His brother, Harry Emerson Fosdick, was even more renowned as a preacher and for his Sunday afternoon radio talks. At one point in his career, he delivered a sermon that was so controversial he was labeled as a heretic and forced to resign from the First Presbyterian Church. He later became the pastor at Riverside Church, a church built especially for him by John D. Rockefeller Jr.)

Raymond Fosdick needed someone whose primary responsibility would be to conduct research, and given the prodigious research Mina had conducted for her master's thesis, she was certainly qualified. He hired Mina to assist him full time in writing the biography of John D.

Rockefeller Jr., a contemporary whom he had known for forty-five years. Although it was always understood that her function would be that of research assistant and that Raymond Fosdick would be listed as the author, Mina was so skilled as a writer that she actually wrote fourteen of the twenty-three chapters. Raymond and his wife, Betty, became two of Mina's closest friends. Although the Fosdicks were the same age as Ruby and Albert Pendo, and although they did not have children of their own, they did not function simply as surrogate parents. "Mina had a beauty, a love of life, a curiosity to learn new things, an ability to have the most wonderful conversations about so many topics that simply endeared her to us," Betty Fosdick recalls. "She was thirty years younger than I, but we had a wonderful relationship. She was the closest friend I ever had."

The three years that Mina spent working with Raymond on the biography, from 1951 through 1954, afforded her an extraordinary opportunity to observe the way that the richest family in the world lived. "I've had to learn to stop making 'rich-as-Rockefeller' jokes," she told her brother, George. Raymond's project was being financed by a grant from one of the Rockefeller foundations, so he was able to pay Mina relatively well. For the first time in her life, she was earning a good salary and doing work that she enjoyed. She could easily afford the rent on a room at the Evangeline, a women's residence on the East Side of Manhattan—leaving her extra money to indulge in her passion for clothes. Mina had an expense account for her work on the Rockefeller biography, but even though she was not spending her own money, old habits died hard. She wondered in a letter to her parents whether the information she gathered on a trip to Williamsburg, Virginia, was worth the one hundred fifteen dollars the trip had cost.

John D. Rockefeller Jr. spent most of his life giving his father's money away to causes he deemed worthy. As a result, one of Mina's primary responsibilities was to research and write about some of the most spectacular philanthropic enterprises ever undertaken. She gathered information about Rockefeller's contributions of both money and time to such projects as the restoration of Versailles, The Palestine Archeological Museum, the Oriental Institute at the University of Chicago, The Cloisters, the restoration of Williamsburg, the Philipse's Mansion in Tarrytown, Washington Irving's home in Sunnyside, the American Academy in Rome, Chartres Cathedral, the American School of Classical Studies in Greece, the procurement and donation of the land on which the United Nations is built, the Rockefeller Institute for Medical Research, the Harvard Business School, along with hundreds of other "lesser" activities and donations.

John D. Rockefeller Jr.'s life, as it unfolded during the three-year project, affected Mina very deeply. She was awestruck, of course; in one of the few letters to her parents that has survived from this period, she described meeting Rockefeller:

Mr. Chorley's secretary came up to tell me that Mr. Rockefeller was visiting and would like to meet me. I went down and shook hands. He is the most cordial polite man to meet and completely simple. We only exchanged a few words about Williamsburg and then he left, but it was very exciting to me. We had met briefly before but I don't think he remembered. Everyone who works for him is so deeply devoted to him.

Mina was also deeply affected by his modesty and his refusal to take credit for his actions, preferring instead to see himself as a medium through which larger purposes could be served. The incident that best exemplifies Rockefeller's reluctance to garner praise for his generosity occurred in 1927 on his visit to Versailles and is described toward the end of the biography:

He had given a large sum for the restoration of the palace, and as usual he was deeply interested in the details of the work. Reaching Paris, he immediately motored out to Versailles, but arrived unannounced at four o'clock in the afternoon just as the visitors' gate was being closed. When informed by the guard that he was too late to be admitted, he accepted the situation philosophically and motored back to Paris. However, he was apparently recognized by someone in Versailles, and harassed officials were soon tracking him to his hotel. The story was headline news in all the newspapers in France, and no action on his part could have so endeared him to the French people. An American millionaire allowing himself, without irritation or protest, to be turned away by a guard at the gate of Versailles, when he had given $2 million for its restoration. (420)

Mina's background as a miner's daughter was particularly useful to her in researching and writing "The Colorado Strike," the eighth chapter of the twenty-three-chapter book. Rockefeller had surprised the entire country when he declared his support of the laborers' demands for better working conditions:

> I have never believed that these things should be provided for working men and women either as a result of chance generosity or deliberate paternalism. Quite aside from the fact that, in my judgment, they represent the soundest economic policy, they are due the employee as a matter of common justice, required by the basic fact that man is a human being first and a member of industry afterward. (181)

Mina also wrote the chapter dealing with Rockefeller's religious upbringing and beliefs. Despite her background, interest, and training in religion, elements that served her well as she researched and wrote the chapter, she still found Rockefeller's literal interpretation of religion "deadening." He had been brought up in a household where dancing, card playing, and especially drinking were strictly forbidden. He grew up hearing the temperance lectures being delivered by the Loyal Legion Temperance Society in New York, an organization to which he and his sisters belonged, and he proudly claimed in a letter to his grandmother that he could recite from memory: "The Price of a Drink," a poem that concludes with the lines:

> The price of a drink, let him decide
> Who has lost his courage and his pride,
> And who lies a grovelling heap of clay,
> Not far removed from a beast today.

In a letter to Priscilla, written shortly after the book was published, Mina noted that she "was saddled with a couple of terribly dull subjects, particularly parks and religion. . . . I remember when I was immersed in [the family's] letters and records—I used to emerge from JDR, Jr.'s apartment completely fed up with anything that even vaguely smacked of religion."

The perks of the project far outweighed the occasional tedious topics, however. Mina's trip to Williamsburg, the one during which she met Rockefeller, was just one of many for which her expenses were paid. Mina, Raymond Fosdick, and Florence Bauer, a secretary, did most of their research and writing in a Manhattan apartment provided by the Rockefeller Foundation specifically for the project. In addition, Mina was often required to spend time in the Rockefeller apartment suite in Manhattan or at the family estate, Kykuit, in Pocantico Hills, in Westchester County. In both locations, she reviewed family letters and records while sitting among some of the finest paintings, rugs, tapestries, and antiques in the world, including the collection of priceless Chinese porcelains, described by experts as one of "unsurpassed magnificence." (The collection was later donated to the Metropolitan Museum of Art.)

Mina was particularly struck by the extraordinary limitations placed upon Rockefeller as a result of his prominence and wealth. The biography describes the two occasions in his life when he was not immediately recognized as the son of the richest man in the world:

> There was the time at Seal Harbor, for example, when a grand piano was being moved into his house. "Hi, Mac," called one of the workmen to him, "give us a hand," and Mr. Rockefeller delightedly obliged. "Now we gotta find Rockefeller," said the workman when the job was done. There was the time, too, when he stopped to converse with some boys in swimming. "How's the water?" he asked. "Pretty good," said one of the boys, "but the kids won't let your pants alone if you leave 'em on the beach. If you want to come swimming tomorrow, I'll come with you, and Francis can watch our pants." (423)

At the end of that paragraph, Raymond Fosdick concluded, "[T]here was an element of seclusion about his life, a kind of loneliness imposed by his own name and the symbol of power for which it stood" (424). Mina was less circumspect in her assessment of Rockefeller, an assessment offered in one of her letters to Priscilla:

Actually, I developed a real fondness for JDR, Jr., and even dream about him as a little boy, yet he is not a man with whom one identifies. Somehow he missed some of the major human wrenches and this told in his personality—not in an ugly or unpleasant way but in a way that makes one always ask afterward, "What was it I missed in his character? What was it that wasn't there?" But one knows that Shakespeare would not have put him in a play.

During the time that Mina was working with Raymond on the Rockefeller biography, she often went to the New York Public Library to do research. During one of those visits, in July of 1953, she met the man whom she would marry less than two months later. She described the meeting in a letter to her parents, postmarked August 18, 1953. Three-quarters of the way through her letter, however, it seems to have occurred to Mina that she had not yet explained what had become of Dan, the man whom her parents thought she was still dating. In the same paragraph in which she told them that her new boyfriend, Don, was anxious to travel to South Dakota to meet them, she briefly explained why she had ended her relationship with Dan, making no reference whatsoever to his jealous and violent behavior. It was the beginning of the inevitable role reversal children undergo in their relationship with their parents; for the rest of her life, Mina did everything she could to prevent Ruby and Albert from knowing anything about her life that would make them concerned or unhappy.

Dear Folks,
I am late in writing you because I have something very wonderful to say and I wanted to have the time to say it well. It's really a very simple thing I have to say—just that I am in love. I met him only a few weeks ago, but it seems already that my whole life is different. I never expected such a thing to happen to me at this late stage in the game [Mina was twenty-nine years old], but here it is—and as Mina Jeanne would say—I waited until the last minute. Let me tell you about it from the start.
I went to the public library one afternoon several weeks ago and was sitting at the microfilm machine looking at sections of *The New York Times*. In order to work there one has to sign his name and his employer. I had done this and then gone over to start work. Shortly after I had sat down, a young man sat at the next machine. "Excuse me," he said, "but I couldn't help notice that you work for Raymond Fosdick. I am working on my dissertation in history and one of these days I am going to contact him to see if he remembers anything about Judge Murphy. Do you by any chance know?" That started the conversation. We talked about Mr. Fosdick. Then this young man told me about his dissertation—that he was completing his doctorate in American History up at Columbia—that he teaches in a boys' private school

in the city—and so on. He wasn't a handsome man—not, I suppose, what you would call good-looking at all, but he seemed very nice and when he asked me if I would like to go out for a soda, I very gladly said yes. We talked for about an hour, during which time I learned that his name was Don Shaughnessy, that we both loved books and teaching, that his background had been very much like mine, that on the subject of religion, he had no definite conclusions and no church affiliation but that he was concerned with such matters, and I had the feeling that he was interested in me. When we finished, I hoped very much that he would see me again.

He did—a few days later. He met me after his class and we walked and talked until one o'clock in the morning. I met him the next night for dinner and again we walked and talked and realized even then, although nothing was said, that this was a very special event. The next evening, we had dinner and went to a movie with some good friends of his—a doctor and his wife from Chicago. When he came to call for me that evening he looked almost frightened, and before we even left the lobby of the Evangeline, he said, "There is something which I must tell you—now. I have been at the library all day, trying to work, but I couldn't. I sat on the library steps watching the pigeons and thinking about you. Finally I met a friend of mine and talked to him. I just had to talk to someone about you. What I'm trying to say is that I am very much in love with you." At that point everything inside me sort of took a major dip into measureless space and all I could do was smile somewhat insipidly. Later on in the evening, after we had left his friends, we walked up Fifth Avenue. Then we crossed over to the East Side, and at the corner of Madison and 60th, he said, "Mina, will you marry me—not right this minute or next week. But eventually?" I said "Yes."

Since then, we have met every day and everything we learn about each other only makes us more certain that we are right. But we are not going to be too rash. We have set December as the date because he will have a short vacation then and he wants to take me to Cuba for a honeymoon. He has already bought a diamond ring and I should have it soon. Isn't it crazy and fantastic and wonderful? I have never been happier in my life. He wants very much to have me finish my doctorate and I hope it will be possible because we are both so fond of teaching. His salary is not large but with the two of us working, we will have plenty. His age—this is so strange—he was born on March 13, 1924 in Queens—the very same day that a placid little baby made her

Mina and Donald Shaughnessy at the wedding dinner given for them by Priscilla and Alan Brandt, 1953. Courtesy of Priscilla and Alan Brandt.

entrance into the world via Lead, South Dakota. And strangely enough—he is also left-handed!

I have talked with him so much about South Dakota and about you and he looks forward to coming home with me and becoming part of the family. This has been difficult for Dan, of course. But as you knew this summer, matters had become so difficult with us and I have waited so long and there had been so many quarrels. I know now that it would have been a mistake and we were both fortunate to realize it finally. I become very sad when I think of it for we came to know each other well, and I shall always have a concern and admiration for him. But he was not the right person. I only hope that he will be able to find a girl who can really help him and give him the things that he needs.

Now I must stop, although I could go on and on. I want you to be as happy as I am and not worry about whether I am being impulsive or cuckoo. Write to me right away—both you and Dad—and tell me what you think. That is, after you get your breath back.

Love,
Mina

George Pendo recalls that he and his parents were exceedingly pleased for Mina, thinking that "a New York man" would suit her taste and intelligence, and assuming that there would be plenty of time for them to meet Donald Shaughnessy and to get to know him better. That was not the case, however. A few weeks later, Mina telephoned her parents to let them know that she and Don had decided not to wait any longer; enough time had elapsed to convince them that they wanted to get married in New York. Six weeks after writing the letter in which she told of meeting Don for the first time, she again wrote to her parents, this time explaining the details of her wedding day. Clearly, she was ebullient. Although none of her family members made the trip to New York, Priscilla Weaver and Alan Brandt prepared a celebration of great intimacy and warmth, just one of the many extraordinary expenditures of time and effort they made for Mina during their lifelong friendship.

September 28, 1953

Dear Folks,

I said I would write on Saturday, but Saturday and Sunday passed and no letter, but I'm sure you understand. But now it is Monday night. I went to work this morning—sort of walking on clouds, but managed to get a bit done, and tonight I want to write you about the wedding, which was almost perfect and would have been if only you could have been here too.

On Thursday night my dress was finished—late—the girls wouldn't let me do a thing, not even sew a button on, so I sat and waited while the last stitches were being taken. It looked beautiful and there was a hat made out of the same material. A tweed, as I believe I mentioned. (Enclosed is a sample.) The stuff was over $5 a yard but I only needed a few. I'll bring it with me at Christmas. That night I kept imagining what the wedding would be. I even got a bit scared about the whole thing—wondering if I was doing the right thing, wishing there were someone to talk to. I finally called Don and talked with him. He listened and consoled me—said it was natural for me to feel afraid, and that if I wanted to wait we could easily do so. But after talking to him I wasn't afraid any more and plans went on.

I didn't sleep much that night. On Friday I went to work in the morning and then took the afternoon off. Bought a gift (leather gloves) for Priscilla and Don got a tie for Alan. At quarter to six we met Priscilla and Alan at Alan's radio station. There we got into a car—a bright yellow roadster loaned to Alan by friends—and we drove out to Manhattan Beach [Brooklyn], about 45 minutes from New York. We arrived at the home of Dr. Wahl—a very comfortable place, and his wife and two children were there waiting for us. We talked for a while very comfortably and pleasantly. Then Priscilla and I went into the bathroom to make a few last minute preparations. We came into the living room and the ceremony began. It was very simple but moving. Dr. Wahl recited the vows very solemnly and clearly but without a slight tinge of affectation. We quietly said "Yes" and then he pronounced us man and wife. It didn't seem to me that anything had changed, and I kept trying to persuade myself that I was now a married woman. Don was very quiet and just kept holding my hand and looking at me. We had a double ring ceremony which is what he wanted. Afterward Mrs. Wahl had some refreshments prepared for us and we stayed to talk and take pictures for a while. When we got outside Alan and the two children and Priscilla threw rice at us and it felt like a regular wedding. Then the four of us got in the car and started back to Manhattan. When we arrived in New York, Alan and Priscilla told us not to come right up to the apartment but to wait for a few minutes until they had a chance to go up and turn on the lights, etc. When we entered the apartment we found a little miniature bridal bouquet on the door, and as we walked in they snapped a picture of us. Inside the place was all decorated for the occasion. Alan had had access to all of the radio station's recordings and he has a machine that plays on indefinitely. The bridal music was playing as we came in and then throughout the evening there were beautiful romantic songs in the background. When we stepped into the living room we found a beautifully decorated table set for four. Tall white candles circled by white and red roses, white linen cloth, crystal dishes and glasses, a bottle of champagne. Alan had gone to Louis Sherry's—the big bridal planning people who make up the decorations for those mammoth weddings you read about—and had had them design everything for a party of four. There were white match books with the initials P and S engraved on them for Pendo-Shaughnessy. White boxes with little bits of cake in them with the same engravings (he got an extra set for you and I will send it to you). A lovely wedding cake was in the middle. It was all very beautiful and I hope the pictures do it justice. On the long marble coffee table were many gifts—almost all of them from Alan and Priscilla—vases, glasses, ash trays, at least ten beautifully wrapped gifts which they had chosen with the utmost care. Both Don and I were completely overwhelmed with it all and didn't know how to thank them. It must have cost a great deal, and although Alan has a good income, it still seemed a great deal for them to do. They said they had thoroughly enjoyed it and had been planning it for weeks. Don told them that he appreciated it, especially because it had made me so happy. After we had eaten and talked and opened the presents, we took a cab back to my new home. At the door Don told me to put down the packages I was holding. Then he picked me up and carried me across the thresh-hold. Fortunately he is big and strong and seemed to have no difficulty at all. It was all completely wonderful and I felt like laughing and crying at the same time. And Don was every bit as happy as I. It would have been worth waiting until I was forty—although Mina Jeanne was persuaded I had waited until the last minute!

The next day we had the quite unromantic job of getting my belongings moved from the Evangeline. Don had gotten a moving firm to help us and the whole thing took only a few hours. The living room is now filled with boxes of books and suit cases which we expect eventually to get emptied. On Saturday evening we had intended going to a movie on Martin Luther but instead we took a walk and sat in the park. Then we bought some ice cream and came home. On Sunday we had our first big dinner in the apartment—roast lamb which Don fixed. It was delicious and we had fun getting it ready. After we were all ready to put it in the oven we discovered we didn't have a roasting pan so we had to put part of it in one pyrex baking dish and part in another with a pan below to catch the drippings. But it tasted wonderful for all that. I made the gravy—enough for an army, but good tasting anyway. That evening we listened to a radio production of *Macbeth* and then read and talked and planned the courses we would be taking this semester. It all sounds rather uneventful but we were both completely happy and almost surprised that so much contentment and peace could belong to two people.

That takes me up to the present. We had a very nice wire from Wes and Leon which I have answered and I think I have written all the letters you suggested so I am up on my thank you notes at present. Nothing has come yet from the Lead friends but I imagine we will be getting some gifts before long. Tomorrow I begin one of my classes. Will be going to class Tuesday, Wednesday and Friday and one class on Saturday morning. Don is glad I am going on with my work and doesn't seem too worried that I will be neglecting my domestic duties. If I find it too much of course, I will cut down on the outside work.

I was thinking that it would be very nice if you would drop a note to Alan and Priscilla thanking them for their contribution to the wedding, etc. Don't if you don't feel like it but I know it would mean a great deal to both of them. You might say something like this: "Mina has told me how much you did to make her wedding a very special memory. We were sorry not to be able to be with her but were also greatly comforted by the knowledge that she had such wonderful friends to be with her and to make the event of her marriage such a festive and satisfying experience. Please accept the thanks of both Mr. Pendo and me, and should you ever come out South Dakota way, be certain that a warm welcome awaits you." Sincerely yours, etc. You could begin it "Dear Priscilla and Alan," but address it to Mr. Alan Brandt. Hate to bother you with this, but it is one of the few ways I know of expressing our gratitude.

Now I have to stop. We wanted to go for a little walk by the river tonight and if I don't stop now we won't get started, I'm afraid. Will write soon and keep you posted on the trials and tribulations of a very green housewife. Do you have some recipes you would like to send? I could use them if you have time.

Love, Mina

Given the Midwest customs of the time, the great distance, and the cost of travel, it was not surprising that Mina did not return home to get married, nor was it unusual that her parents did not attend. Furthermore, she considered herself too old for a large or formal celebration. She had never given her mother instructions; she trusted her implicitly to do what was proper naturally and without prodding. Clearly, Mina felt some discomfort, or at least some concern, that her New York friends would not understand her parents' absence and might interpret their behavior as unusual, even cold.

There may have been another reason Mina decided to get married in New York without her parents first having the opportunity to meet Don. Both Priscilla and Betty Fosdick have described Don Shaughnessy as a "real New Yorker" who said exactly what was on his mind and who preferred to have the last word. It was no secret that Albert Pendo was a "real Midwesterner" who also said exactly what was on his mind and who insisted on having the last word. Mina had always adored her father, despite the fact that he was often brusque, rude, even obnoxious at times. If Albert and Don did not get along, she would be left in the untenable position of disappointing her father or ending the relationship with Don. She wisely decided to avoid such a possibility, and in the end, events proved her right. Norma Pendo, George's wife, remembers that by the third or fourth visit to South Dakota, Don informed Mina that he would not tolerate her father ordering him around the ranch and assigning him chores. Although they managed to maintain a relatively cordial relationship, the two men were, in effect, too similar to ever become friends. (Don's admiration for Ruby grew with each visit, however; he loved her wit, her kindness, and her friendly nature.)

Mina's concern that school might interfere with her "domestic duties" and her request for recipes for "a very green housewife" are almost painful to read today; this, after all, was the woman who would direct one of the first, and certainly the most challenging, Open Admissions programs in the nation and whose speeches, essays, and book would inspire thousands of teachers to reconsider their role and function as educators. Given the time and culture in which Mina lived, however, many of her actions were radical by most standards: after high school, she had "gone east" to Chicago to attend college; she had traveled to New York to pursue a career in acting; then she had married a man whom she had known for less than three months.

Mina and Don never took the honeymoon to Cuba mentioned in Mina's earlier letter to her parents; they quickly realized that it would be imprudent to use what little money they had for such a luxury. Instead, they used their energies and resources to further the educational and career plans they had made together. Don would complete his dissertation in history and Mina would begin taking courses at Columbia toward a Ph.D. They were perfectly happy remaining in New York, in Don's apartment on the Upper East Side. Mina, it seems, had found precisely what she wanted: someone who was well educated, well read, a good conversationalist. Betty Fosdick remembers how happy Mina was as a result of her marriage:

> Mina loved being with Don. They took long walks and bicycle rides around Manhattan together and had conversations about politics, edu-

cation, history, the economy. They were both liberal in their political thinking. They truly preferred talking and reading together to anything else. Don was brilliant and a great conversationalist. He had been born in Queens, the son of a New York City policeman, and Mina came to understand the politics and culture of New York and its boroughs through Don. It was a happy time for Mina, and you could see it in her face. She was more beautiful than ever.

Mina and Don traveled to South Dakota during Don's winter break in 1953, and apparently their first visit as a married couple went well. George recalls that Don amused the Pendos and their friends with stories of New Yorkers and New York expressions. "Chutzpah," Don explained to his rapt South Dakota audience, "was the young man who had just murdered his parents, pleading for mercy with the judge because he was an orphan." Don's relationship with Albert got off to a cordial start, and Don was charming and attentive to Mina's mother, whom he liked immediately. He even began talking about buying land adjacent to the Pendos' ranch, which now exceeded eighteen hundred acres.

Mina and Don may not have been considering a move to South Dakota simply because they wanted to be near her family. Teaching jobs were exceedingly hard to find in the Northeast, and Mina and Don were struggling financially. Mina wanted to teach at the college level, but she was beginning to discover just how difficult it would be to find a full-time job, particularly without a Ph.D. Although she had indicated in a letter to her parents that she would be taking classes toward a Ph.D. four days a week at Columbia, her transcript indicates that in 1953 and 1954 the only course she registered for was Medieval Latin, presumably to satisfy the language requirements for the degree.

There is no grade entered on the transcript for the Medieval Latin course; one suspects that Mina, given that she had just gotten married and that her work on the Rockefeller biography was not yet complete, decided to abandon her attempt to earn a Ph.D. at that time. It was a decision that would haunt her for the rest of her career.

Mina may have discontinued her studies for other reasons as well. In the mid-fifties, it was not uncommon for women who were recently married to sacrifice their interests for those of their husbands, and this could very well have been the case with Mina. In fact, in a letter she wrote to Priscilla Brandt in March 1954, Mina joked: "I look forward to the day when we will both sit down over a martini, after five years of happy incompatibility, and chat with real bourgeois oblivion about recipes and diapers."

And in a letter written to her parents a little more than a year after she was married, Mina wrote: "Don went to a class at Columbia tonight where he presented his first chapter on the history he is writing. He just called to say that it was well received and Professor Nevins (probably the chief American historian today) commended him on it and told him to keep up the good work. It is always nice to get such encouragement."

Mina had not abandoned her own interests entirely, however, for in the same letter to her parents, she informed them of Raymond Fosdick's praise for her work. Directly after the line describing Don's accomplishment, she wrote, "Which reminds me, I asked Mr. Fosdick to write a letter of recommendation for me so I can have it on file in the placement bureau in case we need to use such things for future jobs." As usual, Mina did not want to seem too proud of her own accomplishments, thus the "which reminds me" transition. Raymond's praise of her work, which far outweighed the praise given to Don by his professor, was presented as little more than an afterthought. She did, however, quote the entire letter:

I obtained the services of Mrs. Shaughnessy through the Placement Bureau of Columbia University and she came to me with excellent recommendations. She has now been with me for two and a half years as research associate, and I cannot speak too highly of her performance. She has rare gifts in gathering and ordering material and, in addition, a really distinguished literary style. Moreover, she is a delightful person to work with, cooperative, conscientious, and intellectually at home in many diverse fields.

In a long lifetime I have worked with many associates and assistants. I do not recall any whose qualities have seemed so adequate and satisfactory as those of Mrs. Shaughnessy.

Mina's plans to pursue a Ph.D. were put on hold for another reason. Donald Shaughnessy had been hired to teach history in Rome for a year, and they were both ecstatic over the prospect of living and working abroad. Furthermore, as Mina watched some of her friends from

South Dakota and New York settle into the domesticity that was so rampant in the fifties, she may very well have begun to question her own educational and career plans.

Yet Mina's devotion to her new husband and her willingness to give up work if it interfered with her domestic duties did not eclipse entirely the desire for independence and autonomy that had brought her from South Dakota to New York. In the letter to her parents, dated October 16, 1954, in which she repeated Raymond Fosdick's praises, she wrote: "When we come back from Italy, Don wants me to take off a year from work and get my courses out of the way for a doctorate. We'll see when the time comes. I don't think I could get used to the idea of someone supporting me. He would love to do it but I sort of like to work on my own."

In 1954, Priscilla suddenly departed for Europe in order to escape the problems and pressures arising from her relationship with Alan. They wanted to get married, but religion continued to be an issue. Alan arrived at Mina and Don's apartment late one evening and, as Mina explained in a letter she wrote the next morning to Priscilla, "spilled out the things that were pressing on him." Alan could not bring himself to ask Priscilla to make a statement agreeing to an "identification with the Jewish religion," yet he knew that "from the point of view of his family, this ritual would signify to them" that Priscilla "was not afraid or ashamed to be a part of their group." Mina's advice to Priscilla was to consent to Alan's request—and in the process be exposed to "the rich heritage, the simplicity and the beauty of one of the world's great religions." Alan remembers that this reference was simply one indication of Mina's "fondness for all things Jewish. We used to tell Mina she was a 'pro-Semite,'" he recalls. "She learned everything she could about Jewish customs and traditions, and she was a quick study in picking up Yiddish expressions and phrases—she knew precisely when to use them."

The last paragraph of Mina's letter to Priscilla offers a glimpse of Mina's own state of mind shortly before she married Don. In explaining to Priscilla how easy it had been for Alan's view of the matter to "become distorted," she explained her own circumstances:

Lest I sound smug . . . I had only to project back a few months to Don's and my courtship and remember with what fear and misery I finally confessed to Don a totally insignificant imperfection in myself, fully expecting him to fold up his tent and vanish. Oh how serious and world shaking it seemed to me—and with my arsenal of rejection complexes I had built an amazing fortification against my own happiness.

As the Fosdick project neared completion in 1955, just months before Mina and Don were scheduled to leave for Italy, Mina, along with Raymond Fosdick, Florence Bauer (the secretary on the project), and Don, spent long hours each evening proofreading and editing the 475-page manuscript. Betty Fosdick remembers that at about this time Mina began to bring Don along on her visits to the Fosdicks' country home near Newtown, Connecticut, a beautifully restored and decorated two-hundred-year-old farmhouse surrounded by fields, streams, and orchards. "At first," Betty recalls, "we would extend a formal invitation, but as the friendship deepened, Mina felt comfortable asking if she could come the next weekend. If one or two weekends passed without a visit, we would ask when they were coming." The Fosdicks became one of the cornerstones of Mina's life. She trusted them and confided in them. Although she formed many close friendships in New York, she felt a particular kinship with the Fosdicks; she knew that they understood her. Both of them had been raised in small towns as Mina had, and they possessed a sense of privacy and circumspection that was very similar to hers.

Betty recalls that Mina and the Fosdicks would occasionally spend time in the library of the house, where there was a small electric organ. "Mina was a Lutheran, Raymond was a Baptist, and I had been brought up as a Methodist. The three of us would sing hymns as she played the organ. These were hymns we had all grown up singing. We were quite a sight, I'm sure, but it was just for fun. We were greatly amused by the words, and by our ability to remember the words, but that didn't stop us from doing it again and again."

During this period, Mina wrote a long letter home describing the progress of the Rockefeller biography and their plans for Italy. She had asked Raymond to refer to her by her maiden name in the preface, and she explained why: "The references to me will be in my maiden name. Funny, I resented the idea of using any other, because after all it was you who are responsible for anything I have done. Don agrees, so that is nice. Besides, 'Mina Pendo' is an awfully nice looking name. Did I ever tell you how much I like my name?"

Mina and Don departed for Italy on August 24, 1955, aboard the *Independence*. They had barely been able to scrape enough money together for the passage, but Priscilla Brandt remembers that they were both ebullient, realizing that whatever happened to them "it would be an adventure to remember." Priscilla missed Mina terribly during the ten months' absence and saved all of the letters Mina sent to her and Alan, thirteen in all. Read together, they provide a humorous, self-effacing account of Mina's difficulties with the Italian language and customs, and a gradually increasing appreciation of Italian culture, art, and architecture. Because she could trust Priscilla unconditionally, she also expressed her most intimate feelings about Don, and although the relationship between Mina and Don began to change soon after they returned to the United States, it is clear from these letters that her year in Italy with Don was one of the happiest of her life.

Mina was homesick within hours of their sailing. She wrote to Priscilla, "My spirits drooped for several days and I kept thinking about our friends, hoping that we would be as close when we return as when we left. Please, please keep in touch with us and share all the things that are happening to you." Mina told Priscilla that she felt "very old" as she watched "a number of young Fulbright students being cosmopolitan and exchanging collegiate shibboleths." Mina and Don went out on deck as they passed the Azores, "a wonderful sight," and on the sixth day of their trip, they "opened up your bottle of chianti wine and drank to the dregs." Mina described Don's behavior to Priscilla and Alan:

You would love Don. He drinks glasses of table wine and orders only Italian food, which so far has consisted of various shapes and colors of noodles covered with tomato sauces that reek of garlic and onions. The ship's cook has, I fear, a rather stereotyped conception of Italian food. Now in Spain, I suppose Don will burn out a few tonsils eating hot peppered dishes. But he has a grand spirit, and I shall love him tonsils or not.

Mina's homesickness continued even after she and Don landed in Spain. "Oh how good it was to get your letter! I had no idea I would have such nostalgia for home." The circumstances of their arrival probably did not help to lift her spirits. The "trustworthy" agent whom they had contacted from New York was "inclined to fleece us heartily": he had hired a private chauffeur, given them a lower-than-official exchange rate, thrown in extra fees, and warned them against traveling to Tangiers because of rioting. Mina and Don managed to escape from the agent and fly to Tangiers (where there were no riots). They went to a bullfight and Mina "felt like crying—it was such a slaughter and I'm afraid I cheered at one point when the bull almost got the matador." Don was managing "remarkably well" on his high school Spanish, while Mina "smiled at everyone she saw and said 'Buenos Dias.'" Hearing a few words of English from an old Greek man whom they met left her "wishing for roots instead of change." During their one-night stay in Naples, Mina was

tired and depressed and mad that I couldn't understand a thing on the menu except spaghetti. I wanted desperately to have a big fried fish but under *pesce* I couldn't interpret a thing. Ended up with what looked like spiders and octopus tips. Poor Don was patient and sympathetic (he said later he could hardly keep from laughing) while I delivered my tirade upon being a tourist in Italy.

Their arrival in Rome on September 14th did not improve Mina's spirits. She felt as if she "were simply in another New York except we couldn't speak the language." She and Don were living in a hotel near the Spanish Steps, and the cost of the hotel and meals was draining their scant resources. She was having trouble finding her way around because "everything, as you know, ends up in a piazza or a palazzo and it takes a while to get oriented. In addition, the drivers are madmen who scatter pedestrians like chickens every time they tear down the street." Mina found the people gracious, however, and she described for Priscilla and Alan her attempt to locate one of the Dante Alighieri language schools. One of their friends called the operator to get the number of the school and she replied, "with some dismay, 'Oh, he dead long time.'"

Mina described one incident in particular that led her to realize that "Rome is potentially an intriguing city":

The other day we took a ride with another couple from the school. Went by carriage through the Borghese Gardens and on the way we saw a girl—tightly clad as all these wonderfully bosomed females are and walking alone, as if out for a turn about the park. The fellow with us—in a kind of playful innocent and breezy manner—waved as we passed, whereupon the lady took a firm stance and proceeded to masturbate in pantomime. We all stared incredulously while she continued the display until we were out of sight, although other cars were passing by regularly. I have never seen anything quite like it. It was the sort of thing you would dream about doing in a nightmare and then thank god after you woke up that it was a dream.

Mina took a pragmatic approach to finding an apartment that she and Don could afford. She explained to Priscilla that although she had been able to find "several vacancies in the Bronx section of the city," she was "determined to find the Greenwich Village section of Rome."

The school where Don was teaching, the Overseas School in Rome, was "in a chaotic state with no one quite knowing what he is supposed to teach and not enough rooms for the students." Mina's own situation was no better. In a letter written early in October, she complained to Priscilla of the weather: "the rains came some days ago—drenching, dripping, constant rain"; of her new apartment: it was too large and expensive but it was all they could find; of her health: "I got sick the week before and was in our dreary hotel room for four days, creeping out once a day to get some sort of sustenance (and just try to ask an Italian waiter for milk-toast)"; of the cooking arrangements: "I have only two weak little gas burners to cook on and a totally unpredictable electric oven which also runs up the electricity bill like fury; of the shops: "you buy everything in the wrong place and canned goods—except for tomato and pea soup—are nowhere to be found"; of their financial situation: "I think I shall have to try to hunt up some sort of work so that we will have at least enough to get us where we're going when we return. The whole financial picture depresses me greatly and I try not to meditate upon it too much." These inconveniences were minor, Mina explained; she was unhappy to be in Rome for other reasons, and she tried to describe them to Priscilla. Given Mina's great fondness for Henry James, one must wonder if she recognized some of his most "American" characters—Daisy Miller and perhaps even Henrietta Stackpole among them—in herself:

[T]hings are not improved by the fact that so far I feel a fundamental lack of enthusiasm for Rome. I won't go into the details now.

Part of the response is of course due to my own inadequate acquaintance with art and architecture. And a part is related to the behavior patterns of the people—they are so overt in their vanity, in their sexiness, in their anger (I have never seen people put on such demonstrations!) and while I can maintain up to a point the anthropologist's point of view, I am ultimately backed up against my own deep-rooted prejudice against what they seem to be. I have seen no evidence as yet of what everyone said we would discover—the art of living. Rome is a crowded, quick moving city where people seem just as neurotic about acquiring and displaying material wealth as they are in New York. But it has that depressing stratification of society which seems so much more permanent and merciless than in America. As for sight seeing, I am beginning to wonder how much one sees because he wants to say he has seen it and how much from genuine curiosity. Today we packed a lunch and hiked along the Appian Way—sounds wonderful, but except in the part which is under improvement, the cars dash by so madly that one cannot relax. Once away from the traffic, we looked at the ancient remains of tombs, enjoyed the quiet, and then had lunch. But I have so little of the sense of the historic—I can't seem to get worked up about the idea that a thing is terribly ancient. There is one fountain which I have come to like very much—Bernini's fountain of Triton. It has been different every time I have looked—but in between the times I look at Triton, there is marketing, cooking, budgeting, and cramming into streetcars (which are far worse than New York's during the rush hour).

I know this sounds terribly morose. But I take some comfort in the fact that Don has had many of the same responses that I have had. The cold marble floors of the apartment have already taken their toll and we are both coming down with colds—a fact which may account in part for my sour travelogue. As a matter of fact, neither of us has felt particularly healthy since getting here—a combination of diet and exhaustion, no doubt. But please don't scold us—we're just terribly provincial, we know, and a bit set in our ways. But so far, we just don't *like* Rome, the way sometimes, for reasons that stem way back to the whole complex of experiences that constitute your life, you don't like a painting or a book or a person. Naturally we will do the very best we can to change our minds, and of course we shall get all the museums and monuments off our consciences.

By mid-October, Mina's spirits had lifted considerably; "You will be pleased to know," she wrote to Priscilla, "that I am rallying." In the same letter, dated October 16, 1955, Mina described many of their activities—along with a renewed appreciation of Priscilla's friendship.

Your grand letter arrived this morning. I've read it twice and have gone about talking to you steadily. What a luxury it was to have you to talk to and how often do I meditate upon the miracle of friendship (if I sound like St. Francis, excuse it, but *some* of this country has to rub off on me). But it is miraculous that you can get to a point in a relationship with another human being who is bound to you by none of the more overt obligations of family, tradition, or law that offers so much freedom. The knowledge that I have bored you, exasperated you, interested you, and sometimes helped you and that we have been able to share some of the most important human experiences with a good degree of honesty is one of the most enriching thoughts I have. Oh how I hope that we settle in New York when we return. If only a teaching job will come through for Don somewhere there. We can always go west in the summers.

Mina described a visit to the Vatican, to "rooms that are seldom open to the public," arranged by a friend from Don's school; she even saw "a little pond where Il Papa fishes." She spent an entire morning looking at the five Bernini sculptures at the Villa Borghese, and then went to the hairdressers.

Had my hair cut (not short) shampooed, set, and my nails done (first time in my life and they are gorgeous!) all for $1.60. I felt like Cleopatra and I shall do it every week. Just around the corner from the apartment. Don—what a good man he is—said I looked beautiful and it was the first time in Rome that I haven't felt like a flat-chested old prune.

Mina and Don had found a housekeeper who did everything, including,

talking patiently with me in my monosyllabic and ungrammatical Italian. . . . I sit there with my little dictionary in hand stumbling through little sentences. How completely different it is to learn a language this way. The other seems so artificial now. Of course I grab any word that slightly resembles what I'm after; I gesticulate; and I persist. At this point I'm getting a real hunger for the future and the past tense, but I haven't braved it yet.

The real reason for Mina's rally, however, was probably the fact that she had found a part-time job, arranged through the offices of Raymond Fosdick. Although she complained about the nature of the assignment and the fact that it kept her from her own writing, it satisfied her desire to be productive, to earn money, and to be independent.

As for work . . . I have this rewriting job. But what a pain. I try to devote most of my afternoon to it (Don gets home at 4:00) but it is so awful. An assistant pastor's recollections of his experiences at Riverside Church—badly written and permeated with that sort of limp and pallid good will which one associates with assistant ministers in Protestant churches. I have done very little except read it and stew over the impossibility of making anything decent out of it. But we will need the money. I think one of the things that has been weighing me down is the feeling of pressure—self-inflicted, of course—in connection with my own writing. But with marketing, sight-seeing, and this afternoon job, I haven't the time. Several times, I have sat down and said, "Now be creative. You have exactly two hours." But nothing comes. The only thing I have felt like doing was—it's sort of funny—writing little rhymes that would go in an alphabet book for a child. I don't know what on earth started me on that, but each day I take a letter and think of something to write a few lines about. It gives me that sort of refreshed, tender feeling I have felt on occasions with young children. I think I got the impulse to do it from seeing the Raphael galleries at the Vatican. The walls are decorated with what they call "Grotesque"—delicately painted patterns with all sorts of flowers, fruit, leaves, birds, fantastic animals, arabesques, candelabra, etc. . . . There is a charm and strangeness about them that I associate with children.

Mina's desire to write rhymes for children was perhaps not as odd as she thought. She loved children. Each of her letters to Priscilla ended with special love for Priscilla and Alan's first child, Mia, and Priscilla had just informed Mina that she was expecting her second child. Mina was devoted to her niece, Mina Jeanne; she sent her notes and presents and referred to her at least once in every letter home. Furthermore, she was giving much thought to whether she and Don would have children. Priscilla had written to Mina that she and Alan were considering naming their second child, if it were a boy, Damon. Mina responded that Damon "is in itself a beautiful name" but was concerned that the child's contemporaries might shorten it. "Now what will happen to Damon?" she wondered.

I have come upon two names I like very much, but perhaps they are a bit irregular. Troy, and Cam. Also Mark, but then I may use that myself someday if I can swing Donald over to a new point of view! (Don't mean to put it all on his shoulders—I'm sort of betwixt and between and I can't see it until we get financially more secure.)

Mina still found time to read. She informed Priscilla that she had read much of Hemingway, liking him because "his prose was spare and clean, and his sentiments undecorative." Next, she "took up Virginia Woolf and read her essays in *The Common Reader* and *Mrs. Dalloway*. But that was all for medicinal reasons. Now I am getting functional. Finished last night Pater's *Renaissance*—and found it extremely helpful and stimulating. Have been reading a good history of Rome, and another book on art."

Mina's Italian was improving slowly, but she wondered what she would do with much of the vocabulary she was learning in her class: "fish hook, fig tree, pen knife, mouse, ant, etc. But still don't know how to say 'Quit pushing, you big baboon,' or [having overcome her reluctance to make references to the Rockefeller's wealth] 'Who do you think I am—Rockefeller?'"

Shortly before Priscilla Brandt learned that she was pregnant with her second child (a boy, whom she named Damon), she wrote a long confessional letter to Mina expressing a deep dissatisfaction with her life, in particular the fact that she had done so little with her acting training. Priscilla's doubts were fueled, in large part, by the fact that Patricia Neal, a fellow classmate of Mina and Priscilla at Northwestern, was enjoying enormous success on Broadway.

Mina responded to Priscilla with sensitivity and concern; the letter reflects as much about Mina's perception of her own situation as it does about Priscilla's. Mina was thirty-one years old at the time, and it is clear from her response to Priscilla that she, too, had given much thought to her future. Her advice to Priscilla reflects a deep understanding of what could be accomplished if one realized that success in any field begins in the recognition that dissatisfaction is a "necessary prelude" to any work worth doing. Mina's primary purpose in writing to Priscilla was to comfort her best friend, but it is evident that she had recognized her own lack of "essential boldness"; the letter served not only as an admonition to Priscilla to recognize her talents and use them but as a declaration of what Mina intended to do with her own life as well. The writing itself is exquisite, an example of her prodigious talent—talent that, as a result of her own lack of "essential boldness," had thus far been kept hidden: first in the choice of a master's thesis topic most likely suggested by an adviser who could use the information for his own research; next in the failure to demand recognition for her contribution to the Rockefeller biography and, at the time this letter was written, in undertaking the task of rewriting the "limp and pallid" recollections of an assistant pastor in order to supplement her and Don's income.

Dearest Priscilla,

I am sorry to have delayed so long in answering your letter—a part of the time I was in bed with a cold and the rest of the time I guess I have been trying to sandwich in household duties, sight-seeing, family correspondence, and a little work on the manuscript I am supposed to be rewriting. I expected to have a great deal of free time this year, but instead it seems to be cluttered with innumerable little tasks.

I have been going through something of the same mood that you describe in your letter—the feeling as you say, that the days are closing in and the big decision hasn't yet been made. I have tried to understand what is at the root of this anxiety—whether it is founded on some sort of legitimate need, or simply a vague, destructive way of treating one's general dissatisfaction with the world and oneself. Certainly it has been a persistent ghost with us both, this conviction within us that we ought to be doing something beyond what we are doing, that there should be more unity to our efforts, and more direction. Instead our energies are splattered over innumerable projects and responsibilities—

almost all of them important and rewarding, but none of them ever quite satisfying that deep desire for "a place in the sun," perhaps, or more accurately, for some modest little channel through which one can communicate, with skill and form, his own impression of reality. To the extent that we desire this sort of communication, that we long to share our own impression of the world, and that we desire to do it through some more formal medium than the everyday associations of life provide—I think our dissatisfaction is legitimate and, in fact, a necessary prelude to any work of art no matter how small or how grand. I am sure that this is a very large part of your own motivation and that in undergoing these periods of anxiety you suffer as an artist, not simply as a neurotic.

But, to quote our friend Thomas Gray: "Full many a gem of purest ray serene / The dark unfathom'd caves of ocean bear: / Full many a flower is born to blush unseen, / And waste its sweetness on the desert air." So much more is needed besides the temperament. The craft must be learned, and there must be a current of values and ideas that are stimulating to the artist, and there must be an audience. Even Emily Dickinson—the greatest recluse of them all—wrote for a small audience of friends and thirsted after their encouragement, and then she wrote, quite self-consciously, for posterity. In acting, of course, the audience must exist physically in one place at a specific time—and that complicates matters horribly. But it is a problem of circumstance and can be dealt with more easily than others. As I think back on our long friendship and try to analyze objectively your talents, I would say that on matters of creative sensibility, dramatic skill, and the necessary coordination of body and voice quality—you have superior ability. I think that beneath your feelings of inadequacy, you believe this too. But you lack boldness. You lack the kind of trust in your own abilities that can sustain the artist through all kinds of frustrations and can provide him with a kind of aggressive confidence that can even over-ride his shyness and his inclination to retreat under fire. I believe this is a terribly important quality, not only for its practical benefit, but also because it gives the artist more freedom to create and to get at the center of his own unique response to reality. You question, in your letter, whether you *can* act. I think you are asking the wrong question. Of course you can act—and with a kind of sensitivity and delicacy that Pat[ricia Neal] will never have. You know yourself that countless actors and actresses have gone much farther on far less. But you betray your own gifts by not believing in them, and like children whose parents reject them, your gifts recoil into the shadows of your consciousness, restricted and inhibited. Your concern over the "lush" party and your feeling that you were unable to summon up a conversation are, I think, peripheral matters that would automatically be solved if you were functioning in your own craft. Brilliant or profound conversation is one kind of creative activity; that it may not be yours, any more than oil painting or trapeze artistry, is of no great importance, *providing* your own channel of expression is not closed up.

I firmly believe that if you had the boldness that your talent deserves, the other difficulties could be overcome. If you could somehow put aside the question, "Do I or do I not have the ability?" and accept as a matter of faith that you do and then grapple with practicalities—how to study, with whom, what to try for, how to go about it, etc., treating your talent like some precocious child who only needs an opportunity. Like a child, too, it will misbehave at times and refuse to perform at others, but that is no justification for you to put it out for adoption. Success has no predictable pattern. Some flower late and others early; some are prodigal with their gifts, and others invest them with fastidious care; some are bastards and some are saints; some glance only the surface of reality, and some plunge deep into its center. But success is not rationed and for every sensibility that gains enough freedom to express itself in the universal forms of art, there is an eager audience. You have not made the picture big enough and you have made yourself too small.

I am not trying to be didactic. It is only that I have the same problem and am trying to grapple with it also. There are rational explanations for why we lack this essential boldness, and we have both delved sufficiently into our childhoods to know in at least a general way what they are, and no human being is free all the time from the blight of insecurity. But there is much that can be done, I believe. You speak of the necessity for action—and I think this is a sound impulse. To begin doing something, even if it is not terribly exciting.

I hasten to add that I do not think the solution of this particular problem assures one of happiness. Great artists have often been miserable human beings—not, I think, because they were artists, but because they failed to solve their other dilemmas as well as the particular problem of creative expression. You and I are both fortunate in having done so well in the choice of husbands—that is the key relationship. Isn't it amazing that we get a whole other human being for ourselves? But then one's contentment is measured, I suppose, by the number of knots and wrinkles he is able to iron out of his psyche, and the problem of a profession happens to be one of your knots. If you never solve it, life will not be wretched—only streaked with these days, and sometimes weeks, of restlessness and dissatisfaction. But it seems to me that the chances of your solving it are too good to be missed. The years have brought you much more confidence than you once had, and I see no reason why that should not already be reflected in your work. I hope you will begin to act right away in faith. It is very hard to persuade someone that God exists if you do not believe it yourself.

I hope this letter does not sound like the assistant pastor at River-side Church. I have thought much about what I wanted to say and I have written it in an attitude of genuine concern that you waste no more time conjecturing upon your abilities. I believe and have always believed in your ability as an actress, as have many others. It is a matter of faith, my fair skeptic, and from that will spring the works. Oh dear, I do sound like the pastor.

More, in a later letter, about our lives. Meanwhile, my love to Alan and a spurt of faith to you.

Love, Mina

Mina's next letter was less optimistic, perhaps because, as she explained to Priscilla, she had just finished reading the second volume of Ernest Jones's biography of Freud:

I agree completely with what you say about striving vs. struggling, and I liked the little poem. These things I have believed for a long time, but oh the lag between reason and action. Striving is perhaps an almost instinctive struggle that man makes toward self-fulfillment, and struggling is what he does when he is afraid of himself or others. But one cannot change motives ass-backwards—forgive the expression—but has to dig deep to find what feeds the motives and once having found the hidden springs there is a chance for change. . . . How I sympathize with Milton's Lucifer when after all his titanic struggles, he finally reaches earth only to discover that he has brought his hell with him. So it seems to me, that while each year has brought me new insights and perhaps a kind of wisdom, the effect of this upon my life as a whole has been simply to change the patterns of my neuroses but not the neuroses themselves. I play the same record, but now on high fidelity! And yet I cannot complain too severely. I manage to maintain a daily equilibrium in the midst of all the paradoxes and imperfections, and I sustain the fundamental relationships with a certain degree of maturity. I function, in other words, like a fairly normal body with its quota of weaknesses and imperfections.

Mina *had* finally "grappled with the practicalities" in terms of her writing career, as she had advised Priscilla to do in terms of her acting career, and in the same letter, she informed Priscilla of the results:

I received word two days ago that I had been awarded a scholarship to the Salzburg Seminar for its session (one month) on writing and publishing in the U.S. It is a seminar designed to introduce European intellectuals to various aspects of American culture—economics, publishing history, etc. and it has a series of seminars, each devoted to one of these subjects. For each session there are specialists who come as lecturers—among them in the past were Professor Billington, [Henry Steele] Commager, Saul Bellow, John Ciardi, Randall Jarrell, Alfred Kazin, Karl Shapiro, Edmund Wilson, etc. The session on writing begins this Sunday and I leave this Saturday for a month. I shall be in Dwight Macdonald's seminar on magazine writing and am looking forward to it immensely. Then too, since only three Americans are allowed to come, it means I shall be meeting some interesting Europeans; the competition for scholarships among them is fairly stiff so there should be a good selection.

In addition, in another letter, Mina informed Priscilla that she had submitted an essay to *The New Yorker,* but she exhibited little confidence in the piece. Mina assumed that "they must be sending the rejection slip by boat," and although Raymond Fosdick had promised that he would "give it a boost" if she submitted it to *Harpers,* she no longer thought it was very good. (Mina would never be published in *The New Yorker,* but shortly before her death, an article describing her work at City College; her book, *Errors and Expectations;* and an award she received, a proclamation from President Carter, was published in the magazine.)

While Mina was in Salzburg, she decided to travel to Yugoslavia for a weekend to visit the town from which her grandfather, Rado Pendo, had emigrated. The Pendo cousins gave her a warm welcome, preparing a feast in her honor and photographing her in a traditional Croatian costume that they had provided. Although none of Mina's letters to her parents from this period have survived, Ruby and Albert saved the pictures that she sent from Yugoslavia. George remembers that Albert was proud and pleased that she had taken the time to visit his relatives and that they had been so gracious to her. (Years later, Mina would recall for her colleagues at City College an incident that occurred on the train. She was trying to communicate with a priest whom she had met on the train, and when they made a stop at Dubrovnik, Mina said, in rather formal Italian, "I don't know where I am going." "Don't be anxious, my child," the priest replied, "neither does anyone else.")

The Salzburg Seminar itself, however, was not what Mina had expected. Apparently, the "interesting Europeans" turned out to have far less interest in American culture than in listening to themselves talk. She enjoyed meeting Dwight Macdonald and found him most amusing, particularly his farewell address—offered after he had a few drinks—when he told a room full of foreign "intellectuals" that he had long looked forward to meeting the best and the brightest that Europe had to offer. "And I still do," he said. (Mina did not maintain contact with Macdonald after the seminar, but many years later, in one of those odd reversals of position and fortune, they would again meet. When she was at the height of her career at the City University of New York, some friends of Macdonald, whose heavy drinking and outspokenness had alienated him from the editors and publishers for whom he had written for many years, managed to get him a full-time teaching position at John Jay College of Criminal Justice, a division of CUNY.)

In June 1956, shortly before Don and Mina were scheduled to return to the United States, the biography of Rockefeller, entitled *John D. Rockefeller, Jr.: A Portrait,* was published to good reviews. Priscilla mentioned the book in one of her letters to Mina, apparently making a reference to Raymond Fosdick being listed as the sole author. "It was perhaps not completely just to minimize my part in the book," Mina replied, but it was as much my fault as his, and now it does not loom terribly important to me, and I hope it doesn't to him. . . . At any rate, for your information—and in confidence—I wrote chapters I, II, III, IV, VIII, (oh yes, the courtship and marriage section in Chapter V), IX, a good part of X which was softened and somewhat altered by RBF[osdick], XI, XV, XVI, XVII, XVIII.

Mina had written half of the book, but she did not demand attribution because of her sense of fair play. She had been hired by Raymond as a research assistant, and he had every intention at the outset of writing up the material she gathered—one could hardly blame him for the fact that she presented the material in the form of polished prose; the Rockefeller Foundation had given him—not Mina—the grant to author the book. In Mina's mind, a deal was a deal.

No matter what she believed (or how she rationalized), however, it turned out to be a bad deal for Mina in terms of employment. When she returned to New York, she applied for scores of college-level teaching positions. Had she been able to identify herself as the co-author of the biography of one of the most prominent and wealthy men in the world, a biography published by Harper & Brothers, she may very likely have had an edge over those other applicants. As it was, the only job she could find when she returned was that of an editor at McGraw Hill—she was hired, no doubt, precisely because of the "research" and "editing" she had done on the Rockefeller biography. In this instance, Mina was exhibiting the same lack of boldness for which she had so gently upbraided Priscilla.

And Mina—like Priscilla—was not concentrating on her art: "Instead," she had written, "our energies are splattered over innumerable projects and responsibilities." She had been unable to concentrate on her own writing in Italy because so much of her time was being spent on the Riverside Church project, an assignment she undertook for no other reason than her need for income. Mina's financial situation was certainly not as bad as her year in Wheaton when she ate Jello three times a day, but it was bad enough to sap her creative energy. She would eventually benefit from these circumstances, however. "The craft must be learned," she had written to Priscilla. Mina was learning her craft thoroughly and well: in addition to the writing courses she had taught at Shelton College, she had participated fully in the research and writing of a major biography; she had converted the Riverside Church memoirs into readable prose; she would spend five years at McGraw Hill, responsible not only for the editing of major books but for training and overseeing other editors. Few if any basic writing teachers entering the field when Mina did in the mid-sixties (or even today, for that matter) had such thorough training in their craft—even, or perhaps one should say *especially,* those with a Ph.D.

In one of the last letters Mina wrote to Priscilla before she and Don began their Atlantic crossing, she described their evolution, or as she termed it, "a conversion" to Italy. It was a conversion that would have pleased Henry James.

We have gone through all the stages: the initial disillusionment, the dysentery, the disgust, and then gradually the conversion—to what, it's hard to articulate. Rome didn't bend an inch for us; it didn't seem to care, or else it cared the way some grand indiscriminate goddess would, quite oblivious to the thousands of strangers who have come to seek her out. We bent instead and I think we changed. I only know that we feel a kind of warmth for Rome and for Italy which we have not felt for our own native cities.

Mina and Don vowed to return to Italy someday, but for the moment, finances were their main concern. "We shall be broke when we get back and will have to start all over earning money," Mina explained to Priscilla. Don had decided to "abandon the academic camp" and look for a position with the State Department. She would try to "get some work right away." Although Mina and Donald Shaughnessy had fallen in love with Italy after all, they were ready to go home. Home, they had decided, was New York, and although Don would live for years at a time out of the country while working for the State Department, and although there was still an occasional mention of building a home in South Dakota, New York was where Mina would spend the rest of her life.

CHAPTER THREE

Experience and Dedication

Soon after Mina and Donald Shaughnessy returned to New York on August 30, 1956, they rented an apartment on the Upper East Side, at One Gracie Terrace (not far from the official residence of the mayor of New York City). Within months, they both found jobs: Don teaching history courses at Columbia University, Mina at McGraw Hill, where she would remain for five years. McGraw Hill's employee newsletter described her position as that of "supervisor of editorial training and assistant to the editor-in-chief, Editing Department, Book Company."

Although Mina continued to apply for college-level teaching positions, she was happy at McGraw Hill. Her work was time consuming and demanding, but that was precisely the type of work she preferred. She often brought work home from the office to meet deadlines. One suspects that she learned a lot not just about writing, but about writers. Similar to her work rewriting the memoirs of the assistant pastor, Mina was editing (read "rewriting") the prose of people who were widely known and respected in their fields but whose writing skills were exceedingly weak or who were unwilling to devote the time and energy necessary to produce readable prose. Ten years later, when more and more underprepared students began to enroll in college, critics of Open Admissions, both in and out of academia, declared that these students did not belong in college because they could not write. Mina would know better when she began to teach and later to direct programs for these students: for five years, she edited the writing of some of the most prominent scientists and engineers in their respective fields. If they could not write well after having attended the best universities

Photograph taken by McGraw Hill to be used in its company newsletter, 1957. Courtesy of George Pendo.

in the country, why should students who had just graduated from some of the worst high schools in the country be expected to have adequate writing skills upon entering college?

Mina liked her co-workers, but she liked the position at McGraw Hill for another reason as well: it gave her an opportunity to read and learn in many fields. "The book I'm working on now is a psychology book," she wrote to her mother in April 1958. "It is called Developmental Psychology [and] traces the human being from birth through old age and discusses the various influences and problems associated with each of the major periods. Should be quite informative." Although Mina complained in the same letter that she was "struggling through the long and involved bibliography, trying to see that commas and periods are in the right places," Priscilla Brandt remembers that Mina found the topics of most of the books she edited informative and interesting, and she often referred to them in conversation. "Mina had always loved to be a student, and this was the next best thing to going back to the classroom."

Priscilla also recalls that Mina was finally feeling financially secure, "after years and years of struggling and worrying." In fact, Mina and Don could now afford to send small gifts of money to Ruby Pendo, and this pleased Mina, who was terribly worried about her mother.

Soon after Mina returned from Italy, she visited her parents and was able to see for herself the enormous amount of work and financial investment required to run a ranch. She realized that her mother, miles away from her friends in Lead, needed to get away from the ranch and that she would enjoy intellectual stimulation. Mina encouraged her mother to take a course at Black Hills State College and even left a check so that she would not use finances as a reason not to register. When Ruby informed her that she did not have time to take the course, Mina insisted that she keep the check anyway.

Mina knew that Ruby had made an enormous sacrifice in moving to the ranch, for Albert's sake. She was away from her friends, those women in Lead with whom she had played bridge and attended church functions for so many years. Furthermore, the weather was brutally cold in the winter, and the roads were often impassable because of snow. By this time, Don's relationship with Albert had begun to cool, but he and Mina sent little gifts of money to Ruby with practically every letter—including on one occasion a five-dollar bill to be used to replace the tubes in the television set. At about this time, the Pendos had a telephone installed at the ranch, at Mina's insistence, and with the agreement that Mina and Don would pay for it. However, the concept of "long distance" was still so new (and expensive) that she only called her parents on special occasions. In 1977, Mina noted in an interview about basic writing:

> It sometimes occurs to me that maybe the telephone wasn't such a good invention. So much is done orally in today's society. People used to write so many notes to communicate with each other by the written word. Even if they weren't very skilled at it, at least they did it. Or there is the person who can be called upon to write the condolence letter or some kind of formal ritual message. I found even in my personal life, now that telephones are available, I write home much less than I used to. Also, I know much less about what is going on at home because you communicate a very different kind of information when you have access to letters.

In fact, the letter quoted below, dated December 16, 1958, is one of the last letters that Ruby saved from Mina as their use of the telephone increased. The only other letters that exist fall into that "formal ritual" category, written to mark special occasions.

Mina was often frustrated with the quality of information she obtained through telephone calls to her mother. It was not so much a "different kind of information" but a *lack* of information. Ruby simply never adjusted to the telephone: she was uncomfortable with it; she resented the lack of privacy—they shared a party line; and as George remembers, she could never countenance "the expense of it." Furthermore, Ruby was quiet by nature, as was George. (Mina was more like her father, who was outgoing and talkative.) Frequently, after a frustrating conversation with her mother in which Mina would be able to get information about the weather or about old friends and neighbors but not about her parents' health or financial situation, she would call George at his home in an attempt to get more information or clarification. "George was little help," his wife, Norma, recalls. "He was as taciturn as his mother on the phone." Often Norma would have to get on the line to assure Mina that her parents were fine.

Mina made a special effort—whether in writing or on the telephone—to provide her mother with detailed and amusing descriptions of her life in New York because she knew that such descriptions delighted Ruby. Donald Shaughnessy had made some important political contacts through his work at Columbia and had become acquainted with Henry R. and Clare Boothe Luce. In December 1958, Mina wrote a six-page letter to her mother, describing in great detail an evening she spent with Mrs. Luce, wondering "where one goes on the social ladder after he has dined with the Luces!" "You will be wondering about our social weekend. Friday evening . . . we had dinner with Mrs. Luce (he had to be in Detroit). It was quite an exciting affair." Mina described, for her mother's benefit, the color of the walls and carpets in each room, the menu, the quality of the service, even the silver and china. Ever the clotheshorse, Mina paid particular attention to Mrs. Luce's clothing and jewelry, particularly her pearls:

She has a fair, clear skin and penetrating blue eyes and grey-white hair. She was wearing a black silk dress with a cape effect in the back. A double strand of pearls—beautiful, limpid things that sort of glowed. She had large diamond earrings and a matching diamond pin, and an enormous garnet (I think) ring surrounded by diamonds. Despite all the jewelry, the over-all effect was one of simplicity, and she was quite easy to talk with.

Mina explained that they talked for hours about politics (a topic about which Don was "a natural"), until she realized that it was already midnight:

Mrs. Luce told us to stay a few more minutes, but I was certain she must be tired. . . . So we said goodnight. Somehow she seemed lonely, and despite her charm and wealth, I felt somehow sorry for her. She has no children or family, of course, and perhaps that is why. She had a daughter who would be about my age, but she was killed in a car accident about ten years ago. When we left I went to shake hands with her and instead she kissed me on the cheek and said, "Good night, child." Sad, don't you think?

In an almost unconscious contrast, Mina went on to describe her full schedule for the next few days: theater on Christmas eve with the Fosdicks, Christmas dinner with Priscilla and Alan, lunch with the secretary with whom Mina had worked on the Rockefeller biography, a possible trip to Washington, D.C., with Don, another dinner the next weekend, but "nothing ambitious." Mina may very well have been contemplating the circumstances of her own life at this time: her relationship with Don was changing—they were growing farther apart, and earlier that year, she had undergone a hysterectomy at Columbia Presbyterian Hospital after the discovery of precancerous cells.

As a result of her hysterectomy, Mina and Don did not have to decide whether they would have children. Priscilla Brandt remembers that Mina's doctor told her that she could probably have one child and then have the surgery performed, but Mina was too afraid to wait. At about this time, Priscilla recalls, there was talk of adoption, but Mina was "the one who was anxious to proceed, not Don."

Mina's marriage to Donald Shaughnessy was not developing into a relationship of trust and friendship, and she realized at this time that she did not want to be financially dependent on her husband. Betty Fosdick remembers that even though she and Mina trusted each other implicitly, Mina was discreet and circumspect when talking about her marriage. Her natural sense of reserve and privacy would allow her only to say, even to close friends, that her marriage "wasn't disastrous, it just wasn't successful."

For the next twenty years, friends and acquaintances would wonder why Mina and Don did not get a divorce, and some of them have suggested possible explanations. Mina's background certainly contributed to her decision: George Pendo and Betty Fosdick believe that she was raised in a time and in a tradition when people simply did not get divorced. Others believe that during the early sixties, a period during which Don was unable to find work, Mina was reluctant to get a divorce out of a sense of loyalty. Then, when he found a satisfying and challenging position with the State Department, he was stationed in other countries for extended periods of time—sometimes for as long as four years—and this arrangement seemed to suit them both. Mina once described her relationship with Don to a colleague as one in which "we had separate interests and followed different paths." Given her admiration for the work of Henry James, one could make comparisons between Isabel Archer's behavior in *The Portrait of a Lady* and Mina's behavior: Mina preferred to keep the problems that existed in her relationship with her husband to herself, and she refused to view the situation as an insurmountable tragedy.

Mina's inability to have children, coupled with her decision to "have separate interests and follow separate paths" from her husband, are crucial factors, however, in any consideration of her motives and performance as a teacher and writer and in the influence she would have at City College and at CUNY during the period of Open Admissions. Everyone who met or worked with her expressed amazement at her ability to work so hard, with such dedication and without the least resentment of the time and energy she devoted, until she had completed a particular assignment or project. Her work was the central focus of her life.

Mina had learned to work very hard as a child; as an adult, her work would become a source of enormous satisfaction to her. Her work as a teacher and as a writer became the outlet through which she could express her creativity and intelligence. And as a teacher and later as an administrator, Mina would finally develop the kind of trust in her own abilities about which she had written to Priscilla, "the kind of trust that can sustain the artist through all kinds of frustrations and can provide him with a kind of aggressive confidence that can even over-ride his shyness and his inclination to retreat under fire." The domestic arrangement—including the happy housewife and mother scenario—that she had referred to in letters to her mother and to Priscilla early in her marriage was no longer a viable alternative. Mina began to develop and to exhibit a strong sense of independence and an even stronger ambition to succeed. In fact, it was at this time that she asked Clare Boothe Luce for permission to write her biography. Although Luce declined, for reasons of privacy, it was clear that Mina had overcome her shyness and "inclination to retreat."

In fact, Mina's confidence in herself developed to such a degree that by the time she became the director of the Instructional Resource Center of CUNY in the mid-seventies, her friends and associates had nicknamed her "The Countess" because she demanded, and got, almost everything her students needed. "She was the countess of our teaching," Irving Howe once explained, "the aristocrat of our egalitarianism" (2).

As a fifteen-year-old girl, Mina had written to her parents the night before a declamatory contest: "Oh how I do want to win." But she knew she would have many other opportunities. Now, however, Mina was thirty-four years old and had come to terms with the fact that, for all practical purposes, she was on her own. She was acutely conscious that her parents were aging; even if she wanted to, she could not turn to them. Furthermore, she did not want them to know the extent of her alienation from her husband. George Pendo remembers that when Mina visited, more and more often without Donald, she "made it seem as if everything was just fine," and it was not until the mid-seventies, after her mother's death, that Mina would bring another man with her on one of her visits to the ranch.

In 1961, Mina finally found her entry into academia. It was, however, through the back door. She resigned from McGraw Hill to teach composition and literature courses at Hunter College. The position was only part time, and it was in the General Studies division where classes met in the late afternoon and evening. Betty Fosdick remembers that Mina would meet with her students after class and sometimes not get home until after 11 p.m. Betty also remembers that this was the beginning of "Mina's blue period," because "she would arrive each weekend at our house in Connecticut and spend hours and hours grading the stacks of essays written in those ubiquitous blue books."

In addition, at this time Mina embarked on another freelance writing project with Raymond Fosdick, with whom she had worked on the Rockefeller biography. The Rockefeller family had donated $325 million over a sixty-year period to a fund called The General Education Board. Much of the funding had been used to improve schools in the South, particularly the schools whose student population, because of segregation, was African American. The trustees of the program asked Raymond to write a history of the board, and he described Mina's help on the project in his introduction: "For a period of months, I was able to secure the assistance of Mrs. Mina Shaughnessy who visited various educational centers in the South and whose penetrating comments gave fresh perspective and enabled me to bring the story up to date" (ix). The book, entitled *Adventure in Giving: The Story of the General Education Board,* was published in 1962. This project earned no more fame or recognition for Mina than the Rockefeller biography had. However, the information and insight she gained about the history of education for blacks in the South and about trends in educational practices and policies would prove invaluable when she joined the faculty at City College and was placed in charge of the Open Admissions program. She already knew what had worked—and what had not—in the education of generations of minority students in the United States.

While at Hunter, Mina encountered what can be described as the "first wave" of underprepared students—almost a dress rehearsal for what she would face six years later when she joined City College. The General Studies program admitted students who would not necessarily have been admitted to the daytime degree-granting programs whose students were mostly white, middle-class New Yorkers with high school averages of 85 percent or above. As a result, Mina came to know, for the first time, those "nontraditional" students whose numbers would swell by the end of the decade. While many of the students who would later attend City College when she began her work there in 1967 were members of minority groups, most of the "underprepared" students whom she taught at Hunter beginning in 1961 were of Italian and Irish descent—the children of laborers, factory workers, and civil service employees. When critics of Open Admissions made a connection between race and skills, Mina knew better. When she described her students in the introduction to *Errors and Expectations* as "strangers in academia," she was referring of course to the students with whom she had worked at City College, but she had gotten to know these "strangers," even though very few of them were members of minority groups, six years earlier in her evening classes at Hunter College (3).

It was also at Hunter College where Mina had her first exposure to the resistance of many academicians to the right of underprepared students to attend college. During her time at Hunter teaching writing to students whom she would later identify as "basic writers," she worked with Gerald Willen, a professor in the English department, and developed a close friendship with him. However, on the subject of basic writing, Willen reflected an attitude that Mina would encounter hundreds—perhaps even thousands—of times during her career. "Quite frankly," Willen recalls, "Mina and I didn't agree professionally on what it was that she was doing":

> The crux of our disagreement was that I never did feel . . . that remedial work should be done in a four-year college. My pitch to Mina was that remedial work was certainly necessary. Mina thought that it could be done in four-year colleges without any harm being done to their educational objectives. . . .
>
> We never came to blows over the issue, and certainly it didn't affect our friendship. If anything, it was something that we would kid each other about.

Willen's argument was one that Mina would hear again and again from faculty, both at Hunter and at City College. She would describe the proponents of this argument in *Errors and Expectations* as "teachers unready in mind and heart" (3) to face their students, but at the time she began to teach at Hunter, it was difficult for her to balance the needs of her students—and her conviction that they were capable of doing the work—with her desire to be accepted in an academic institution. As a result, she played down her dedication to these underprepared students and kept her observations about them to herself. "I never knew very much about the nature of her work," Willen recalls; "whenever I asked, she said I wouldn't be terribly interested."

Nor was Mina prepared at this time to abandon the more traditional concerns and interests of an English instructor. She wanted a full-time position at Hunter College, and she knew that she would have a far better chance to obtain one if she exhibited an interest in literature rather than an interest in students who, according to many faculty members, were damaging the reputation of Hunter College. Mina succeeded in balancing her priorities. She spent hours and hours of her own time working with her students, but she also submitted essays about literature to academic journals. In addition, she began to write poems during this period, and she continued to do so for the rest of her life—Donald Shaughnessy found more than forty poems among her papers after she died. She did not date most of her poems; therefore, it is difficult to determine precisely when each was written, but one can speculate in many instances on the basis of the topic itself. (One can assume, for instance, that "Returning to New York from San Juan" was written after Mina and Don spent two weeks there in January 1962.)

Mina knew that she had to play the publish-or-perish game, and many of the poems she wrote at this time were about suitably serious and literary topics. She wrote two exquisite poems about Milton, for example, one of which was published, but her students—and their struggles—were making their way into her poems as well. "Evening schools are not for winnowing," was the title she gave to the following poem:

> They are a way of reviving the spirits of those
> who would otherwise be staring at blank walls.
> They make chinks in the walls through which the
> untalented, the unlucky, the maimed can look.
> Occasionally a student of talent and persistence
> will break through but generally there is no such
> melodrama, merely those glimpses into a green land.
> A jazz musician, burned out at 19, falls in love
> with Daisy Miller; a subway conductor reads Words-
> worth on the night shift; a blond receptionist with
> silver eyelids and frosted lips weeps when she
> hears T.S. Eliot's poetry read in class.
>   And there was that mountain of a girl—
> let me call her Miss Schlapfel—with the most
> remarkable gift for misspelling I have ever
> encountered. . . . [poet's ellipsis]

Miss Schlapfel appears once again in another poem and finds a happy ending in the second stanza:

> But one night as she steered that awesome bulk
> Across the creaking desert of the floor,
> She stopped, or teetered, at the classroom door

And fumbling shyly through literary names
Blurted out with love, "I sure am hooked on James!"

In 1964, having taught part time at Hunter for more than three years, Mina accepted an offer to teach full time at Hofstra University, a four-year private college in Hempstead, Long Island. This new position would entail a ninety-minute commute from Manhattan to Long Island, but the inconvenience was worth it: finally, she would be a full-fledged member of an English department, with a day schedule—she would even have her own office. Mina continued to teach part time at Hunter in the evening for another two years, however, in the hope that, even without a Ph.D., her fine reputation would have an impact on the selection process and she would be offered a full-time job there.

At Hofstra, Mina taught freshman composition, advanced writing, advanced grammar, and a course entitled Sophomore Survey, and she worked as hard as she had at Hunter and at Shelton. She enjoyed the collegiality at Hofstra and made many friends. Here Mina first met Alice Trillin, whose husband, Calvin Trillin, would later achieve great recognition as a writer. Alice and Mina had the same relationship at Hofstra, and later at City College, that Mina and Priscilla had had at Northwestern and during their early years in New York. Alice was as beautiful and as intelligent as Mina, and they shared a deep concern for their students. In fact, it was Alice who had obtained a grant from the Samuel Rubin Foundation to set up a program called "Project NOAH" at Hofstra. Through this project, both Alice and Mina were able to tutor minority students. Alice recalls that when she and Mina would drive back to Manhattan at the end of the day, "we often talked about the 'patterns' of mistakes the students seemed to make, and about how interesting it was to tutor these students." And in Alice, Mina also found a fellow clotheshorse: they would browse in stores for hours on end, sampling perfume and trying on clothes. Like Priscilla Brandt, Alice Trillin would become one of Mina's closest friends.

It was also at Hofstra that Mina met Marilyn French, who would later earn wide fame over the publication of *The Women's Room*. Their friendship deepened quickly: in Marilyn, Mina found not only a good friend in whom she could confide, she found an intellectual much like herself. They spent much time together (particularly, Mina noted in one of her letters to Marilyn French, on "the long, vacant ride home

on the good old Long Island Rail Road"), read each other's unpublished work, talked endlessly about literature, and discussed the possibility of co-writing a textbook about Shakespeare's works. French was
one of the few persons to whom Mina showed her poems in draft form.
Her poetry was never as accomplished as her prose, but like everything
else she did, she took it very seriously, revising over and over until she
achieved the precise meaning she intended. Mina's Hofstra students crept
into her poetry just as her Hunter College students had. She sent a copy
of "On Re-reading a Sophomore Report on Shakespeare's *Hamlet*" to
French, knowing that she would recognize her students—and herself—
in the poem:

> an arrow   a plumed hat   an awkward *caveat*
> a dusky skull   a leaky flask
> the deadly jawbone of an asp,
> each atom falls in special ways and   shapes
> a grapefruit   a giddy girl   a haughty race of Gauls
> is not the answer
>
> the ape moved to tears   godhead
> bears the weight of years upon the mount
> the bush   the lotus   the blooming
> of our shame   a burst of sour trum-
> pets,
> all the same
> is not the answer
>
> ether and ore   we strut upon the floor
> with inclination and obsession
> whether/or   this cruel profession
> defies the law of rarity
> is not the answer
>
> dare I   dare we   oppose
> assault a cloud of atoms
> to be   a what?   a shroud?
> and end up like my old man?
> it's out of the question.

It was during this time that Mina wrote "Reason under the Ailan-thus," an essay describing the protagonist in *Washington Square,* and her behavior and relationship with her father and with her suitor. Mina's title was an intended allusion to O'Neill's *Desire under the Elms* (but she would later tell a friend that no one but she had ever figured that out). The essay was published in 1967 in a collection entitled *A Critical Edi-tion of Henry James' Washington Square,* edited by Gerald Willen at Hunter and published by Crowell. The essay offers a sound and interesting in-terpretation, particularly of the behavior and motivation of the two male characters, and it even includes a reference to Milton's Eve. But the essay is interesting for another reason. One can see, through Mina's disappointment in Catherine's character and behavior, her preference for another type of character—and for another type of life. "Perhaps then the simplicity James objected to in *Washington Square* was more than technical," Mina observed:

> Perhaps it came from a barrenness in the material itself, from the absence of some fine exuberance or vitality that would give even Catherine a real brush with life. James gave us a novel about a place, as his title suggests, but not about people *living* in that place. Patience, duty, reason—these are ways of controlling and ordering life. What we want—and what James would provide in the sensibilities of his "richer" heroines and in the setting of older cities—is the encoun-ter of heroic characters with the force, the allure, the risk of life it-self. (252)

Mina's attraction for James's later female characters reflects the deep-ening complexity that her own life was undergoing. George Pendo remembers that although Mina was still his best friend, he sensed that there were elements of her life which she kept to herself—not because she did not trust her family, but because she understood that they lacked the emotional and intellectual frame of reference needed to understand her life in New York and her unconventional relationship with her husband. "Mina would keep it simple when she came home," George recalls:

> She didn't want us to see that she had changed. She wanted us to be comfortable with her, and she was afraid that if she talked too much

about the people she was meeting, the places she was going, the books she was reading, her own writing, we would act differently toward her, and she wouldn't get to see us the way we really were. And that's primarily what she wanted when she came home: to return, just for a little while, to a very simple style of life.

Mina's desire to "keep it simple" at home was reflected in other ways as well. Although she was devoting large amounts of time to her poetry during this period, she did not share her poems with her family. Rather, she sent them copies of the children's stories that she was also beginning to write at this time, stories about gypsies and haunted houses and injured fawns, all of which were published under her maiden name in *The Golden Magazine,* a popular monthly children's magazine. Mina knew that her family would not know what to make of her poetry, particularly with the many references to Milton's and Shakespeare's and Chaucer's characters, but she knew they would understand her children's stories and could read them to her niece, Mina Jeanne.

Albert and Ruby Pendo's life on the ranch consisted of excruciatingly hard work, with very little relief. Knowing this, Mina did not want to seem too intellectual or cosmopolitan to her family. Ruby kept journals from 1955 until 1975, recording the family's activities and the many duties performed and purchases made to keep the ranch running. They were short jottings, made in pencil next to a date, often no more than one line long. The notations she made for five months in 1963, representative of her years on the ranch, indicate the stark contrast between Mina's life and that of her parents. There are entries indicating the days on which Ruby was called to substitute teach, entries mentioning six-foot snow drifts, entries indicating the depth to which Albert and George had dug for a new well (while Ruby went without water), entries indicating that the temperature had dropped to eighteen degrees below zero and remained there for days, and entries indicating the number of cows and calves that had been vaccinated on a particular day. The tenor of Ruby's life seems even more harsh when one realizes that, at the time she made those entries, she was sixty-seven years old.

During a visit that Mina made to South Dakota during the summer of 1966, she wrote the following description of her parents to Marilyn French:

Some of the buildings on the ranch in Spearfish, South Dakota. Courtesy of George Pendo.

My parents are well. Dad has a hard time with arthritis but he manages. Mom is not the pioneer type but I think she is perhaps stronger. When I am with them I have moments of almost complete well-being. I think at those moments we will never die and there will never be bad news. Then, at the moments when I see this cannot be, I am unspeakably sad. I am not home long enough to analyze their frailties—although I suppose I know them quite well.

It was during this visit that Albert and Ruby informed Mina that they had placed the title for the original 240 acres in her name. If she ever wanted to return home, she would have a place to come to. Mina and Don would occasionally talk about building a house on the property, but nothing ever came of it. She did talk about the property to her friends in New York, however; Janet Emig remembers that Mina would make sketches of the house she wanted to build when she retired, including the wide front porch that would face the Black Hills.

Mina never romanticized her parents' life on the ranch to her friends; in the same letter to Marilyn French, she described the ramshackle nature of the house and the patio:

I am sitting on the patio, but when I say that you will imagine the wrong thing—probably a cool modern brick affair looking out on the plains and cattle and cowboys. But this is a rather slap dash patio. I carried big stones for it for weeks one summer and then the cement mixer came and filled her up. And then it rained, rained, rained. And here it stands—or slants, rather—attached to a run-down house with cement on one side, shingles on another, and tarpaper on another. Inside it is clean and homey and without decor, has that miscellaneous quality, that clutter of lived-in places. The whole place is somewhat run-down. My father loves used, broken-down, discarded things. He likes to fix them up. But he lacks the time and the patience, and he is driven by a hundred visions of what he would like to do. Result: we have yards of junk. I have become fond of it.

But Mina also described for Marilyn French the magnificent surroundings she enjoyed on her visits:

Beyond this little spot of clutter is the land, stretching north in plains until you reach the bare mountains in North Dakota and rising in the south almost abruptly into hills thick with evergreens. I hike a great deal in the hills. Start out in the morning with a canteen and my lunch. Reach the high ridge by lunch, then follow the spine of some mountain until it leads me back home. And during those walks I seldom have a single thought. Wordsworth would be shattered.

Betty Fosdick remembers that each time Mina returned to New York from South Dakota, "it would take her awhile to readjust to New York. On each visit, she noticed that her parents were aging, and it worried her. She knew her mother was working too hard for her age, but she felt helpless to do anything about it."

In June 1966, when Albert Pendo was sixty-six years old, he was admitted to the hospital in Rapid City for prostate surgery, and the doctor ordered him to remain in the hospital for ten days. But "on the third day," Mina wrote to Marilyn French, "(he rose again from the dead and . . . .) he got up early, dressed, and announced to the doctor he was leaving. And did. He is doing well out of pure spite." Although Mina was able to joke about the incident in her letter, it actually upset

Mina pausing during a hike along the ridge above the ranch. Courtesy of Marilyn Maiz.

her so much that she called the doctor from New York to confirm that her father was okay. Not only had he checked himself out of the hospital seven days early, he had walked almost a mile from the hospital to George and Norma's house, where he announced that he needed to get back to work on the ranch.

Mina went home in August to see her father; his illness had made her even more sensitive to the possibility that each visit might be the last occasion on which she would see her mother or father. It was during this visit that Mina first suggested that she tape-record her father's anecdotes and memories about his life, particularly his childhood. "We took his stories for granted," George recalls, "because we heard them so frequently. But when Mina came home on visits, it was as if she was hearing them for the first time, and she wanted to preserve them. She never did get Father to sit down and talk into a recorder, but he seemed to like the idea. He was flattered that someone valued his experiences, and he loved to talk."

In September 1966, Mina returned to her full-time teaching position at Hofstra, but she did not continue to teach part time at Hunter. For two years, she had juggled a full daytime teaching schedule on Long Island while teaching one or two evening classes at Hunter in Manhattan. She was not doing it for the money but to maintain her visibility there. "Mina wanted a full-time position at Hunter in the worst way," Betty Fosdick recalls, "but she finally realized that no matter what she did, without a Ph.D. she wasn't going to get one." A position at Hunter

Albert Pendo on the ranch. Courtesy of George Pendo.

College carried a certain prestige in the City University of New York system's pecking order, second only to teaching at City College further uptown, followed by the other four-year colleges in the other boroughs—Queens, the Bronx, and Brooklyn—then the two-year colleges. (In 1973, after Mina had earned a national reputation in the field of basic writing, she was finally offered a position as director of the Writing Center at Hunter. Although she did not accept the position, the offer gave her great satisfaction.)

Mina remained at Hofstra for only one more year. In 1967, she and Alice Trillin were offered full-time teaching positions at City College. The summer before, City College had inaugurated a Pre-Baccalaureate Program for low-income students who needed further preparation for college, and as the number of students in the program grew, so did the need for instructors with experience teaching such students. Alice had been reading about the new program in newspapers and journals, and in November 1966 Herbert Kohl published, in *The New York Review of Books,* an essay entitled "Teaching the 'Unteachable,' The Story of an Experiment in Children's Writing." Alice discussed the essay with Kohl, and soon after, she went to see Leslie Berger at City; he hired her on the spot. Alice then told Mina about the article, and Mina also went to see Berger; he hired her immediately as well. Berger, a psychology professor who had helped to design and inaugurate the program, would eventually become one of the deans responsible for overseeing the rapidly expanding remedial programs being inaugurated not only at City College but at the other CUNY divisions as well with the advent of Open Admissions. He had already heard about Mina's work with underprepared students through Alice, and he had spoken with her at several conferences. "She had such a presence," Berger recalls, "even in those very early years."

> There was her beauty of course—people were simply attracted to her; they wanted to be near her. When you spoke with her, or when she made presentations, she held her head up high; she looked people in the eye; she was in control not because she possessed power but because she helped us realize that power wasn't the issue in this new venture, it was a compassion for these students and a knowledge of how we could teach them that was needed. Mina had that, right from the start. And she never lost it.

Berger was also one of the first administrators at CUNY to realize that advanced degrees and publications were not the type of credentials needed to make the Pre-Baccalaureate Program, and later the SEEK and Open Admissions programs, successful. "The English department at City College was one of the most elitist in the country," Berger recalls.

> We had some of the most prominent scholars in the world in that department, but their role had been to teach a very different kind of student than the ones who were being admitted to what we came to call the Pre-Bac program. Mina didn't have a Ph.D. (and that would become a problem for her later when enemies of Open Admissions tried to keep her from being promoted), but she had what we desperately needed: experience and dedication.

Berger remembers being particularly impressed by the similarity between Mina's references from both Hofstra and Hunter; it proved that she was the perfect candidate to help students who would never have been admitted to City if it were not for this special program. Allan Davis, the chair of the English department at Hofstra, wrote: "Mina has that rather rare gift of being genuinely concerned for the inadequately prepared writer, and she seems to have developed a very special ability to make such students progress in this complicated business of communicating." And Gerald Willen, despite his reservations about the work Mina was doing at Hunter, had nothing but praise for the way she was doing it:

As a teacher, I am convinced, Mrs. Shaughnessy is among the best we have had in the School of General Studies at Hunter. Her former students continue to speak of her with affection and admiration; many of them had planned to take further courses with her and keep asking if and when she will be back on the staff. . . .

She is most dedicated and conscientious, taking upon herself extra work, holding frequent conferences with students when according to the terms of her contract she was in no way obligated to do so, and supervising the correcting of papers (particularly those of poorly prepared but otherwise able students) in a very careful and understanding way. When she left Hunter . . . I was aware—as were all my colleagues— of our having lost a colleague, a friend, and a teacher who was as close to being irreplaceable as any single person is.

Mina was officially informed on April 10, 1967, of her appointment as a lecturer in the Pre-Baccalaureate Program to begin on September 1, 1967, by Edmond L. Volpe, the chair of City's English department. In that same letter, Volpe informed her that Anthony Penale, director of the program, would be in touch with her. Mina would have the summer of 1967 to relax and to prepare for her courses. However, in June 1967, Penale suffered a heart attack, and although he would eventually be able to return to teaching, returning to work within three months to direct an experimental program was simply out of the question. Volpe, on Berger's recommendation, wrote to Mina offering her the directorship. Alice Trillin remembers Mina telling her that "she was terrified of taking on the SEEK writing program." Alice remembers "reassuring her, not really sure myself whether anyone could do much with the program, but knowing that if anyone could, it would be Mina."

The Pre-Baccalaureate Program at City College had been voluntarily inaugurated in September 1965, offering remediation, counseling, and stipends to 109 black and Puerto Rican students. The program quickly expanded, was renamed SEEK (Search for Education,

Elevation and Knowledge), and immediately began to engender resistance and hostility from many of City College's faculty members who believed that admitting students on the basis of ethnic or racial quotas rather than academic achievement would destroy City College. At the time Mina was hired to teach in and administer the SEEK program, more than 600 students were enrolled, and that number would grow precipitously within the next two years.

Mina visited Anthony Penale in the hospital (they quickly became good friends), and within a week of that meeting, she wrote a letter to Edmond Volpe accepting his offer and promising to do her best.

Mina did do her best: she devoted all of her formidable intelligence, experience, discipline, and energy to the SEEK students through her teaching, through her administration, in her writing, and in her presentations—and she did so despite great resistance to her work, resistance that often took the form of personal attacks. Mina Shaughnessy was such an inspiration to so many people, particularly the younger faculty members at City College and throughout the CUNY system, that critics of Open Admissions nicknamed them "Mina's minions." Her contributions were recognized by some of the most formidable intellectuals in the country. Irving Howe would say of her after her death: "Whatever is good in this battered university of ours, whatever we still have of the genuine and sincere, found its embodiment in her work. As long as she was there battling for her people, one kept some faith" (2).

CHAPTER FOUR

The House That Mina Built

*M*ina Shaughnessy began her City College career in 1967 as she began most things: determined to work as hard as necessary to succeed. She knew her job would not be an easy one; there was the inevitable confusion that arises when a program is first getting under way, coupled with her unfamiliarity with the machinations of City College.

Mina was well grounded, however, in New York City's politics, a result not only of her fifteen years as a resident but of the knowledge she gained through her marriage to Donald Shaughnessy, a knowledge that would be invaluable to her in her work at City College. Although Don was a staunch Democrat (as was Mina), he supported John V. Lindsay, the Republican candidate for mayor of New York City, and in 1966, when Lindsay was elected, Don was given a job with the administration. Through him, Mina gained an intimate knowledge of the ins and outs of New York City politics. Furthermore, Don had been born and raised in New York City and understood almost intuitively the way that ethnicity affected so many things that happened in the city, where struggles for political power usually involved Irish, Italians, and Jews; blacks were just beginning to enter the fray.

In the early 1960s, an unusual permutation of city politics had evolved at City College and in the other divisions of CUNY over the years: the vast majority of City College students were Jewish, while at Brooklyn College and Queens College, there were larger numbers of Irish, Italian, and Asian students—a reflection of the population of each of the boroughs. When SEEK and Open Admissions programs were instituted in the CUNY system, a far higher percentage of black stu-

Mina and Donald Shaughnessy in the Brandts' apartment. They had stopped by on their way to a dinner at Gracie Mansion with Mayor John V. Lindsay, 1966. Courtesy of Alan and Priscilla Brandt.

dents enrolled in City College than in the other four-year institutions, reflecting the far higher percentage of blacks living in Harlem and upper Manhattan. Mina's work with the students at City College was always guided by principles of justice and fairness, but she knew that most of the decisions made affecting those students were for political—not pedagogical—reasons.

During her first month at City College, however, Mina was far less concerned with the politics of remediation than with the logistics. In a two-page, single-spaced memo written to her chair, Edmond Volpe, on September 22, 1967, she outlined the progress she was (or was not) making as she got the English component of the program started. The program was being touted as a "grand" and "revolutionary" experiment in increasing the numbers of black and Puerto Rican students at City, but it was Mina who was in charge of the details. "I won't bother you with all the crimps and clanks and near-breakdowns in the machinery of registration," she wrote, but "the right students now seem to be meeting the right teachers in the right classrooms, and for that I am grateful—and a bit surprised." In fact, Mina was still unable "to get the total Pre-bac registration." (The title of the program had officially changed from Pre-Baccalaureate to SEEK in 1966 when it became part of a statewide program; however, many of the people at City continued to refer to it as "the Pre-bac" program simply out of habit.)

Mina proceeded to outline her progress in the area of procuring tutors and scheduling lectures. Ever the pragmatist, she had decided to work in "a few central lectures" on such standard problems as "organization, verb tenses, fragments, etc." In this way, she could be certain that "all students have instruction in those problems that are often neglected or are skimpily treated by teachers who want to get on with the discussion of great big ideas."

Mina had already begun to sense the resistance toward the program on the part of many of the faculty members in City's English department. "I have persuaded most of the Pre-bac teachers to attend the English department faculty meetings," she wrote to Volpe, "but they clearly feel unwanted and uncomfortable. I hope something can be done this year to reduce that feeling. Unfortunately, Professor Lavender omitted me from your agenda at the orientation meeting. He did give my name and then added, with the smile of a professional mourner, that everyone wished me well."

Mina had other concerns as well.

And while I am being negative, I must again bring up the subject of office space. Everyone is aware of the space problem; the disgruntlement rises more directly from the fact that every teacher in the regular English program has some kind of office space whereas not one teacher in the Pre-bac program has any office space. The counseling time that is worked into the teachers' schedules is not an adequate substitute: no one can reach the teachers by telephone except in the evenings, and the teachers, in turn, run up their telephone bills at home; they have no place to "land" when they get to campus; they cannot meet students' requests for appointments; and most important, their contention that they are invisible is seriously reinforced by the failure of anyone to allot them space. Is there nothing we can do and no one we can bother about this?

Along with the memo, Mina sent to Volpe a copy of "Milton," the poem that had been published in the *Hofstra Review* the previous spring. "I attach the Milton poem you asked about," she noted. "I can't quite remember how it felt to have time to read poetry, let alone write it!" Within two weeks of her official start at City College, she had already begun to experience that condition so common to developmental educators: the inability to even read—much less write about—other areas of interest. (Shortly before her death, Mina expressed a strong desire to teach during the summer at Bread Loaf in Vermont so that she would finally have an opportunity to teach a course on Milton.)

Even before Mina joined the faculty at City, many of the faculty members in the English department and from other departments had begun to express their opposition to the SEEK program, claiming that City was abandoning its high standards. Their protests took the usual forms: committees, memos, speeches, editorials, rallies, even entire books devoted to the topic with titles like *The End of Education* and *The Death of the American University: With Special Reference to the Collapse of City College of New York,* both written by City College professors and filled with grave forebodings about the destruction being wrought upon their great and glorious institution of higher learning. "Surely the greatness of our nation rests in large part on the type of men and women turned out by the educational system," Louis Heller wrote in *The Death of the American University.* "As rightly understood by the enemies of the country, if that system is destroyed, the downfall of America itself is imminent. Consequently there can and must be no retreat, no craven capitulation to the anarchists, Communists, and know-nothings who would bring down the society" (12).

However, the opposition took far more personal and threatening forms as well. Mina and the other SEEK instructors were accused of being incompetent; their credentials were questioned; they were made to feel unwanted. City College was no place to teach the fundamentals of writing, many of the tenured professors claimed. "Is this what I'm being paid to do?" asked Geoffrey Wagner, one of the staunchest (and most vocal) opponents of Open Admissions. When he noticed a line of students waiting in the hall to visit the basic writing instructor with whom he shared his office, he exclaimed: "You've brought the slums to my office." Mina often found threatening and insulting notes in her mailbox or scrawled on her office door, and in one instance, pornographic photographs were placed in her mailbox with the word "whore" printed across them.

Mina did not take her detractors personally, nor did she engage in confrontations with them. Her reaction was based in part on the innate respect she held for professors. "Mina really thought that professors were something, with their advanced degrees and publications, even if it should have been very apparent to her that many of them were assholes," notes Leonard Kriegel, an English professor at City who became one of Mina's closest friends and allies. In fact, she was slightly intimidated by professors; she had once asked Edmond Volpe to extend an invitation to several of the professors in the department because, she wrote, "professors scare me." Furthermore, she respected their literary accomplishments. "Mina may have become the most successful advocate Open Admission students ever had," Les Berger recalls,

> but that does not mean that she was abandoning her own background in literature and her passion for it. Mina loved Shakespeare, Chaucer, Milton, Henry James—and she wanted her students to love them as well. She and the other members of the SEEK program spent endless hours putting together anthologies of black and Puerto Rican writers, fully recognizing the legitimacy and importance of such literature. But Mina was not abandoning the traditional canon; she was trying to develop ways to bring the canon to her students.

One of her poems reflects this concern:

> The blue books are passed out. Then the examination questions. And the scribbling begins:
> the skin stretches white over the knuckles, eyes
> look out occasionally from pathetic isolation.
> Could they be writing about the pilgrims of
> Canterbury with such stern faces? Could King Lear
> ever arouse such dispassionate busyness?
> No—surely this has nothing to do with Lear.
> But suppose some student should, now, in this
> room, accidentally grasp Lear's terror, feel the
> burn of that great pessimism. Would the scribbling
> stop? Would he, perhaps, sit there weeping all over
> the blue book?
> And would I give him an A?

Mina's reaction to the criticism she and the SEEK students received also stemmed in large part from the realization that confrontation was probably the least effective way to proceed as she sought to make City College a place where the professors would be willing, as she later explained in *Errors and Expectations,* "to make more than a graceless and begrudging accommodation" to the students' "unpreparedness" (293). Instead, she adopted a far more effective method, one that she described to a man who had written to her asking advice about setting up a basic writing program. First of all, she advised, be prepared to work harder than you've ever worked before. Next, develop a camaraderie among all the people assigned to teach basic writing: let them get to know each other, enjoy each other's company, and learn from each other. Make sure there are enough meetings and discussions for this to take place. In addition, try to recruit people from the senior faculty because that is where some of the best teachers are often found, and they will become the most effective teachers in the program not simply because of their experience, but because of the knowledge and influence they have on campus. But most important, she said, make it look like you're having fun.

Faculty members who worked with Mina recall the way she applied those principles to her work at City, to such good effect. In 1972, Leonard Kriegel published a book entitled *Working Through,* in which he described his work with Mina in the SEEK program. (Her philosophy and actions had such a profound impact on him that he dedicated the book to her.)

> The SEEK teaching staff was directed by a woman who had joined the department that September [1967]. She was one of the few people I had ever met who had actually thought about the problems involved in teaching essentially noncommunicative students how to write, how to grasp the idea that communication itself required logic and assertiveness. . . . Time and again during our staff meetings, she would force us to concentrate on the problems of teaching these students. From her point of view, they were the beginning and end of our academic responsibility and purpose. Whenever any of us turned away from these problems to speculate on the meaning of the program, she would gently but forcibly bring us back to our students. . . .
>
> She had a single thought in mind: to educate. She had little patience with political rhetoric, but she had great tolerance and an enormous feeling for the SEEK students. . . . Although she wished to guard the program from those intent on preaching diatribes, she realized that it was essential that our students change their images of themselves and of their capabilities. Wary of any tendencies toward

illusion and self-deception in herself, she would not tolerate them in others. For her, mastery of the art of communication was revolutionary. . . . She wanted to give her students the power to command language, to say what they meant. . . .

Her sense of what was real kept her sane and made her an effective teacher and administrator. While some of the teachers in the program discussed who was and who was not a racist, she moved quietly through the immediacies of City College. She was able to drive herself with incredible diligence, and she shamed others into making the effort their students required of them. (172)

Mina's tendency was always to learn from others—"she was the most careful listener I have ever known," Janet Emig recalls—and to share knowledge and information. From the outset of her career at City, Mina conducted faculty meetings in order to share ideas, experiences, and information. Blanche Skurnick, who joined the faculty at City while still completing her Ph D in literature at Columbia, remembers the high quality of discussions at these gatherings:

As a black woman, I decided to teach courses at City for the very specific purpose of helping the people who had until that point been systematically deprived of an opportunity to attend college. Mina had this uncanny ability to attract teachers to the program who were intellectuals and who were committed to teaching—not always a priority at the college level.

Mina appealed to these people because she was an intellectual, and she was the first person any of us had ever met who was making a formal, scholarly inquiry into the teaching of "basic" writing. She read linguists, grammarians, sociologists. She was particularly interested in William Labov's sociolinguists, in Otto Jesperson's grammar, in Janet Emig's landmark study of the composing process of twelfth graders. And she read existing and emerging studies of Black English. Mina was taking an intellectual, research-oriented approach to teaching writing.

I cannot begin to understand where Mina found time to do the reading she did during that period. She then measured these ideas and research against the writing of our students and brought some of them into the structure of our basic writing courses, such as formal one-on-one student-teacher conferences (these were weekly and required), and into the Writing Center.

As she amassed her own database from our students' writing, she met with us and urged us to read what she was reading. That is not to say she dominated the discussions at our meetings. She had hired talented people to work with her, and she drew them out. Pat Laurence, Ann Petrie, Barbara Quint Gray, Sarah D'Eloia, Betty Rizzo were all doing interesting and innovative research and testing existing ideas in practice, and Mina constantly encouraged them to write about their findings.

One of the best results of these meetings was that they got us out of the grind of teaching and grading, and they prevented us from feeling isolated. In academia, teaching composition is work for junior faculty. But with Mina we understood we were on the cutting edge of work with broader social relevance that cried for scholarly inquiry.

Patricia Laurence had also recently joined the faculty while completing the requirements for her Ph.D., and she remembers the importance of the meetings to the success of the program:

During those early years, there was a core group of people [some of them would later become members of the first editorial board of the *Journal of Basic Writing*] who built the curriculum that had to be created in response to the new linguistic needs of the students. In addition, no books existed in the field, so we created modules of instruction, and we created a writing center.

In those years, we were changing institutional structures and ways of thinking about linguistic problems; we were figuring out how to remedy the problems of students whose linguistic habits, caused either because of ESL or dialect or poor early training in the high schools, so they could enter the mainstream of courses.

Mina held this all together. She was very single minded, very dedicated. Various people in the group gave birth to their children during this period, and many of us were in doctoral programs at the time. We all led very complicated lives. Mina was freer than we were in many senses; she was at a point in her career where she was ready to move into something with commitment. The combination of this commitment with her personal charm, along with the timing of Open Admissions, contributed to her success. When she began, she was thrust into a position, she rose to it, handled it, worked very hard, and structured a program that earned credibility in a terrain that was ready to disbelieve and be critical.

But we didn't see ourselves as revolutionaries or as establishing a new paradigm. We were too busy, too close to it all, to perceive it that way. And we kept a sense of humor through it all. We had one module committee that we named the "S" committee because we worked on the *S* inflection for at least a year; we once figured out that the letter *S* in the English language probably cost the City of New York at least a million dollars.

Ann Petrie also worked with Mina, and she, too, recalls the influence that Mina had on everyone who came in contact with her:

I was hired as an instructor because I was a creative writer, along with other writers such as Erica Jong, Joseph Heller, and Israel Horowitz, but there I was stuck in this elite little program with elite students to whom I was supposed to teach creative writing when I became aware of this group of passionate, interesting, young, brilliant people connected with the Open Admissions program, and there was this amazing woman, Mina Shaughnessy, in the middle of it all. They would talk about ways of teaching with a passion and motivation I had never seen before.

Everybody says this, I know, but Mina Shaughnessy changed my life. She was one of the most charismatic people I have ever met, and her interest in the students was so far above the politics swirling around her. Her motives were genuine; that's what set her apart. She insisted on high standards and helped us to develop the pedagogy to achieve those standards—and everything she did was so that the students would have a chance. It was that simple.

After I was "retrenched" (most of us were laid off during the budget cuts in the mid-seventies), I began to work in film and spent a year producing a documentary about Mother Teresa. It was then that I began to realize that there are certain qualities that these people with vision have. I noticed that Mother Teresa has a certain kind of fearlessness stemming from an inner faith, and this translates into a kind of charisma that is absolutely irresistible. And as I spent time with Mother Teresa, I began to be reminded of Mina's behavior—it was the same fearlessness, the same willingness to do whatever had to be done.

Barbara Quint Gray, who had also been hired by Mina to teach basic writing, remembers being impressed by Mina's devotion to her students, given the amount of administrative work with which she had to contend. Gray recalls one incident in particular which helped her to appreciate Mina's intense involvement with the students in the SEEK program. Gray had invited Mina to a dinner party and asked her to bring a bottle of wine. "I can't do that," she replied, explaining that she was trying to live on the same amount of money that was provided to the SEEK students through their stipends. "Not only can't I afford to buy a bottle of wine on this budget," she told Gray, "I'm not sure I can afford to eat dinner at all. I'm grateful to friends who offer to feed me."

This is not to say that Mina behaved like a zealot, however. In fact, she abhorred political rhetoric. Ed Quinn, who worked with her at City and who would become one of her closest friends and allies, re-called her reaction at a rally they attended together:

> I remember being with Mina at a demonstration in the late sixties or early seventies. I can't remember—it was either anti-war or pro-open admissions—one of these two. (There were a lot of rallies in those days.) In any case, it was one of those in which the sentiments were unimpeachable but the language dreadful. Mina submitted to about three hours of that really bad rhetoric and then she said, "On a day like this the only thing you want to do is to go home and read Nabokov."

Mina believed that one way to discover what the students should be taught in the SEEK program was to discover what they would be expected to know when they took courses in other disciplines. She encouraged the basic writing faculty to audit these classes, and when she later wrote the section on academic vocabularies in *Errors and Expectations,* she drew on the research conducted by Valerie Krishna and Gerald Kauvar. "The[se] authors were City College writing teachers who took introductory courses," Mina explained in a footnote,

> one in biology and the other in psychology. As students in the courses they experienced the language tasks of each subject and observed the experience of other students. Their reports attempt to describe the language "problems" in each subject and to recommend ways of helping students cope with what seemed to them a formidable academic task, even for college teachers. (219)

Mina surrounded herself with strong allies—tenured professors who had been in the English department for many years—and they quickly became friends as well. Len Kriegel and Ed Quinn, a Shakespearean scholar who would later become chair of the English department, would, Quinn recalls, often "run interference for Mina." Les Berger, the dean who had first invited her to join the City faculty, and Theodore Gross, who would succeed Edmond Volpe as chair of the English department and later become a dean of the college, were staunch supporters and admirers of her work. Although Volpe admits that he "resisted all the way" the implementation of the SEEK program, it was Mina who was able to convince him "that it was the right thing to do."

> I was chair at that time, and she saw me as the point person to make this program "legitimate." She would make an appointment, arrive at my office at that time, and we would talk. She had to work very hard; I was not an easy subject at all. I had come from the Columbia University literature tradition; I had recently published a book on Faulkner, and I was not anxious to lose the respect I had in the department. So here she was with this enormous charm and attractiveness—she was never coy—and she would begin to show me some of the students' writing from their blue books and discuss the observations she was making about the way they wrote and about the way they were learning. It all made perfect sense as she described it to me, so I began to support and defend her right to continue to do this.

Other conservative members of the faculty were not so easily converted, however. When Gross replaced Volpe as chair of the English department in 1970, he remembers that Mina's efforts were still being largely ignored, and in some cases denigrated, by many of the tenured members of the department. During the summer of 1970, Mina, as director of basic writing, hired more than forty full- and part-time faculty members to keep up with the growing numbers of students who were enrolling at City College. Each student was required to take one or more of the three sequential basic writing courses that Mina and her colleagues had designed in an attempt to place the students in courses to suit their needs and current level of competency. Gross recalls:

Mina was one of the few faculty members on campus during the summer; she was working harder than anyone else at City, yet she knew that her work was being disparaged by these traditional, tenured full professors who dominated the English department. Mina's beauty and poise kept them from confronting her directly, but they made it clear to her in so many other ways that she was unwanted, that they perceived her work as destructive to the institution. She had a great sense of humor, she radiated charm and confidence through it all, but I remember one phone call after a particularly bad day. She called me about ten o'clock at night and said, "I don't need this job, you know." But that was the only time she complained, at least to me.

When Mina began at City, two-thirds of the courses being offered by the English department were in literature, and one-third were in writing. Two years later, it was exactly the reverse. Imagine the reaction of this very conservative department as we hired more and more writing faculty—and Mina was the one who was seen as "responsible" for this change. There was so much resistance.

The effect of Mina's beauty on her success simply cannot be ignored. Almost twenty years after her death, it is often the first thing people comment on when they are asked to discuss Mina Shaughnessy and her work. They describe her blond hair, her blue eyes, her exquisite cheekbones, her poise, her clear and pleasing voice. They remember her beautiful clothes and her make-up. Her beauty was all the more striking to people because, as Len Kriegel notes, "In the academic world, we are not supposed to care about such things. But Mina cared, and the effects were exquisite. She once told me that one of the most important decisions she made each day was which perfume to wear." Ed Quinn remembers walking into the faculty dining area one day in September 1967 and seeing Edmond Volpe sitting with Mina. "She was easily the most beautiful woman any of us had ever seen in that room, and I, and I suspect many others, made it a point to get to know her." As Patricia Laurence says, "At City, there were the women who worked with Mina, and there were the men who were enchanted with her."

Les Berger remembers when he first met Mina. "It's hard to describe the effect she had on us," he recalls, "now that the feminist movement has made us so much more aware that our responses could be perceived as sexist, but to put it simply, she was strikingly beautiful."

She would hold her head up high, look people in the eye. She would never get into a struggle or an argument. Even the elitists on campus didn't tangle with Mina directly—she somehow managed, with her appearance and her demeanor, to rise above the petty behavior that so many people were engaging in at that time. And there was that theatrical training. Mina may have been depressed, disgusted, overwhelmed—who knows what emotions she felt during those tumultuous years—but she never showed them in the "arena." She "performed" for one of the toughest academic audiences in the country at that time, and the performance was always flawless.

Mina made it look easy, Les Berger recalls, but in actuality, "she was probably working harder than anyone else on the campus," and this made it difficult for her to maintain contact with her friends. During this period, Priscilla Brandt remembers she and Mina would often go for weeks without seeing each other, and when they did get together, "Mina always had a stack of blue books with her." Mina's already close relationship with the Fosdicks continued, but Betty remembers that Mina's weekend visits to their Connecticut country house were one of Mina's few sources of relaxation. "Mina was under enormous pressure at the time; she was clearly overworked and bearing great responsibility." Betty also remembers that Mina would arrive carrying, along with a bunch of flowers or a bottle of wine, "stacks and stacks of blue books to be graded."

During the summer of 1970, the Fosdicks invited Mina to join them as their guest on a two-week trip they were planning to take to Greece. Raymond had suffered a heart attack in 1968, and Betty remembers that they all realized it could very well be his last visit to Europe. Mina needed the rest desperately, and she enjoyed being with the Fosdicks. Betty remembers one incident from the trip in particular that pleased Mina very much:

On one of our trips to the Peloponnesus, we visited the restored theater of Epidaurus. The acoustics were such that when standing in the center of the stage, those in the upper rows could hear a pin drop. To prove that this was true, we took turns reciting some favorite passages. Raymond recited Shakespeare, Mina recited Chaucer; and I recited some Homer in Greek.

Betty still remembers how she and her husband laughed when Mina asked after the recitation: "Are we the same three people who sing those old-time hymns together in Newtown, Connecticut?"

In 1971, Donald Shaughnessy, who had left the Lindsay administration several years before as a result of major disagreements over policy and practices, began to work abroad for the State Department. He was sent to Vietnam, where he remained until 1973, and he was reassigned to Zaire, after a short visit home, until 1977. About once a year, he returned to the United States on leave, and during these periods he and Mina would travel to South Dakota to visit her family or they would vacation in places like Mexico, Puerto Rico, or the Bahamas. During these years, Mina lived alone in a small but comfortable co-op apartment she and Don had purchased on the Upper East Side. She developed a particularly close friendship with the couple who lived in the apartment directly below her, Alvin Schlesinger, a prominent New York judge, and his wife. The three of them often went out to dinner. "We knew that Mina was married," Judge Schlesinger recalls, "but Don was very rarely home, and that seemed okay with the both of them." When the Schlesingers purchased a new piano, they gave their old one to Mina. Judge Schlesinger remembers how much the piano pleased her; she played it practically every evening when she arrived home from work.

Soon after joining the City faculty, Mina asked Edmond Volpe to invite Marilyn French to join City's faculty; the expansion of the SEEK program was creating job openings, and Mina was anxious to fill them with people who would not view basic writing "as a college contagion ward" (*Errors,* 290). When French declined, Mina was disappointed but not surprised. "You can't blame me for trying," Mina wrote to her. In the same letter, Mina described the difficulty of her work at City, one of the rare occasions when she admitted to anyone that she was feeling overwhelmed. In this letter, she seems to have come to the realization, perhaps for the first time, of the permanent and profound change her position at City was having on her life:

I am writing from under water—way down deep in a churning, murky, frenzied world full of sentence fragments, and sweet, betrayed students, and memos and suspicious colleagues. Hofstra had its faults, but looking back I see that it was a rather simple place. And I remember you—the luxury of our talks together. I remember how we had read some of the same things and how we talked about them almost as if we were essays. And how there was time for drinks—and the long, vacant ride home on the good old Long Island Railroad. I remember it all—but it was long, long ago. . . .

Well, as you can see, I am going mad. I cannot imagine keeping up with the many demands this job makes and I am too busy to contemplate the outcome. Strange, but I simply cannot imagine what it would be now to *not* think every day about black and white. . . .

It is midnight and I have a stack of papers. Let me know when I can see you.

Mina was so consumed with her work at City that it was becoming more and more difficult for her to separate her professional life from her personal life. She planned lunch and dinner dates, attended theater and ballet, went to parties and out for drinks, had small dinner parties at her apartment, but she did these things more and more with other people who were involved—even consumed—with the SEEK program. She maintained her friendships with people outside academia, but Priscilla Brandt remembers that Mina began to compartmentalize her life at this time, suspecting that her friends would not be able to understand what she was doing at City College—or why she was doing it.

Alice Trillin, with whom Mina had taught at Hofstra, had also been hired to teach at City College. She and Mina worked closely in the SEEK program, and their friendship grew. Alice gave birth to two daughters, and Mina "adopted" the girls. Alice remembers that she would often arrive at the Trillins' Greenwich Village apartment and inform the girls that she had just met a fairy princess on the street. Pulling trinkets and toys from her pockets, she would explain that the fairy princess had asked her to deliver them to the girls.

In 1971, as SEEK enrollments continued to expand, along with Mina's responsibilities, she was able to hire an assistant, Marilyn Maiz. Her area of specialization was statistics (a useful skill for evaluating the efficacy of the program—as well as for the tedious function of arranging schedules and room assignments). Although Marilyn was more than twenty years younger than Mina, they developed such a close and enduring relationship that Mina came to rely on Marilyn's unconditional friendship for the rest of her life, especially during her long, final struggle with cancer in 1978.

In addition, Mina was finally given approval to hire a secretary. After interviewing several candidates, she hired Dorethea McGill, who still remembers the day Mina called her to inform her that she had been hired. "I remember her friendly, encouraging voice over the phone, saying 'I think we will work well together, don't you?'" McGill worked for Mina for more than six years, a period during which McGill came to understand "just how magnificent Mina was."

Because I was African American, some of the students would initially express their doubts to me about whether or not this lady with the blond hair and blue eyes was "for real." Their concerns were justified, of course. If you came up the hard way, as these students did, with so much racism, you begin to think that white people aren't interested in you. But Mina got that straight very fast. For her, there was no black and white. She was simply not affected by race. She never patronized, and she never discriminated. She didn't see color; she saw need. She saw kids who had been disadvantaged, kids from poor neighborhoods, kids who needed someone to help them. She took so many students under her wing, helping them with their work, giving them money, lending them books, taking them to lunch, calling them at home, that it amazed me that she got any work done at all.

But she got enormous amounts of work done. I believe that woman worked in her sleep. And boy could she delegate. Once she asked you to do something, that was it. She just assumed it would get done. She didn't look over your shoulder. And she defended us against criticism or bullying. Once, when someone "important" insisted on seeing her rather than speak to me about something, Mina very calmly explained that I was in charge of that particular issue, that in fact she knew very little about it.

We were doing serious things, and we were overworked, but Mina always had time to talk about our families and our problems. After my daughter died suddenly and unexpectedly of an aneurism, Mina helped me get through that very terrible time, giving me time off, calling me at home, helping me with paper work and official matters. I took custody of my two grandchildren, and when I couldn't get my grandson into a school near work for a couple of months,

Mina simply said, "Bring him here; I'll teach him reading and writing, and Marilyn will teach him math." And that's exactly what they
did. That boy learned more in two months than he had learned all
year.

And there was fun in that office as well. Mina would often practice her ballet steps in front of us. She was graceful and beautiful, of
course, but she thought she was clumsy and would laugh at herself,
and before you knew it, we would all be laughing, too. Mina was
right. We did work well together.

Shortly after Mina joined City, she met Adrienne Rich, whose
reputation as one of the foremost poets in the country was already secure. Rich had been asked by Edmond Volpe to teach in City's renowned
creative writing program, but she was already teaching at Columbia.
However, after the assassination of Martin Luther King Jr., she decided
to apply for a job in the SEEK program at City. She joined other prominent writers, among them Toni Cade Bambara, Paul Blackburn, and
June Jordan, who were committed to serving those students who had
"traditionally been written off as incapable of academic work."

Mina valued Adrienne Rich's friendship; she drew strength and
reassurance from her absolute devotion to the students and to the cause
of Open Admissions. When Mina wrote to her during the summer of
1969 to confirm that she would again be teaching two sections of writing for the SEEK program, Rich responded that she would be most
happy to teach and enclosed with her letter a quotation that she had
copied from *Letters and Papers from Prison* by Dietrich Bonhoeffer, a
German clergyman who was executed for his resistance to Hitler. Mina
saved the quotation in her files; given the often tedious and unpleasant
nature of Mina's job at City, she must have welcomed Rich's recognition of the heroic quality of the work that she was doing.

As long as goodness is successful, we can afford the luxury of regarding success as having no ethical significance; it is when success
is achieved by evil means that the problem arises. In the face of such
a situation we find that it cannot be adequately dealt with, either by
theoretical dogmatic armchair criticism, which means a refusal to
face the facts, or by opportunism, which means giving up the struggle
and surrendering to success. We will not and must not be either
outraged critics or opportunists, but must take our share of respon-

sibility for the molding of history in every situation and at every moment, whether we are the victors or the vanquished. To talk of going down fighting like heroes in the face of certain defeat is not really heroic at all, but merely a refusal to face the future. The ultimate question for a responsible man to ask is not how he is to extricate himself heroically from the affair, but how the coming generation is to live. It is only from this question, with its responsibility towards history, that fruitful solutions can come, even if for the time being they are very humiliating. In short, it is much easier to see a thing through from the point of abstract principle than from that of concrete responsibility. The rising generation will always instinctively discern which of these we make a basis for our actions, for it is their own future that is at stake.

In 1972, Adrienne Rich wrote an account of her teaching experiences at City. Entitled "Teaching Language in Open Admissions," the eighteen-page essay describes not only the trials that the teachers and students endured—budget cuts, small, poorly ventilated classrooms, the effects of tracking begun "at kindergarten (chiefly on the basis of skin color and language)," the responsibilities the students carried in addition to school, the cruel resistance to the students' presence by many on campus—but the privilege and pleasure they experienced as well:

> What has held me, and what I think holds many who teach basic writing, are the hidden veins of possibility running through students who don't know (and strongly doubt) that this is what they were born for, but who may find it out to their own amazement, students who, grim with self-deprecation and prophecies of their own failure or tight with a fear they cannot express, can be lured into sticking it out to some moment of breakthrough, when they discover that they have ideas that are valuable, even original, and can express those ideas on paper. What fascinates and gives hope in a time of slashed budgets, enlarging class size, and national depression is the possibility that many of these young men and women may be gaining the kind of critical perspective on their lives and the skill to bear witness that they have never before had in our country's history. (67)

Adrienne Rich remembers why she so valued working with Mina at City College: "It never occurred to Mina that the teaching of basic writing could be a mere task," she recalls. "She seemed far more concerned that the poets and writers then being hired to teach basic writing were imaginative enough, responsible enough, lucid enough, to benefit the students." Rich also remembers the way that conditions changed—for the worse—as the Open Admissions program expanded:

> When I first went to teach at SEEK in the late sixties, conditions were better, less crowded; there was more money for SEEK itself. After Open Admissions, the overcrowding was acute. In the fall of 1970 we taught in open plywood cubicles set up in Great Hall; you could hear the noise from other cubicles; concentration was difficult for the students. I also remember teaching in basement rooms, overheated in winter to a soporific degree. My feeling was that the message was being sent that the new students were being no more than tolerated at CCNY; but also, of course, I could only respect their tenacity, working part time, with families, traveling for hours on the subway, and with barely any place to sit and talk or read between classes, none of the trappings of an "intellectual life" such as the Columbia students enjoyed a few miles downtown. Mina fought for space in every way she could.

Rich also remembers the meetings Mina conducted with other members of the SEEK faculty, the way that she dealt with those not directly involved in the program, and the way that she interacted with her students:

> In SEEK, we were working in an overall awareness that language can be a weapon of domination and oppression, or a liberatory tool. Mina often gave lucid, beautifully structured, yet expressive articulation to this understanding, both in our meetings as a group and in my personal encounters with her. She was certainly adept in the politics of knowing how to win support for policies and programs, but I'm talking about politics in the larger sense.
>
> Mina had a strong sense about the idea of "failure." She often suggested that in teaching language it might be the teacher who "failed" the student, in a double sense. Not because she believed (far from it!) in lowering standards or "letting them pass." But she did believe that teachers can use language in authoritarian, dominating ways, calculated to "write off" certain kinds of students. And that most of us highly skilled writers and teachers had absorbed some of those tendencies in our education.

One of Mina's favorite books was *Letter to a Teacher by the School-boys of Barbiani*. Barbiani was a small, poor village in Italy where in the fifties and sixties a young priest had established an alternative school. He wanted to demonstrate that the dropout rate from state schools of poor and working-class students was not a result of their lack of capability for schooling but of antiquated pedagogy, class arrogance, the "failure" of teachers licensed by the state schools. The book is close in spirit to Paolo Freire's *Pedagogy of the Oppressed* but was written and put together by the students themselves. Mina urged us to read this book.

Mina was able to get along with and address herself to a wide range of colleagues, but embedded racism and intellectual arrogance aroused her ire. She was grounded in her experience as a South Dakota-born daughter of immigrants, who had made her way to the big city, sold cigarettes in a night club, used her looks to earn an education. Perhaps she understood experientially that if you looked a certain way (tall and blond and beautiful, or black or Puerto Rican) you could be perceived as "dumb."

Mina was effective in the classroom because she met each human being as such; there were no stereotypes in her head and this was evident in how she responded to questions, gave instruction, met students outside of class. She also had a wonderfully lucid and structured mind, a passionate love for literature, and a genius for ordering material so that it could be readily absorbed by someone coming newly to it. Her whole stance was reassuring. She never seemed to "wing" it or glide along on charm or personality. She *was* grounded, and I think students felt and trusted that.

Marilyn Maiz has saved Mina's copy of *Letter to a Teacher,* and Mina's passion for the work she was doing is evident in the phrases and sections she either underlined or copied into the inside cover:

Besides, we should settle what correct language is. Languages are created by the poor, who then go on renewing them forever. The rich crystallize them in order to put on the spot anybody who speaks in a different way. Or in order to fail him at exams. (12)

I tried to write the way you want us to. (15)

We do not linger over every mistake in grammar. Grammar is there mainly for writing. One can get along without it for reading and speaking. Little by little one gets it by ear. Later on, it can be studied in depth. (16)

The most important tools were in their hands: motivation, belief in a capacity to break through, a mind already underway on linguistic problems. (19)

People who get no criticism do not age well. (20)

Teachers are like priests and whores. They have to fall in love in a hurry with anybody who comes their way. Afterward there is no time to cry. The world is an immense family. There are so many others to serve. (35)

Whoever is fond of the comfortable and fortunate stays out of politics. He does not want anything to change. (87)

To get to know the children of the poor and to love politics are one and the same thing. You cannot love human beings who were marked by unjust laws and not work for better laws. (87)

It is language alone that makes men equal. That man is an equal who can express himself and can understand the words of others. Rich or poor, it makes no difference. But he must speak. (90)

True culture, which no man has yet possessed, would be made up of two elements: belonging to the masses and mastery of the language. A school that is as selective as the kind we have described destroys culture. It deprives the poor of the means of expressing themselves. It deprives the rich of the knowledge of things as they are. (100)

Teachers are not deeply concerned, or not concerned at all, with the human predicament, with the problem of creating a world and a society in which all men in their many ways may lead good, rich and human lives; but are busy producing or collecting knowledge and skill to be sold like any other commodity to whoever will pay the highest price for it. (166)

One of Mina's first students at City College was Lottie Wilkins, an African American woman who "was supposed to become a secretary, but then the SEEK program started." Lottie and Mina developed an extraordinarily close relationship, and many of Mina's friends believe that Lottie came closest to being the child that Mina never had. Nowhere is Mina's dedication to the SEEK students more apparent than in the interaction that occurred between her and this student. They first met in a summer basic writing course that Mina taught in 1968, and Lottie remembers that Mina "was just the most amazing teacher I had ever had":

> She would sit you down if you had a problem writing and try to figure out what exactly was going wrong. You didn't have to be bright to earn Mina's attention, you just had to be willing—she would do absolutely anything to get you to the next step. The minute students mastered something, subject-verb agreement, whatever, and we'd master it by completing the zillion practice sheets they had developed in the writing center, then you'd be expected to stay in the writing center and teach it to someone else. As the program developed, Mina managed to get us paid as tutors for doing this under a work-study program.
>
> Very few of the students were aware of the politics that existed at the time, but because I worked in the center and because Mina and I were growing closer, I saw and heard a lot, maybe even more than Mina saw and heard. I would overhear conversations, and the general feeling was, When is she going to go away and take her program with her? When will she let us get back to running our college the way it's supposed to be? Why doesn't she realize that these kids don't belong here and we should not be expected to teach them how to write?
>
> You have to remember that, as Mina's constituency, we were absolutely helpless—most of us didn't know what was going on; we could barely write; when we were not with the SEEK faculty we were made to feel unwelcome and inept—very much like second-class citizens. Mina fought for us. She wouldn't let anyone stand in her way—she was fighting on two fronts: trying to figure out how to teach us while trying to figure out how to get the college to let her and the rest of the SEEK staff do that teaching.
>
> I fell in love with Mina right away, probably because of her beauty and fairness. I'm still not sure why she fell in love with me, took me under her wing so to speak. She followed my progress all through City. I remember once when I got a C in a political science course, she sat with me and went over the papers I had written line by line,

showed me where I needed tighter analysis, clearer thinking. She never offered pity or condescension. When we finished that session, I realized I was lucky to have gotten the C.

Mina was fascinated by my relationship with my mother; she wanted to know how my mother had instilled in me a desire to learn. That's the way Mina operated—she'd find out how and why things worked for students and then try to duplicate it for other students. She knew how poor I was. I had never shopped in a store below 149th Street and Third Avenue; I didn't even know there was a world beyond that. Mina showed me that world. She would take some other students and me to plays on Broadway—she was so dignified in her behavior toward us—no condescension whatsoever.

Then as graduation approached and I started to talk about the possibility of law school, Mina really got into gear. The next thing I know she's on the phone, writing letters, arranging interviews and loans, and presto—I'm accepted into Columbia Law School. That's when she took me to Bloomingdale's. I remember how scared I was, but Mina realized that there were some things I had to know and have before I started at Columbia. She bought me some perfume and other little things; she was trying to teach me to be comfortable in a strange environment. I still cannot walk into Bloomingdale's without thinking of Mina.

Throughout law school, Mina kept in close touch and helped me over some very rough, uncomfortable places—I was probably the poorest student in my class. Then again as graduation approached she was back on the phone, this time to her good friend, Judge Alvin Schlesinger. Before I know it, I've got a clerkship. I was so naïve at the time that I didn't realize how rare and valuable these positions were—I had gotten used to Mina and her magic wand.

In 1989, when I was elected to be a civil court judge in Bronx County, Mina would have been proud of me, but I wouldn't have been a "specimen" to her, an example of *her* success. She would be equally proud to know that I married my childhood sweetheart and have two wonderful children.

Between 1967, when Mina first began her work at City, and 1972, extraordinary changes occurred in the SEEK program, in the college, and in the CUNY system. The precipitous growth in the number of students being admitted to the SEEK program exacerbated even further the strain being placed on City's budget and caused those who were opposed to the SEEK program to fight even more vociferously for its removal. In April 1969, SEEK students and their supporters began a protest, occupying the entire south campus, demanding greater minority representation and stronger support for minority students. Scores of accounts have been written about this period at City, describing in great detail the demands made by the Black and Puerto Rican Student Caucus; the formation of Faculty for Action, a group of white professors who sided with the students' demands; the closing of the college; the destruction by fire of the Finley Student Center; the arrival of two hundred police officers to stop the violence that erupted after the college reopened; and finally, the resignation of Buell Gallagher, City College's seventh president.

Jean Campbell, a SEEK student who had first met Mina in 1968 and who had become extremely close to her, remembers the way that Mina reacted to the riots and shutdown:

> As a black woman, I saw those protests and strikes as a way for people like me to change things, to gain the power and control we needed to get an education. But Mina and I were at loggerheads about this, and we were careful to avoid talking too much about the issues exploding around us. As long as we could get on campus, she refused to cancel her classes. Mina had decided that she would practice her "politics" in the classroom, not on a soapbox. She told us that she was providing the SEEK students with the tools to think, to write, and to read; that was the greatest contribution she could make. From anyone else, perhaps this would have been hard to take, maybe even impossible, but there wasn't a black or Puerto Rican student on that campus who didn't know that it was Mina Shaughnessy who fought hardest for the SEEK students. In fact, when some of the buildings were occupied, the students did a lot of damage in some offices—but not Mina's. She was the best thing that ever happened to us, and everyone of us knew it.

Those protests, and others like it across New York City, ultimately resulted in 1970 in an Open Admissions policy that guaranteed every student who graduated from a New York City public high school a place in one of the two- or four-year divisions of the City University of New York. The result at City was an increase in the SEEK population to more than thirty-five hundred students. Jean Campbell remembers that during this period, Mina was "absolutely exhausted":

I worked in Mina's office part time, and I remember that she worked constantly. When she wasn't teaching or advising, she was working on schedules or in the writing center. As if that wasn't enough, she was constantly working on reports and studies. When I would ask her why she worked so hard on her research, given all of the other things she had to do, she would say, "I'm going to produce the research that is needed to prove that these students can learn, and I'm not going to let anything or anyone interfere with what I am trying to do." There were thousands of blue books in her office and at her apartment. We would make jokes about them, but I swear she knew where every blue book was, maybe even what was in each one.

When we got really close, I began to call her "Lady." A lot of the other students called her "Shaughn." She would tell me to just call her Mina, but I explained that the word *Lady* was special to me— you had to be just the right kind of person for me to call you that. After that, she let me call her Lady all the time. Sometimes I would change it to "Miss Lady" [Campbell also had a nickname for Toni Cade Bambara: "Miss Black Loretta Young."]

"Lady" was only one of the nicknames that Mina acquired during these years. Marilyn Maiz recalls that people began to refer to her as "'the Countess,' with great affection and approbation. It wasn't because she looked like a countess, although she did," Marilyn recalls:

It was because of her ability to get what she wanted from administrators and bureaucrats at City and CUNY. She would decide that the program needed something, or that someone needed funds to attend a conference, or that something special had to be done for a student. At first, we would tell her she was crazy to think that an exception could be made or that it could be done at all, but then before we knew it, Mina had gotten precisely what she wanted. In fact, as her career progressed at CUNY, we elevated her to "the Queen." She would just smile—if she was going to use her charm for anything or anyone, it was going to be for her students.

Some of the research to which Jean Campbell referred—and those stacks and stacks of blue books—would eventually result in *Errors and Expectations,* but during 1970 and 1971, in addition to teaching and administering the largest Open Admissions program in the CUNY system, Mina was preparing a research proposal and several reports requested by the college's administration. She had spent an entire summer developing a graduate-level course in composition that she would teach the next fall to the writing instructors in the SEEK program. In addition, she was frequently being asked either to make presentations about City's basic writing program or to explain the program to visitors from other institutions. Mina's City College personnel file bulges with letters and memos thanking her for her time and praising the expertise she exhibited in her presentations, along with notes from various deans, provosts, and presidents of City informing her that they had received great accolades about a particular presentation or address.

Despite such recognition, however, in 1970 it was still necessary for a waiver to be granted in order for Mina to be promoted from instructor to assistant professor in the English department—because of her lack of a Ph.D. In addition, Ted Gross, who was chair of the department at that time, recalls the response of the tenured members of the English department faculty to Mina's promotion application. (At that time, nontenured faculty members did not have a vote in promotion or tenure decisions.)

> I remember when Mina's name came up in one of the meetings—
> she had become eligible for her first promotion; the response was
> overwhelmingly negative. They opposed her in every way they could:
> that she didn't have the terminal degree was a big issue. "She teaches
> verb endings," I remember one of the faculty members saying. They
> claimed that the department was being destroyed. I remember standing up in the middle of this storm and defending Mina—one of the
> things I'm still most proud of in my career. "This woman is probably working on the single most important subject in this university," I said, "and you're telling me she shouldn't be given a promotion because she doesn't have a Ph.D.? You've got to be kidding."

When Mina's promotion was finally approved, she mentioned it in a letter she wrote to her parents, making only the most oblique reference to the resistance many of the tenured members of the faculty had exhibited:

As I mentioned, I have been promoted to assistant professor, which I'm sure doesn't sound like much of anything, but for some silly reason it is a hurdle very difficult to get over if you don't have your Ph.D. I hope no one stops it further on up, but anyway, it was good to have the full endorsement of the Department, which is one of those rather traditional and strict departments on matters of the Ph.D.

Somehow during this tumultuous period of Mina's professional life, she managed to find time to write a twenty-page essay entitled "Teaching Basic Writing," sometimes referred to as "Some New Approaches toward Teaching." The essay, which was published by CUNY's Office of Academic Development in a collection of essays entitled *A Guide for Teachers of College English* and reprinted in the *Journal of Basic Writing* in 1994, can be seen as the beginning of the observations and theories that would eventually evolve into *Errors and Expectations*. More important, however, it reflects her thinking as she and her colleagues tried to develop the curriculum for the three levels of classes being instituted for the basic writing students. Mina lamented the fact that writing teachers often "expect (and demand) a narrow kind of perfection which they confuse with the true goal in writing, namely, the 'perfect' fit of the writer's words to his meaning." She had come to recognize, through her students' attitude, behavior, and writing, that

teachers have not only ignored the distinctive circuitry of writing—which is the only source of fullness and precision—but have often short-circuited the writing activity by imposing themselves as feedback. Students, on the other hand, have tended to impose upon themselves (even when blue-book essays do not) the conditions of speech, making writing a kind of one-shot affair aimed at the teacher's expectations. Students are usually surprised, for example, to see the messy manuscript pages of famous writers. "You should see how bad a writer Richard Wright was," one of my students said after seeing a manuscript page from *Native Son.* "He made more mistakes than I do!" Somehow students have to discover that the mess is *writing:* the published book is *written.*

A writing course should help the student learn how to make his own mess, for the mess is the record of a remarkable kind of interplay between the writer as creator and the writer as reader, which serves the writer in much the same way as the ear serves the infant who is teaching himself to speak. No sooner has the writer written down what he thinks he means than he is asking himself whether he understands what he said. A writing course should reinforce and broaden this interplay, not interrupt it, so that the student can use it to generate his own criteria and not depend upon a grade to know whether he has written well. The teacher can help by designing writing situations that externalize the circuitry principle. The teacher and the class together can help by telling the writer what they think he said, thereby developing an awareness of the possibilities for meaning or confusion when someone else is the reader.

But if the student is so well equipped to teach himself to write and the teacher is simply an extension of his audience, why does he need a teacher at all? The answer is, of course, that he doesn't absolutely need a teacher to learn to write, that, in fact, remarkably few people have learned to write through teachers, that many, alas, have learned to write in spite of teachers. The writing teacher has but one simple advantage to offer: he can save the student time, and time is important to students who are trying to make up for what got lost in high school and grade school. (4–5)

This lengthy essay provided the first exposure for many people at City College and in other divisions of the CUNY system to Mina's literary style, and they were immediately struck by the grace and clarity of her prose. Adrienne Rich recalls that *all* of Mina's writing was exquisite:

In a field, English composition, where deadly subhuman academic textbook writing abounds, Mina was a remarkable literary stylist. Many of us who were members of the SEEK staff remember even her office memos as having a grace, a liveliness of language which was not a self-conscious English professor's wit, nor false poetry, nor phone colloquialisms; it was rather the style of a woman who loved language enough never to use it without pleasure.

In July 1971, Mina attended the York Conference in England, where she met James Britton, along with almost every other then prominent figure in the field of composition studies. Her election in 1972 to the National Council of Teachers of English's Committee on the Teachers' Right to Teach further expanded her growing national role and visibility.

Beginning in early 1972, Mina also began to meet on a regular basis with faculty members from other CUNY institutions, many of whom were either directing the writing programs or the writing centers, and all of whom were experiencing the same difficulty dealing not only with the academic needs of their students, but with the strong and often hostile resistance of other faculty members. She drew on the work and discoveries of these colleagues as well in *Errors and Expectations.*

These meetings, which continued throughout the years when Mina worked on *Errors and Expectations,* were the beginning of what would later evolve into CAWS, the CUNY Association of Writing Supervisors, but initially, Ken Bruffee recalls,

> It was a sort of floating craps game of anywhere from three or four to eight or ten people from around the city. I called some people in CUNY to find out if any of us knew anything about what we were supposed to be doing, and everyone told me that Mina Shaughnessy at City College seemed to have a handle on things. We'd meet in restaurants and have a cup of soup or coffee, and we'd talk.

Eventually, the group decided to come together "as a study group of sorts," and Bruffee remembers discussing such books as Richard Sennett and Jonathan Cobb's *The Hidden Injuries of Class* and Ruth Benedict's *Patterns of Culture:*

> We were ranging pretty widely in our reading. I have a note in my journal from this period, for example, to read Suppe's *The Structure of Scientific Theories,* also Sanford's *American College,* and Wilson's *College Peer Groups,* in addition to some mention of reading about "behavioral research." We quickly realized that everything we were doing at our own institutions was being done in grungy faculty rooms or basements, and there was a tremendous amount of labor and confusion involved. I had become known at Brooklyn College as "Mr. Open Admissions, the Destroyer of Western Civilization." Mina wasn't faring much better at City, neither were Bob Lyons and Don McQuade at Queens, or Harvey Weiner at LaGuardia. The group later expanded to include many others, and we eventually began to push the MLA and NCTE to begin to at least recognize our existence.

Janet Emig, who was at Rutgers University at the time and whose study *The Composing Processes of Twelfth Graders* had been published by

NCTE in 1971, was also included in this group of faculty members. She and Mina developed a close friendship; in addition to the meetings, which usually took place every Friday afternoon about three or four o'clock, she and Mina began to meet at other times as well. Emig remembers "many Thanksgiving dinners together after the annual NCTE convention."

More and more, Mina was being recognized as an expert, perhaps *the* expert on basic writing, and her work at City College was further recognized in spring 1972 when she was chosen as one of the recipients of the 125th Anniversary Medallion of City College. Under her direction, the citation read, "the Basic Writing Program of City College has attained its present stature as one of the outstanding programs of its kind in the country." But in the English department, Mina still held a minority position in her belief that her students had as much of a right to be at City as any other students, and a right to the kind of instruction that would contribute to their success. She was overworked; more and more demands were being made on her time, and educators from across the country were beginning to view her as the one who could provide the quick answers and solutions that would "solve" their students' writing problems. She later described the frustration she was feeling at this time in the introduction to *Errors and Expectations:*

> Here were teachers trained to analyze the belletristic achievements of the centuries marooned in basic writing classrooms with adult student writers who appeared by college standards to be illiterate. Seldom had an educational venture begun so inauspiciously, the teachers unready in mind and heart to face their students, the students weighted by the disadvantages of poor training yet expected to "catch up" with the front runners in a semester or two of low-intensity instruction. (3)

Mina was becoming more and more convinced that unless she was given the time to engage in a systematic study of basic writing, these students would be deprived of the type of instruction they needed to succeed. She explained her position early in 1972 in a twenty-five page proposal to the college administration for released time and funding that would enable her to prepare a comprehensive report "on the basic writing program at City College and on the writing problems of its students." She wrote:

During the long debates that preceded Open Admissions, it was common to hear professors, administrators, and even students refer to the arrival of the new students in the metaphors of disease—of debility, decay, paralysis, contagion, even of mortality rates. "Preparation" for Open Admissions seemed, in such a context, to mean "protection" for the teachers and their "bright" students, those who had been classified by their academic records as "college material."

This concern for what came to be called "maintaining standards" pressed most directly on the remedial teachers of the college, who were charged with the task of transforming within a semester or two their "disadvantaged" students into students who behaved, in academic situations at least, like "advantaged" students. This, of course, was impossible. More seriously, it started things off in the wrong direction: it narrowed the base of responsibility for Open Admissions students to the remedial programs, giving "regular" departments an illusion of immunity from change; it channeled most of the Open Admissions money into remedial programs and into counseling that was aimed at helping students adjust to the college world; but it provided no support for research into the learning problems of the new students (significantly, the only research so far to emerge from Open Admissions has been statistical reports on grades and drop-out rates); and it encouraged remedial teachers, under pressure to produce imitations of the model "bright" students as quickly as possible, to go on doing what writing teachers have too often done before—work prescriptively rather than inductively, removing mistakes without trying to understand them.

This was a wrong direction—not because "bright" students should not be imitated or mistakes corrected but because learning seldom takes place if the teacher has no idea of what is going on in the mind of his student, and the teacher is not likely to be looking there if his eyes are fixed on the model "bright" student. He will be ticking off, instead, the incidences of failure to match the model and making judgments about the intelligence of students who continue to make the same mistakes. . . .

Meanwhile, we are learning that the ability of our students to master written English is hindered less by their deficiencies than by our failure, too often, to understand more precisely what is going on in them when they don't learn what we try to teach. Often, our very formulation of a problem keeps us from understanding it.

Mina was asking for time to sort it all out, to make sense of what she had experienced—and discovered—during the past five years. Her proposal was submitted by City College to the Carnegie Foundation, and in May 1972 she was informed that the foundation would appropriate $46,079 to City College to be used to subsidize her research and writing of "a report on the writing problems of disadvantaged students." Ted Gross informed the department of the grant and announced that Blanche Skurnick would assume Mina's duties for the 1972–73 academic year. A party was held in Mina's honor to celebrate the grant, and it was attended primarily by those instructors who taught with her in the SEEK program. With the exception of Len Kriegel, Ed Quinn, and a few others, the full-time tenured professors did not celebrate her achievement.

A month later, on June 21, 1972, Mina's parents celebrated their fiftieth wedding anniversary. During the previous winter break, she had visited them in Arizona—where they had gone in an attempt to find some relief for Albert Pendo's arthritis. Because of the work involved in preparing to turn the basic writing program over to Blanche Skurnick, however, Mina was unable to travel to South Dakota to be with her parents on their anniversary.

She wrote them a letter instead, telling them that although she could not be with them, she was spending the evening "looking at your wedding picture and the two pictures I took of you in Arizona this year." She saw the faces of "two people who have taken on the world, faced its difficulties, tasted its joys, satisfactions, and its bitterness, too. They are wonderful faces . . . that belong so much together that I cannot see one without somehow seeing the other."

In the last paragraph of her letter, Mina expressed gratitude to her parents for the love they nurtured in her, but she also asked: "What was it that made things work?"

Was it, in part, your assumption that things had to work, that one made this decision once and then stayed with it? I think even more than that, it was a kind of generosity of heart, an impulse toward affection covered a multitude of difficulties. It was the quality that has always made our home a place where people want to come. It was a place with love in it, and that love was generated by you and spread out among your children and your friends. . . . You will be celebrating your marriage— a marriage . . . that started no doubt with all the gossamer dreams of newly weds but did not end there. It became rooted in the real earth and has grown like the strong tree, and I will be celebrating that creation with you.

Perhaps Mina was comparing her parents' circumstances with her own marriage. Her husband was halfway across the world, their relationship reduced to weekly letters and occasional visits. She had no children of her own. But there were strong similarities as well. Mina had found challenge—and satisfaction—in her students; she, too, had "assumed that things had to work" and had "stayed with it," with a "kind generosity of heart."

"In a period of much pedagogic drama and experimentation," Adrienne Rich would later write of this period in Mina's life, "Mina represented an extraordinarily pure concern for the actual learning processes of actual students," while "teaching grammar, inventing new ways to teach it, training teachers, conceptualizing our everyday collective experience, negotiation and struggling with higher administrators, writing grant proposals, dealing with students and staff alike, on the most human and individual level" (1).

CHAPTER FIVE

Toward a More Democratic Educational System

No one was surprised when Mina was awarded the Carnegie Foundation grant, given her expertise and brilliance, except maybe for Mina herself. Les Berger, the dean who had originally hired her, and with whom she had developed a close friendship, recalls that she was nonplussed when she first learned of the award, uncertain if her research plans were adequately developed. "Don't worry," Berger assured her. "In this business, first you get the money—then you get the ideas."

Under the terms of the Carnegie Foundation grant, Mina would be released from her teaching and administrative duties for the 1972–73 academic year, but Marilyn Maiz recalls that Mina worked even longer hours than she had before; given her growing reputation in the field of basic writing and as a proponent of Open Admissions, it was impossible for her to concentrate exclusively on her research and writing. Marilyn recalls that despite these unavoidable interruptions, Mina managed to "accomplish more in a year than most people do in a decade":

> Mina worked harder and more efficiently than anyone I have ever known. Even before getting the grant, she had been thinking about a book for a very long time, keeping notes, classifying and sorting the students' essays, doing library research, reading and studying sociologists, linguists, philosophers. She listened carefully to everyone, particularly the teachers who were working with the Open Admissions students. She knew they were making important observations and discoveries, and she wanted to learn from them.

After Mina was awarded the grant, she was given an office in Shepard Hall at City College, and she was assigned a secretary and a research assistant. She worked in the office from Mondays through Thursdays, then she would often spend long weekends at the Fosdicks' country house working on the book. Initially, she visited some other Open Admissions writing programs at other institutions, but soon she got heavily into the writing.

That's not to say that the attacks on Mina and her work ceased, although she was able to keep a sense of humor about it. I remember one time Mina came into the office after what must have been a particularly heated exchange with one of the conservative faculty members and commented: "These people not only blame me for the presence of Open Admissions students on campus, they seem to think that I gave birth to each and every one of them."

Mina's ability to concentrate was amazing. At about this time, people began to realize her importance; her reputation in the field was growing. Many people wanted to meet with her, to be with her, to be seen with her. They wanted a piece of her, but Mina did not let anything get in the way of her work. If she had a luncheon appointment, it lasted for an hour at most, and then she'd get back to work. She moved quickly from one thing to another; she was very good at that. She did not talk very much about what she was doing or what she was going to do, she just did it.

Even Mina Shaughnessy, despite her extraordinary energy and ability, could not complete the project she had outlined for herself in the one year for which she had been relieved of her teaching and administrative duties, so in September 1973 she wrote a letter to Alden Dunham at the Carnegie Corporation requesting additional funding that would enable her to hire a secretary and to teach a reduced load when she returned to City in fall 1973. The letter details the prodigious amount of work that she *had* been able to complete in one year:

A year ago I began work on a resource book for teachers of basic, or compensatory, writing at the college level. Since that time I have, with the help of a part-time research assistant and secretary, accomplished the following:

1. Analyzed about 4,000 essays by incoming students at City College in order to determine the nature and frequency of their

writing difficulties.

2. Completed one computer study of error frequency at different levels of proficiency.
3. Read extensively in those areas of research that are relevant to my study.
4. Visited colleges in other parts of the country (California, Arizona, and Florida) in order to determine the "transferability" of what we are doing at City.
5. Prepared a seven-page outline of the resource book.
6. Completed two chapters of the book itself. A third chapter is nearly complete.

My own pace as a writer and the size of the task I have undertaken have kept me from meeting the deadline I proposed for myself a year ago. Now that I must return to my full-time responsibilities as director of the Basic Writing Program at City College, I will of course have much less time to give to the work. Nonetheless, I hope to proceed with the writing at the rate of about one chapter a month. By December, I should have completed the analysis of what I am calling the Level 1 writers. This will include six chapters, three of which are virtually done. The remaining six chapters I plan to complete between January and June.

As Marilyn Maiz notes, Mina had the ability to do more work, and to do it better and faster, "than most humans." Nowhere is this more evident than in the work she outlined in her letter to Alden Dunham. She was not simply checking off, identifying, and enumerating errors; her "analysis" of "about 4,000 essays" provided her with the rubric she needed to divide *Errors and Expectations* into "familiar teaching categories," which would serve as "headings for the main sections of the book." The results of her analysis would then enable her to do three things, as she would later explain in the book's introduction: "First, to give examples of the range of problems that occur under each category of difficulty; second, to reason about the causes of these problems; and third, to suggest ways in which a teacher might approach them" (4).

The computer study to which Mina referred was an attempt to evaluate the efficacy of the three levels of writing courses that she and her colleagues had instituted at City. She was troubled by this concept, and the computer study was an attempt to evaluate whether or not clear enough distinctions existed among the writing abilities of the students to justify such a system. In a chapbook that she kept during this period, she attempted to describe the differences among these three levels of writers, wondering if the frequency of errors in various categories was enough to justify such a division. Perhaps the computer study helped her in this regard, but little mention is made of it in her notes. She did, however, copy the following quotation into the section entitled Level 1: "Give me a good fruitful error anytime, full of seeds, bursting with its own correction."

Mina's claim that she had "read extensively in those areas that are relevant to my study" does not begin to describe her level of expertise. Robert Lyons remembers:

> Mina read everything there was to read. That's the first question she would ask any of us when we met: "What are you reading?" She'd jot down the title and that particular book or essay would lead her to two or three other books or essays. There was no legitimate field of composition studies at this time, and Mina was one of the first to realize that because our students were untraditional, then our reading would have to be untraditional as well.

Errors and Expectations contains references to scores of books and articles in the field of linguistics, composition, sociology, and psychology: H. L. M. Abercrombie's *The Anatomy of Judgment;* Douglas Barnes's *Language, the Learner and the School;* Benjamin S. Bloom, J. Thomas Hastings, and George F. Madaus's *Handbook on Formative and Summative Evaluation of Student Learning;* James I. Brown's *Efficient Reading;* Alan Casty's *Building Writing Skills: A Programmed Approach to Sentences and Paragraphs;* Francis Christensen's *Notes Toward a New Rhetoric;* Edward DeBono's *New Think;* Lee C. Deighton's *Vocabulary Development in the Classroom;* Janet Emig's *The Composing Processes of Twelfth Graders;* Charles Fries's *The Structure of English;* R. C. Gardner and W. E. Lambert's *Attitudes and Motivation in Second-Language Learning;* Paul R. Hanna, Jean S. Hanna, and Richard E. Hodges's *Spelling: Structure and Strategies;* Otto Jesperson's *Growth and Structure of the English Language;* Kenneth Koch's *Wishes, Lies, and Dreams;* William Labov's *Language in the Inner City:*

Studies in the Black English Vernacular; Susanne Langer's *Mind: An Essay on Human Feeling;* John C. Mellon's *Transformational Sentence Combining;* James Moffett's *Teaching the Universe of Discourse;* William G. Moulton's *A Linguistic Guide to Language Learning;* Frank O'Hare's *Sentence Combining* and *Sentencecraft;* Sidney J. Parnes's *Creative Behavior Guidebook;* Michael Polanyi's *Personal Knowledge;* Hugh Rank's *Language and Public Policy;* I. A. Richards's *Practical Criticism;* Edward Sapir's *Language;* William Strong's *Sentence Combining: A Composing Book;* Stephen Ullmann's *Semantics: An Introduction to the Science of Meaning;* Richard Wright's *Black Boy.*

The visits to other institutions that Mina mentioned in her letter to Dunham may or may not have helped her in her research. It seems that whenever she visited these institutions, the administrators and directors whom she met looked to her for guidance and instruction, often expecting her to deliver lectures and conduct workshops. It is no wonder that she stopped making these visits early in her research.

In her letter to Dunham, Mina also noted that, in addition to a seven-page outline, she had completed three chapters. In effect, she had completed a third of *Errors and Expectations,* yet her statement to Dunham referring to her "pace as a writer" seems to imply that she believed she wrote slowly.

Although Mina was probably aware early on that she would not complete her proposed project in one year, she was still not willing to give up the meetings and collaborations with other basic writing faculty and directors that she had formed during her early years at City. In many ways, it was these associations and collaborations, as much as her experience teaching basic writing, that would enable her to write *Errors and Expectations.* Several references in her book to colleagues both at City and at other CUNY institutions reflect the importance of these collaborative relationships. Soon after Mina became the director of writing at City, she and several of her colleagues—all younger faculty members who had been hired to teach basic writing—had begun to meet regularly to discuss their work. In 1975, members of this group published the first issue of the *Journal of Basic Writing,* but long before the journal came into being, Mina was inspiring—and being inspired by—the work and discoveries of these colleagues, and she cited them in *Errors and Expectations:* Oscar Chavarria-Aguilar, Sarah D'Eloia, Barbara Gray, Gerald Gould, Gerald Kauvar, Valerie Krishna, Patricia Laurence, Kenneth Libo, Betty Rizzo, Kathy Roe, Blanche Skurnick, and Alice Trillin. She maintained regular communication with writing instructors from other CUNY institutions as well, citing in *Errors and Expectations* the research or teaching innovations of Mary Epes of York College and Marie Ponsot of Queens College.

Mina asked Janet Emig to read the early chapters of *Errors and Expectations* as they were being written—because of her expertise in the field of course—but also because she realized that Emig's experience in completing her pioneering study, *The Composing Processes of Twelfth Graders,* had enabled Emig to understand and appreciate the difficulties inherent in creating a work for which there was no frame of reference. "We were certainly not aware that we were establishing a paradigm because there was no tradition to play against," Emig explains.

I think that's why we were able to give support to one another; Mina knew that I had done my own work in a vacuum. I had ten advisers at Harvard, and they kept failing my work because it was about writing—I had absolutely no support system. Mina was deeply involved in her work, but at the same time she needed people to talk to; she was relieved to know that people like me and Nancy Martin and Jimmy Britton found it of immense interest and importance.

I was so impressed by her brilliance and her ability to work so hard. She had developed this extraordinary system to analyze the students' essays; each chapter took an immense amount of time to write. That book is grounded in actuality. I remember that we'd sit in the graduate center and Mina would read me what she had written. I made comments, of course, but I was absolutely fascinated by what she was doing (it was such a different population than the one with which I had worked; the students were older and far more diverse). I was utterly struck by the level of sympathy and understanding she had for these students—students so different from herself. It's an extraordinarily rare quality among teachers who do not see themselves in their students, and Mina could not possibly have seen herself in her students because her background was so different.

I am convinced that *Errors and Expectations* reflects, more than anything else, Mina's commitment to the infinite possibility of the individual. No one had ever considered this particular student population before; most people at CUNY—and elsewhere—were unused to people of color, the culture was unknown to them. But Mina was totally appreciative of her students' individuality and possibilities.

And then of course there was the eloquence and gracefulness of her writing. Like her appearance, Mina made it all look very easy and beautiful, but I knew better: she worked very hard for everything she accomplished. I was always struck by how overburdened she was; every minute of her day was accounted for. She was so disciplined that she always maintained her writing schedule no matter what else she had to do.

And what most impressed me was her wide background and knowledge; Mina had the imagination to use so much of what she read and heard from others; her connections made perfect sense; they left you wondering why you hadn't thought of that.

It is possible that Mina shared the early drafts of *Errors and Expectations* with Janet Emig not only because they enjoyed each other's company and intellects, but because Emig's experience with her advisers at Harvard was extremely similar to the circumstances Mina was facing at City. Bob Lyons remembers that Mina very rarely confided in anyone about the problems or resistance she encountered at City College; in fact, most people looked to her for assurance and guidance. She may have seen in Janet Emig a kindred spirit: she was female, she had published a groundbreaking study about writing with no support from her graduate advisers, and she was constantly encountering resistance to her ideas at Rutgers in much the same way Mina was at City. Emig remembers that Mina would "let her defenses down" a bit when they were together:

> Mina was performing much of the time; her role had become that of the spokesperson for Open Admissions and for basic writing. It wasn't possible for her to express her concerns and fears aloud; too many people looked to her for guidance and inspiration. But when we were together, a more sardonic side of Mina would become apparent, and I always suspected that I was one of the very few people with whom she could do this.

Most of the people who were associated with Mina believe that they learned from her—they looked to her as the leader in the field of basic writing. They quoted her or cited her work at City in order to initiate change at their own institutions. However, Mina learned from them as well. This is evident in the chapbook she kept in preparation for writing *Errors and Expectations*—a binder divided into nine sections roughly reflecting the book's chapter titles. The notes that she inserted under these various headings reflect an extraordinarily eclectic variety of sources and ideas: quotations from Henry James and James Joyce, from a report of the Kellogg Foundation, from an 1810 report to the Trustees of Columbia College. She reminded herself to refer to a passage from *Jonathan Livingston Seagull;* she quoted Nancy Martin, who said that "confidence is the major element in developing writing"; and she reminded herself to refer to her "notebook of quotations for the definition of university as the fiduciary subsystem of the culture, requiring a degree of skepticism unknown for college students of the past." There is a quotation about television watching outscoring newspaper reading from an essay by Jerzy Kosinski in the autumn 1973 issue of *American Scholar;* there are references or reminders to return to the work of I. A. Richards, Peter Elbow, and Ken Macrorie.

Under the subsection entitled "Writing Habits" and "Proofreading," Mina clipped the top quarter of a page from *The New York Times* containing the following quotation from Jonathan Swift.

> Blot out, correct, insert, refine,
> Enlarge, diminish, interline;
> Be mindful, when Invention fails,
> To scratch your Head, and bite your Nails.

Although most of the entries in the chapbook were written by hand, Mina would occasionally type up notes from a conference she had attended or from a report she had read and tape them into the binder; there is a one-page, single-spaced entry from a Brookings Research Report discussing the difficulty of even collecting, much less analyzing data on the effectiveness of education (a theme that she would develop in the essay "Open Admissions and the Disadvantaged Teacher"). Her notes end with the following sentence: "Perhaps the real world is not organized to generate information about 'production functions'—the relation between efforts expended and results—no matter how skillfully the statistics are collected."

On another occasion, Mina taped into her chapbook an entire page of notes taken at a conference she attended at Staten Island Community College (now The College of Staten Island), at which one of the instructors, David Rosen, described his experiences with Open Ad-

missions students. "Need there be this either/or situation between attitude and skill?" Mina wrote at the top of the page, and she marked
off the following passage:

> My [Rosen's] failures resulted when I felt an obligation to be struc-
> tured and to communicate skills in the old way, passing out infor-
> mation. I really felt that I failed, that [it is] no longer effective learn-
> ing grammar straight from a book or a teacher's mouth. And my
> successes [resulted] when I tried to create an experience in class which
> included information but that also included information for widen-
> ing perceptions of a given space, or a given time, or a given situa-
> tion.
>
> At one point during the semester I came into class and apolo-
> gized that I thought I had short changed [the students] in not teach-
> ing them grammar skills and preparing them for the realities of the
> college at large and that I'd do my best to rectify this next year. After
> the class a few of them came up to me and said they felt very badly
> about my putting myself down because, "We don't think that you
> and the rest of the people in the program realize the effect that you've
> had on our lives. A lot of us would have dropped out in total disgust
> after the first semester. If we had wanted just the skills we would
> have come and told you, but we felt that we were getting in touch
> with what we are as people—which was much more important."

Under the subheading "English I, priorities," Mina wrote about
errors, a topic that so dominated most discussions about basic writing
at the time that she and the other editors of the *Journal of Basic Writing*
would use it as the title of the first issue in 1975.

> The obsession with error is not easy to dispel, particularly if one
> hopes at the same time to work in the correction of errors. Yet the
> alternative of ignoring error—the expectation that fluency and con-
> fidence will reduce the number of errors or provide a reason for caring
> about them—will not work in programs that have but a semester or
> two in which to prepare students for the writing tasks of college.

Mina stapled into the binder a small piece of paper on which she
had written a quotation from Jack H. Mimmis, a professor at Philadelphia Community College. She labeled the paper "Error Strategies" and
reminded herself to "enter [the quotation] under teaching":

Students are as reluctant to drop their academic defenses as teachers are. They have been trained very carefully for at least twelve years to recognize their deficiencies and to develop compensations and excuses for what they consider their inabilities. More important than the excuses, though, students bring with them a complete set of methods they can use to avoid learning anything. Cajoling the students into exposing their weaknesses to the teacher, the contradiction of all they have learned, is not only the greatest innovation of all, it is the essence of teaching.

Mina's decision to place that particular quotation under the subtopic "Teaching" says much about the direction of her thinking at the time, her growing conviction that the arrival of Open Admissions students was forcing an issue that until then had been ignored in colleges and universities—the issue that she would later describe as "a situation in which teaching clearly *had* to make a difference." In another entry under the same subtopic, she recorded one of her own thoughts on the subject: "Students fail to learn less because of their teachers' lack of knowledge than because of their teachers' lack of good will, patience, and hard work."

With the exception of Mina and her colleagues in the basic writing program, no one at City College was writing about the field of composition; in fact, they saw no reason why they—or anyone else—should. Their concerns were "literary." In the English department's newsletter dated January 1972, shortly before Mina began her leave to start her research and writing, the names of those faculty members being promoted were listed along with their publications: of those faculty members who were being promoted to full professor, one was currently completing a comprehensive edition of the letters of William Morris, another was the author of *Nathanael West's Novels* and *Isaac Bashevis Singer,* a third was adapting a trilogy of British novels for the American stage. Of those faculty members being promoted to associate professor, one had written a book entitled *Shaw and the Doctors;* one had completed a book entitled *Medical Malpractice in Medieval England* and had presented a lecture tour of Medieval song; one was writing a study of Harold Pinter; and another had edited a collection of essays on Keats's "The Eve of St. Agnes."

The irony of the situation was not lost on Ted Gross, the department chair. Gross published a three page, single-spaced "Chairman's

Report," beginning on the front page of the twenty-page newsletter, opening with the line: "Let us begin with the hard questions." Although Gross's intention was to present an objective portrait of the department's evolution from the inception of Open Admissions, he was clearly responding to the outright animosity that was being manifested in the English department. And although he recognized and defended the need for instructors who were experts in composition theory—a field in which there were very few Ph.D. programs at the time—his own ambivalent feelings concerning those faculty members who did not possess a Ph.D. became evident.

The very fact that Gross published such an essay is evidence that the animosity engendered by Open Admissions among the faculty at City College was not abating. In fact, Mina's success in winning a grant from the Carnegie Foundation may even have exacerbated the resentment and jealousy felt by those faculty members who were convinced that City College's reputation was being irreparably harmed by the influx of these "unqualified" students and the instructors who were being hired to teach them. Gross wrote:

> What happens to a department that suddenly finds itself offering 50% writing courses, 15% introductory literature courses, and 35% elective courses, when this same department, only two years before, offered 32% writing courses, 16% introductory courses, and 52% elective courses? What happens when older professorial staff, untrained for the new remedial work, have fewer electives as part of their program and must teach in this remedial program? What happens when some of the newer staff, who do not yet possess the Ph.D. and who, in certain cases, may not be interested in publishing criticism and scholarship, dominate a department numerically? And what happens when those who have always had a certain set of "standards" in grading students find themselves appraising work that they find inadequate? What is the ideal degree for a person teaching in this kind of department? What sort of professional expectations should he have? Does the professor, with his Ph.D. in hand, confront the lecturer, with only his M.A., and is a conflict inevitable? Where, finally, is the English department moving in a college whose character is changing more rapidly than ever before?
>
> These questions—and all the others that inevitably follow—vibrate throughout the English department and therefore throughout the entire college; they confront any urban or state university that

no longer adheres to a traditional mode of education or that, in one form or another, commits itself to Open Admissions. The questions go to the root of our profession, for they are a result of historical paradoxes that have suddenly converged and that now assume extremely difficult practical manifestations.

Many of us have been trained for an elitist profession, but we are asked to perform democratic tasks; we have written dissertations on Spenser, but we are teaching remedial writing; we are committed to the book, but the students have been culturally shaped by television and film; we have studied a body of culture that is fundamentally Anglo-Saxon, but we teach many students who are Black and Asian and Spanish; we pay homage to the history of English literature, but we are surrounded by the consequences of American history and the political presence of America; we are in an "English" department, but our work is involved with the literature of the world and with the language that is spoken by Americans. . . .

The frustration that some of our lecturers feel stems from a disparity between what they are teaching and what they are studying, from the pursuit of a Ph.D. that has not accommodated itself to the educational needs that are so apparent to anyone who teaches undergraduates. I do not wish to see the Ph.D. relegated to an anachronism and an irrelevancy that would only further polarize the teacher and the scholar. If we believe in the perpetuation of a humanistic tradition then we must believe in a Ph.D.—but in a degree that is organically related to the world of today. If graduate schools do not modify their curricula in terms of the educational demands made of candidates once they appear in the classroom, then the Ph.D. will deserve to die; and if the Ph.D. dies, replaced largely by some form of "educational" degree, then the heart of humanism will go with it. . . .

There was a time when no one but a professor with a Ph.D. could be granted tenure. Exceptions were extremely rare. Now a lecturer can be given a certificate of continuous employment if he is reappointed to his sixth academic year; but, given our present system, he will remain a lecturer and his professional rewards will be less lucrative than those of the professorial staff. I think it is unwise for anyone in our department to remain a lecturer—not only because his rewards will be fewer but because he will not possess the training that a proper Ph.D. should offer a person who seeks to teach on a college level. Those few people who, for one reason or another, do not complete their Ph.D.s and who are reappointed only because of their excellent teaching, will have to pay the price of having acquired limited credentials: a greater burden will be on them for the rest of their careers. . . . [T]he lecturer rank officially precludes the necessity to publish, and in this department, at least, publication is one important reflection of a person's growth; if an instructor does not demonstrate that growth, I don't believe he deserves to advance—I don't believe he himself would maintain he ought to advance—as quickly as the person who does. These considerations go beyond the official contracts we have made with our profession. At the critical moments in a person's career, you take a man or woman for what he or she represents, no more and no less—and this applies to a "professor" or a "lecturer" or an "instructor."

Gross's remarks reflect the difficulty of chairing an exceedingly conservative English department whose tenured members were unwilling to come to terms with the changes being wrought at City College, of course, but they were also an attempt to reconcile factions which were becoming increasingly polarized. (Promotions had been granted in the past to members of the English department who did not hold the Ph.D., but only rarely, and only to exceedingly prominent scholars such as Edgar Johnson, the renowned Dickens scholar.)

Mina's lack of a Ph.D. was no longer really an issue at City College; she had already been promoted to assistant professor without one, but some of the people whom she had hired to teach the ever-growing numbers of Open Admissions students not only did not possess the terminal degree but were not interested in pursuing one. These new faculty members were young, idealistic, and committed to their students. They spent hours and hours preparing for their classes, meeting with their students, responding to essays. Mina was their idol—a fact that must have been particularly irksome to those tenured faculty members who in the years before Open Admissions had been admired, even fawned over, by the newest faculty members—brand new Ph.D.s in hand.

Richard Sterling, who became director of the National Writing Project in 1995, had not even completed the requirements for a master's degree when Mina convinced him to teach basic writing at City. "Mina had a way of finding us and inspiring us," Sterling remembers. He had begun his education at City as a nonmatriculated evening student and had graduated from City College with honors—what better role model could the students have? Not only was he a fine instructor who spent hours tutoring the students, he was an active participant in transforming the group of writing directors and supervisors into the CUNY Association of Writing Supervisors.

Several faculty members who did pursue a Ph.D. degree were more interested in the field of composition studies than in literature. Tom Farrell, for example, completed a dissertation entitled "Opening the Door: An Analysis of Some Effects of Different Approaches to Educating Academically High-Risk Students at Forest Park Community College [St. Louis, Missouri]." And those faculty members who completed degrees in literature, Patricia Laurence and Blanche Skurnick for example, did so *in addition* to their interest in the field of linguistics and composition.

Mina also published a report in the same English department newsletter; it appeared directly after Ted Gross's. She quoted two sentences written by two Open Admissions students, but instead of pointing to their writing difficulties as evidence of a deficiency in the students themselves (a belief held by a great majority of the English department faculty at that time), Mina went on to proclaim instead that "the broken sentences" of the students

suggest the scope of the failure of the urban school system. (And the word "system" must be stressed, lest the remarkable work of thousands of individual teachers be overlooked.) The sentences also suggest the dimensions of the task the College now faces as it attempts to remove the barriers of undeveloped skills for these students and for many others who, although they may be somewhat more advanced in writing, are still seriously unprepared for college work.

We are beginning to see that the first stage of Open Admissions involves *openly admitting* that education has failed for too many students. For the sentences above are merely symptoms of what has *not* happened during twelve years of formal education.

Mina presented statistics indicating that, despite a common belief on campus that Open Admissions students at City College were overwhelmingly black and Puerto Rican, in actuality "low-income white ethnic students . . . make up about two-thirds of the Open Admissions freshmen with below-80 high school averages."

But for whatever the reasons, here they are—more of the educationally betrayed citizens of New York—and City College has chosen not to take the traditional options of calling them dumb and flunking them out or of suggesting that motivation is a matter of character, not education, and therefore outside the responsibility of school. It is assuming, or learning to assume, their educability at the college level and moving on to the question of what, given harsh limits on time, space, and money, can be done to make Open Admissions succeed.

Mina described the "modest innovations" that had been incorporated into the writing program under her directorship: the writing center, the summer language workshop, and a freshman curriculum that would correlate history, psychology, and political science, describing them as "signs of life, signs that the College is beginning to respond creatively to Open Admissions."

When one watches the flow of students that fills Convent Avenue between classes and senses behind that remarkable variousness of dress and color and contour and talk the shared experience of studenthood, it is hard to imagine anyone who would not wish Open Admissions well. Yet the soothsayers within and outside the college continue to invent statistics to fit their cataclysms. To answer them is pointless. There are no dependable statistics on Open Admissions yet. Even the end-of-semester body counts are meaningless, for they make no distinction among students who transfer, drop out for personal reasons, or actually fail the work itself. Furthermore, no one has decided what success should look like under Open Admissions. What indicators can we devise that will measure self-esteem? How will we chart the routes these young men and women take as they begin to experience the luxury of making choices. . . .

At City College, the most severely pressed of the senior colleges, the number of students in Basic Writing classes has tripled since last fall without any commensurate increase in classroom space. And the budget crises that keep shrinking our staffs and swelling our classes will be as regular as taxes until we find a way of paying for Open Admissions. Without more support, this experiment in education threatens to become an extension into college of the woes of the urban high school. In three semesters, under grotesquely inadequate conditions, we have begun to see how Open Admissions might be made to work. The decision of whether it will be allowed to work now rests with those who have the power to set public priorities.

Mina's "report" was a manifesto of sorts; she was presenting ideas and concerns for the first time in writing that she would repeat in essays and speeches throughout the rest of her career. She tried to take the high road as she described for her colleagues—many of whom she knew did not wish Open Admissions well—the challenges faced by Open Admissions students and by the faculty that was "committed" to serving them.

Mina's concern for the future of Open Admissions stemmed in large part from the budget cuts that were becoming more severe as New York City entered the fiscal crisis of the mid-seventies, but it stemmed as well from a growing conviction that no one inside or outside the university cared about these students. Adrienne Rich remembers that it was during this period that Mina spoke to her about "the political powers of the city and in the country at large." Mina defined these powers to her as

"a cold center" which no human appeal or sense of decency and justice could reach. I think Mina's experiences among college and city administrators and bureaucrats made her more and more aware that there were certain interests which had no intention of implementing a more democratic educational system. We were all learning this; I think Mina, in her particular position, had more opportunities to see it "from inside."

These concerns had an influence on the direction that Mina was taking as she proceeded with her work on *Errors and Expectations.* In her original proposal, and in early references to the book, she described a project whereby she would prepare "as full a description as possible of the entire range of difficulties remedial students have in writing." But now, in her second proposal to the Carnegie Foundation, dated March 8, 1972, she explained that she intended to focus as well on the need for teachers "to confront our ignorance of whole territories of linguistic experience, to look more carefully at the process of writing to understand just how we have managed as a profession to become so unsuccessful with so many students." Enough books had been written addressing the deficiencies of students: textbooks, handbooks, grammar workbooks. Mina would produce instead "a resource book for remedial teachers and administrators, and I would want it to be open about what we know and don't know, the right steps we have taken and the wrong."

The contrast between Ted Gross's report and Mina's report reflects the determination and high-mindedness that so many of Mina's "minions" valued and respected. Gross was still trying to arrive at some sort of accommodation between the old and the new, and perhaps as chair of the department that was a necessary concern. Mina, on the other hand, chose to ignore such issues: the question of degrees and rank had been eclipsed a long time ago for her by the needs of thirty-five hundred basic writing students. The newly arrived instructor who had confided to Edmond Volpe that "professors scare me" was now a force to be reckoned with; even without the Ph.D., Mina Shaughnessy was vital to the department and to the college, and everyone knew it.

Mina would not be eligible for her next promotion, to associate professor, until 1976. However, circumstances arose that led Ted Gross to request that she be promoted three years early. She had been offered the directorship of the Basic Writing Program at Hunter College at the rank of associate professor. Marilyn Maiz remembers that Mina displayed no untoward pride or delight—her modest and unassuming nature prevailed—but she must have been ebullient. She had worked as a part-time lecturer at Hunter College for five years, doing everything she could to earn a full-time appointment. But because of the lack of a Ph.D., coupled with her specialization in basic writing, she was never offered a position. Now, almost ten years later, still without a Ph.D., Mina was being offered a position by the president of Hunter College, Jacqueline Wexler.

Mina used Hunter College's offer to improve her position at City College: if City would match Hunter's offer in terms of rank and salary she would remain at City; if not, she would join the faculty at Hunter and continue to do the same thing she had been doing all along: administer a basic writing program for Open Admissions students—with unparalleled dedication and talent. She was in the midst of researching and writing *Errors and Expectations,* but the position at Hunter would not begin until September 1973, the same time she was expected to return to City. Ted Gross knew Mina's worth to City College, and he wrote a three-page, single-spaced letter to Saul Tousler, provost of City

College, imploring him to match Hunter's offer. Gross's letter indicates just how much Mina had accomplished in her seven years at City College. She had become, in effect, the most prominent expert and spokesperson in the country in the field of basic writing. Gross's request—that Mina be promoted three years early and receive two salary increments—was an extraordinary one, particularly since severe budget cuts were being implemented at CUNY. But Gross's letter offers ample evidence that Mina Shaughnessy was extraordinary as well. One can only imagine her pleasure in reading the letter—a recognition of (and perhaps even a vindication of sorts for) the extraordinary contributions that had often been either unrecognized or disparaged by a large majority of the faculty.

In his letter, Gross explained that, as chair of the department, he and Mina had "struggled with the Open Admissions program of the English department." He had witnessed her talent and dedication during the period when the SEEK program suddenly and unexpectedly became an Open Admissions program:

I remind you of Mina's career at the college to indicate that she served in one of the most sensitive and difficult roles on this campus during the 1968–1969 riots and during the various other crises, before and afterwards, when Presidents Gallagher and Marshak, Provost Schwartz and yourself, Professors Volpe, Buckley and I depended upon her—when we needed her. She has been at the center of the most vexing problems we have all had to confront and has emerged as a leader, a highly regarded member of this faculty, whatever constituency one speaks of—Puerto Rican, Oriental, Black or White; older and younger; radical and conservative; men and women. I think it is fair to say that without her constant support, loyalty, and extraordinary diplomacy, the history of Open Admissions at the City College would have been indeed a different history.

Mina possesses qualities that I have seen in very few members of this college community. She has the ability, on the one hand, of speaking in the most sophisticated and theoretical terms about language and then of turning, with infinite patience, to the pragmatic business of moving a remedial student from square one to square two, of helping young and old faculty members work out their writing problems without the least condescension. There is a spirit of intellectual curiosity and human generosity that flows from her and that creates faculty morale among young lecturers and insecure students; and within the context of this compassion and concern she maintains the most rigorous standards. It is no accident that there has not been one incident resulting from the many problems in the Basic Writing Program—when, in fact—it is potentially one of the most explosive areas of study in the curriculum. The smooth professional character of that program, the style of seriousness, social and educational commitment, of rapport among "professors" and "lecturers" and various types of "new" students—all of these characteristics bear the signature of Mina Shaughnessy.

It is a notorious fact that Basic Writing Programs at other city colleges have "borrowed" her extensively prepared written materials, have consulted with her concerning their own programs, have visited our campus to see how she has been so successful. Her local reputation has spread quickly throughout the country and she is now one of the academic leaders in the whole field of language skills: her leadership at the National Council of Teachers of English, at the 4C's, and her election to the Executive Committee of NCTE indicate the regard with which she is held. . . .

The research on Open Admissions, for which she has received the Carnegie Foundation Fellowship, will result in a book that should be the first fully documented study of the effects of Open Admissions on college students. It grows out of her experiences at City College, out of the long summer and evening hours as well as working days that she has spent so selflessly in Basic Writing, and she should be on this faculty when that book is published. I have seen some of the data that she has accumulated. The early drafts promise to develop into a book of considerable significance in an area of education that is and probably will be the most important field—in terms of the education that American students need. . . .

We have a student body that is desperately in need of language skills. We are blessed by having the most gifted person in our midst to grapple with this issue, to help us retain our leadership in the field of language skills, to set guidelines for other colleges, to educate—if there is one person in an English department of 148 members who is indispensable, she is that person. In the context of the entire college, I would add my own deep conviction that this is a personnel decision of the first priority for all of us.

City College met Hunter's offer; administrators got around the salary problem by changing Mina's title from assistant chairperson of composition within the English department to director of the Writing Program—the same title that Hunter College had offered to her. It took several memos to iron out the details and to define her "new" position "with vastly expanded duties" in terms that would justify the unusual salary increase and promotion, but in effect Mina's responsibilities would not change that much at all—she would continue to be responsible for everything and everyone involved in basic writing at City College.

Obviously, Mina wanted to remain at City College: it was, after all, the place where she had pieced together—sometimes single-handedly—a writing program that is even today referred to as "the house that Mina built." Furthermore, despite the resistance and animosity directed at her because of her position and involvement in Open Admissions, even her detractors had come to begrudgingly recognize her accomplishments, and she had developed close and important friendships at City. Mina had met Addison Gayle at City, one of the most respected writers and poets in the English department, author of such books as *The Black Aesthetic, Freedom and Beyond,* and *The Way of the New World.* Gayle wrote about his relationship with Mina in his autobiography, *Wayward Child: A Personal Odyssey,* referring to her as Nana to protect her privacy.

In addition to those colleagues with whom she worked in the English department, Mina had made many other valuable friendships, with Allen B. Ballard, for example, the highest ranking African American administrator at City College. He thanked Mina in the acknowledgments of his book, *The Education of Black Folk,* for having read and commented on the manuscript and for, as a member of the SEEK staff, "demonstrating . . . that the elitist theory of education rests on the slimmest of reeds—the belief that some are endowed from birth with the ability to learn and that others, of a different skin color, are doomed forever to be separated from that knowledge necessary to survival in the modern world" (vii).

By remaining at City College, Mina could easily continue her friendships with Alice Trillin, Marilyn Maiz, Adrienne Rich, and many others, friendships that extended far beyond a professional relationship. These relationships were particularly important to Mina because she and Donald Shaughnessy spent so little time together. "People would assume that Mina lived an 'all work and no play' existence primarily because she accomplished so much," Marilyn Maiz says, "but she loved to have a good time. Whenever there were department parties, Mina was always the one who danced the longest (and the best); she loved to talk and have fun. She'd invite colleagues to her apartment for drinks or dinner—she loved good stories, and the people at City were very good storytellers."

Alice Trillin remembers that she and Mina worked hard together, along with Blanche Skurnick, Barbara Quint Gray, and Sarah D'Eloia, on a series of videotapes that would be used to teach grammar, but they also spent many evenings and weekend afternoons together, "being friends, confiding in each other, laughing a lot, shopping, talking about literature and people."

Adrienne Rich remembers that she and Mina had provocative conversations about many topics, particularly the growing feminist movement of the 1970s, and she was able "only with great difficulty" to convince Mina to attend a debate at Town Hall featuring Norman Mailer, Germaine Greer, and others. (Janet Emig has described Mina as "breathtakingly nonfeminist.") Mina was good-natured about it, Rich recalls, "but she did not understand any possible relevancy of feminism to her life and concerns, and that debate, really a debacle, of course did not help at all."

Mina's new title, academic promotion, and higher salary did not change the fact that she still needed more time to complete *Errors and Expectations*. She had been at City College for almost seven years and thus was eligible for a sabbatical. Her request was approved, giving her another year without teaching and administrative duties, from September 1973 until August 1974. She requested that she be permitted to continue to work on campus, in the same office she had used during the period of her Carnegie Foundation grant. The Carnegie Foundation had given her the additional funds she had requested, so her working arrangements with a secretary and a research assistant would also remain the same.

Mina did not work exclusively on the book during this period, however, because so much of her time was occupied with committee work. In 1972, she coordinated the Open Admissions Seminar at the 4C's in Boston; in 1973 she became a member of the Executive Committee of NCTE and chaired an NCTE pre-Conference in Philadelphia on Growth in Writing. In 1974, she was appointed chair of the

Research Committee on Reading Problems of High School Graduates, a committee convened by the National Institute of Education, Department of Health, Education, and Welfare.

And it was early in 1973 that Mina began to work on an essay that she would entitle "Open Admissions and the Disadvantaged Teacher." (See Appendix A.) She delivered this address at the 4C's in New Orleans in spring 1973, and it was subsequently published in the December 1973 issue of *College Composition and Communication*. It was the first of Mina's essays to reach a national audience, and the reaction was immediate and intense. From that moment on, she was perceived by everyone in the field as the leading spokesperson for basic writing; requests to chair sessions, write articles, deliver speeches, and visit writing programs began to flood her office—making it even more difficult for her to find the time she needed to complete her book.

"Open Admissions and the Disadvantaged Teacher" is an extraordinary essay; the title itself reflects Mina's conviction that the problems encountered by Open Admissions students stem as much, if not more, from the disadvantages imposed on teachers of basic writing as from the "disadvantages" of the students, and that these problems resulted from the language and behavior of those who opposed Open Admissions. Mina was determined to recast the way Open Admissions would be viewed and judged, no longer in terms of statistics, but in terms of what society was willing to do to save its students—and itself. She was articulating the beliefs that guided the actions of so many other dedicated basic writing instructors, giving them the voice and the inspiration they so desperately needed. City, state, and federal budgets were being slashed as a result of the economic recession that had begun in the early seventies, further exacerbating the conditions under which many basic writing instructors (a growing majority of whom were part time) were working (and which still exist today): too many students crowded into basement classrooms or makeshift temporary quarters, with few if any support services. Furthermore, their work was often viewed with confusion, even hostility, by administrators, politicians, and the public.

Bob Lyons remembers the effect that Mina's essays and speeches had on those teachers who were "in the trenches":

> Mina would write one essay or give one talk, and those who read
> it or heard her would be so inspired that they would be prepared to

work with the dedication that you would associate with a military unit. There was a real call to arms here; Mina called it "cheering the troops," and this suggests that part of her poise and power was being aware of herself doing these things. It was not at all cynical, rather it was simply a consciousness of what she needed to do. To a large degree, her theatrical training really helped her here: she had a double sense of herself—the podium was a stage—she was aware of what needed to be done under the circumstances and how to affect an audience. She was absolutely superb at it. She had her moments, of course, of wondering if we would succeed, but she kept them to herself or shared them with only a few of us; her great poise and graciousness never seemed to be dampened.

Nowhere is Mina's ability to "cheer the troops" more apparent than in one of the closing paragraphs of her essay where she posed the "real" question being forced by Open Admissions (a question that remains unanswered even today):

Open Admissions began as a remedial wing to a few departments on traditional college campuses, but it is now transforming the colleges themselves, exposing far more than the deficiencies of the new students. By probing into the nature of those deficiencies and resisting those who have tried to isolate the phenomenon of disadvantage from the society that caused it, Open Admissions is forcing the real question—not how many people society is willing to salvage, but how much this society is willing to pay to salvage itself.

CHAPTER SIX

Errors and Expectations

*M*ina continued to work on *Errors and Expectations* for the next two years. Marilyn Maiz remembers that throughout 1973 and 1974, Mina would arrive at the City College campus on Monday morning with the pages she had written or typed over the weekend, usually on yellow legal paper. Many of these weekends were spent at the Fosdicks' country home. In fact, when *Errors and Expectations* was published early in 1977, Mina inscribed her copy to Betty Fosdick: "For Betty, my dearest friend, who helped me begin every one of these chapters." She would edit the pages she had written during the train ride from Connecticut to Manhattan and turn them over to Marilyn to be typed.

There were distractions, however; so many in fact that it is a wonder Mina was able to do any work at all on the manuscript. Her mother, Ruby Pendo, had begun to suffer angina attacks, and Mina worried constantly about her mother's health. Her father's arthritis had become so severe that he and Ruby had begun to spend their winters in Arizona. Mina tried to visit them more often and to stay for longer periods of time. She continued to pay their phone bill (they still considered the telephone a luxury) so that she could speak to them on a regular basis.

Janet Emig remembers one particular incident that occurred at this time. Mina had dreamed about one of the rooms at the ranch, a dream that was so clear and precise she could read the names of the books lined on one particular bookshelf. The next morning, Mina called her mother to confirm the accuracy of her dream, and they both marveled and laughed over the incident—Mina had even dreamed the books in their correct order on the shelf. A Freudian could have had a field day with such a dream, but Emig recalls that Mina told her about the incident simply as a means of describing the wonderful relationship she had with her mother and her memories of South Dakota.

Late in 1973, Donald Shaughnessy's assignment in Vietnam ended, and he spent three months in Manhattan with Mina before departing for Zaire, where he would be stationed until 1977. Although Mina continued to work on the manuscript, she and Don could not resist watching parts of the Watergate hearings on television, fascinated by the political machinations. One of the footnotes in *Errors and Expectations,* in fact, cites Wilfred Sheed on the hearings: "Mull the marvelous language, not just the familiar examples but the whole cunningly flaccid tone of it. . . . The bureaucratic mind recoils from the active verbs because they fix responsibility" (86).

While Don was home on leave, Raymond Fosdick died suddenly of a heart attack at his home in Newtown, Connecticut. Betty called Mina and Don immediately, and they spent the next several days helping her make funeral arrangements. Mina was deeply saddened: she had worked very closely with Raymond on the Rockefeller biography and on the history of the General Education Board, and they had developed a deep respect and affection for each other. Furthermore, she realized the loneliness that Betty would now experience. Mina spent even more time with her, determined to provide companionship and friendship when it was most needed. During the spring of 1974, Betty invited Mina to travel with her to Greece once again, as her guest. They spent about ten days visiting many of the same sights they had visited with Raymond several years earlier. Betty remembers that Mina was relaxed and happy on the trip, "a perfect companion in every way," and both of them were quite impressed by the fact that their guide was the same one who had served as a guide for Edith Hamilton.

Although Mina was officially on sabbatical during the 1973–74 academic year, there were still many issues and concerns she had to deal with at the college, and of course there was no way she could avoid campus politics. In 1974, it was decided that a dean would be appointed to oversee the basic education program, including math as well as writing. Ted Gross, who was an associate dean of humanities, submitted Mina's name, confident that she would be appointed by President Robert Marshak. "She was such a logical choice," Gross remembers.

Mina on one of her trips to Greece with Betty Fosdick. Courtesy of Betty Fosdick.

"There was no one in the country, much less at City, more qualified for the job." Gross assumed that Marshak would agree that Mina was the most suitable candidate as well; as president, he had always recognized her contributions to City. In fact, in a 1973 report entitled *Problems and Prospects of an Urban Public University* (an attempt to portray the turmoil that had overtaken the college as "the first positive steps [leading to] an important turning point in the College's history" [12]), Marshak cited Mina's work in developing and directing a writing center "that has attracted the attention of colleges and universities in various parts of the country, and representatives from many of these institutions have visited and plan to create similar laboratories" (24). In addition, he referred to her grant from the Carnegie Foundation as evidence that "the Writing Center plans to begin the research phase of its operation" (24).

Mina wanted the job of dean, of course; in fact, Marilyn Maiz remembers that Mina would talk about someday becoming a college president. However, she wanted the job not simply for the prestige a deanship would bring, but because she knew it was a role in which she could continue to expand the opportunities available to Open Admissions students. Ed Quinn, who had become chair of the English department, remembers that Mina continued to do department work on behalf of the Open Admissions students even though she was supposed to be on sabbatical.

> Mina would spend days, sometimes weeks, preparing reports and memos to justify budget allotments, hiring new tutors or instructors, opening new classes, expanding the writing center, in addition to visits and presentations that she was making more and more frequently as a representative of one of the most well-known and successful basic writing programs in the country. As chair, I must have received fifteen to twenty telephone calls a week asking for information about "Mina Shaughnessy's writing program."

Mina was a natural choice for the job because of her growing reputation; her ability to function effectively in an environment that was hostile to the changes that had been brought about by Open Admissions; her deep knowledge and understanding of the problems Open Admissions students faced, and the reasons for those problems; the recognition, even among her most staunch opponents, that she was not trying to overturn a system but rather to prepare students to succeed in that system; expressions of interest and offers of positions from other institutions; her ability to help teachers become more effective without seeming dogmatic or patronizing; and her fine writing ability. Ed Quinn remembers thinking that there was simply no better fit of position and person. Her brilliance and dedication to the students was important of course, but even more than that, he recalls,

> Mina was effective because she was one of those people who didn't need credit for accomplishing something; that's why she got so much done. She wasn't one to "protect her turf" so to speak; she let us do her fighting for her when it was absolutely necessary, but she didn't play games the way most academicians do in order to get ahead or gain power. She never lost sight of her goal—to see to it that more and more students succeeded at City. And long after it was obvious to everyone that she knew more about basic writing and composition than anyone else in the country, she still had a rigorous intellectual commitment to the field, doing research, still reading and attending conferences and listening and learning.
>
> Mina had paid her dues many times over. She deserved that deanship as a reward, but everyone knew she wouldn't use it in that way—she'd just keep working even harder.

Ted Gross was incredulous when it became apparent that Marshak was going to give the job to someone else at the college, an administrator with far less experience in basic education. Gross recalls a meeting he attended at which the final decision was reached:

> There were one or two people arguing against Mina, claiming that she didn't have a Ph.D., therefore she wouldn't have the respect of people both inside and outside the college; that she was only an expert in the field of basic writing, not math, therefore she wouldn't be sympathetic to the issues of math education. The arguments were so unfounded, so weak, that I could barely contain my anger. Of course I argued that her reputation was so great that the Ph.D. was irrelevant at that point. Furthermore, the Carnegie Foundation grant was an indication of Mina's ability to bring in money from other foundations. She was such a quick study that she had been able to convert what could have been a disastrous situation into one of the most effective and promising Open Admissions programs in the country, so one could just imagine what she would do for the entire area of basic education.

It soon became apparent to Gross, and to many others who were aware of the situation, that Mina was probably not given the appointment precisely because of her qualifications. The political and economic climate of New York City was growing more conservative, and race began to be an even larger factor: many whites were alarmed when critics of Open Admissions declared that the new students were destroying the entire CUNY system. There were many influential people, at City College but elsewhere as well, who associated Open Admissions exclusively with black and Puerto Rican students. (Aware of this perception, CUNY administrators often went to great pains to stress the fact that Open Admissions was also serving white students. In fact, Marshak's report noted that Open Admissions had "opened the door for white ethnic Catholics as well, chiefly of Irish and Italian background.") Marshak knew that as dean of basic skills, Mina Shaughnessy would have drawn even greater national attention to the needs of Open Admissions students, forcing not only educational administrators but other powerful and influential people—politicians, writers, intellectuals—to come to terms with the fact that it was not the students who needed remediation but the system itself. Giving someone like Mina a position from which she could espouse the rights of Open Admissions students would have made it even more difficult for administrators to mollify those who did not believe that City College should use its resources to level the educational playing field in New York City. These minority students were not going to go away, that was clear to everyone, but administrators (who were being forced to make difficult budget decisions) most certainly were not going to provide a forum for a spokesperson and advocate who would use her intelligence, expertise, and charisma to argue—convincingly and eloquently—for the rights of these students.

Mina was severely disappointed, of course, but as always, she kept her countenance, telling very few people how she actually felt and acting as if nothing had happened. Marilyn Maiz remembers, however, that Mina began to realize how little she was actually valued by those in power at City College:

> Mina was always able to accept criticism from those people, primarily professors who had been at City for a long time, who did not believe that Open Admissions students belonged at City College. With just a few exceptions, these professors were open and honest with her about their positions, so she always knew where she stood with them.
>
> However, when the very administrators under whom she had been fighting the good fight for more than seven years and who knew how hard she struggled to make the writing program work didn't give her the deanship, it was too much for her to bear. It was, after all, a grave insult. Mina wasn't a person who got angry very easily, but she was very angry about this. I think it was at this time that she resolved to leave City. If they were not going to make her a dean of an area about which she knew more than anyone else, why should she stay? They didn't value her contributions, and it was now clear that there was no future at City for her.

At about this time, Leslie Berger, who had gone from his position at City College to associate dean for academic affairs for the entire CUNY system, talked with Mina about a new position that was being created at the CUNY administrative offices. Berger and other CUNY administrators had begun to realize that there needed to be a central location, a resource center, where research and resources being produced in the various CUNY divisions could be collected and disseminated, where inservice training for teachers could occur, and where new curricular materials and placement tests could be developed. Every CUNY campus had its own basic writing and math program, and the educators and directors of these programs were often duplicating the same efforts. They were, Berger recalls, "reinventing the wheel at least once a week." Although the position was advertised nationally, with more than one hundred applicants responding, Berger had actually written the job description with Mina in mind, knowing that she was "eminently qualified." She was not as convinced as Berger of her ability, however. He recalls her reaction when they discussed the position:

> Many people knew the "public" Mina, the one who came across as if she was in control. She'd hold her head up high; she had that wonderful bearing; she'd look people straight in the eye when she spoke to them. But Mina and I developed a very close friendship— after all, I had met her in 1966, so we had been through a lot together at City College. She was able to confide in me, and she would often express doubts over her ability to do something. As a psychologist, I understood this need and offered her unconditional support and friendship. I wanted her to take the CUNY job; she was perfect for it. She had already earned the respect and admiration of everyone working in basic education; she had already proved that she could develop instructional materials and train faculty; she wasn't finished with the book yet, but everyone knew that it would be as good as everything else she did.

Mina did finally accept the position, to become effective in spring 1975. In addition to her official title of director of the Instructional Resource Center, she would also be appointed an associate dean of CUNY. In the meanwhile, despite the fact that she had to attend meetings and form committees in anticipation of the resource center's opening, she was determined to continue her work on *Errors and Expectations*.

In December 1974, however, Ruby Pendo suffered a heart attack and remained in a hospital in Yuma, Arizona, for three weeks. Mina flew to Arizona on January 11, 1975, to be with her when she returned

Mina with her mother, June 1970. Courtesy of George Pendo.

home from the hospital. Mina would have gone even sooner, but her husband was home from Zaire for a Christmas visit, and Ruby had insisted that Mina remain with him until he returned to Africa.

Mina wrote an account of her mother's illness, and she recorded their activities during this period:

> I arrived around 10:00 p.m. She looked so small and weak but seemed otherwise herself, as always overjoyed that I was home. I had brought her a new suit and she looked at that, even tried on the jacket and loved it.
>
> Then began our long and careful period of convalescence. We had not been given adequate instruction and felt our way along with the medication. She had several angina attacks during that week. She would begin to feel discomfort and then slowly become very pale and put her head back and occasionally move her hands. It was intense pain. And then, when it was over, she would seem to snap right out and smile and say she was all right. Once during one of these spells, I held her hand and wept and after I asked her if she didn't want me to stay on longer, but she was insistent, even disturbed by

the suggestion. "No, no, my dear, you have your life to live." Yet to me, during those moments, all my life seemed to be there with her.

Mina remained in Arizona with her parents for almost a month, and she recorded several events and impressions of the time she spent with her mother. Despite several more angina attacks, Ruby seemed to be recovering: "Each small trace of improvement," Mina wrote, "more appetite, a day without pain, sitting in the sun—was cause for celebration." Ruby described for Mina the way that she had cared for her own mother during her final illness, but Mina "could never think of what to say when she mentioned this, because I didn't want to accept the analogy." Mina recorded the smallest details of their time together:

> She looked lovely all those days. Her body was agile and her hair was full and pretty. Some mornings . . . I helped her dress; scolding her for moving too fast. She laughed a lot—even about being ill. One day she came upon a saying that went something like this: "Arthritis, indigestion, high blood pressure—old age isn't for sissies." And when I would ask her my constant question, "How are you?" sometimes she'd grin and say "Terrible!" which meant good. She laughed at something Dad did one day. I can see her now sitting in bed, giggling in that irrepressible way.
>
> We used to laugh at her "Grandma" underwear when I got it out in the mornings and at the sorry state of some of her slips.
>
> And she read a great deal—newspapers, *My Antonia*, *Road to Byzantium* and every night read from a Bible. . . . Then she would finish with a little prayer book, which was her custom for years. We never spoke of death but always of when I would be out in March or when they would go back to Dakota. On the day I left, she said it would be sinful to be sad because we had had such a good time and because she was feeling so much better. And then, we sat, the three of us, in the living room on the day I left and chatted. "Bring those slippers out when you come in March and I'll mend them." Other things I don't remember now. I don't remember either what she was wearing, except that she had on a white sweater and a pant suit. Then at the last we hugged and tried not to give way to our feelings. She lay down on the sofa and didn't look out the window to wave. She must have cried, as I did. She used to sit beside the window and wave out.

On the way to the airport Dad and I talked about her improvement and felt relatively good. But just as we got out of the car, Dad said in a broken voice, "You are a noble daughter and you will never regret having come out here to be with Mom."

Mina arrived home in Manhattan on February 5, 1975, and four days later, on February 9, 1975, Ruby Pendo suffered another heart attack and died. She was seventy-nine years old. Mina returned to Arizona the next day and stayed with her father for two weeks. It was at this time she promised her father that she would write down as much as she could remember about her mother's final illness and death; it seemed very important to Albert Pendo that some record be made, a commemoration of sorts. (The passages quoted above are from this ten-page handwritten account.) It is unclear when Mina wrote the description, but George Pendo saved it in the same envelope in which she mailed it to her father, postmarked September 1975, seven months after Ruby's death. Mina tried to remember the names of everyone who visited, but wrote "it is all mixed in my memory now." She recorded that she chose the scripture verses and hymns and wrote some comments about her mother for the Lutheran minister to incorporate into his eulogy. George remembers that, during the wake, people commented that Ruby looked "natural and beautiful," but Mina did not agree: "Mina placed Mother's glasses on her, and that seemed to make Mina feel better."

The last page of Mina's account reflects the pain she was enduring over her mother's death:

> We put her things in order and mourned in our hearts as the memories from her presence, from her loveliness, cut into our hearts and made it seem that there was no end of tears. . . .
>
> What is most painful now is the memory of her unselfishness, of her innocence—reflected in countless events and gestures that reach back over my life. Her dignity and pride. Her enjoyment of clothes. Her quiet excellence in the kitchen. Her cheerfulness. Her strong will. Her tenderness. Her way of contending with disappointment. Her little verses and recipes tucked into envelopes all over the place. Her sewing enthusiasms. Her ways of worrying about money. Her grace—until the very last. Her subtle, womanly way of remembering and doing and taking pains. Gone.

Mina's friends were unprepared for her reaction to her mother's death. They had been aware of her devotion to her mother, of course, and they understood the severity of her loss, but her grief was so deep, so intense, that they were unable to comfort her. Priscilla Brandt recalls that Mina felt enormous guilt over not having done more for her mother while she was alive; in addition, Priscilla remembers that Mina believed she had lost her best friend:

> Mina talked to her mother and about her mother all the time. Every Christmas, she would share with us the steam pudding that her mother had prepared and sent her. Mina was so proud of that pudding and the love and hospitality it represented. Whenever we went shopping, she would buy clothing for her mother—entire outfits. She loved to do things for Ruby.
>
> Mina never discussed her mother in the way that grown daughters sometimes do—accepting and tolerating their foibles. She adored and admired her mother, and she wanted to please her; she wanted her mother to be proud of her. When my aunt sent Mina a note of condolence, Mina replied to that note saying, "She was the perfect mother." She truly believed that.
>
> It was also apparent to Mina that her mother's life had been a difficult one. Mina's father could be hard to live with at times, and she knew that her mother often bore the brunt of his temper and his insensitivity. This troubled Mina enormously; after Ruby's death she wished that she had done more for her mother. Alan and I tried to convince her that she had been a wonderful daughter, reminding her that she had spent practically every school break traveling to see her parents, but Mina wasn't comforted.
>
> She wasn't depressed in the clinical sense after her mother's death, but she was deeply saddened. It was a loss from which I don't think she ever fully recovered.

Mina knew that her mother had felt great pride over her professional accomplishments; whenever Mina returned home, Georgia Jensen, her high school friend, would assure her that she knew, through Ruby Pendo, everything that she had been doing at City College. On May 4, 1975, less than three months after Ruby's death, *The New York Times* ran a full-page article entitled "Capitalizing on Poor Writing," about Mina and her work at City College, describing her work and her commitment to her students (accompanied by a photograph of Mina looking extremely beautiful). She is quoted extensively throughout the article: eloquent, cogent, and convincing comments that enabled anyone who read it to understand not only that the students about whom she was speaking were perfectly capable of "learning what their teachers had learned," but also that she was an extraordinary educator. It was one of the first of many articles and accolades that Mina would receive, but George remembers that she derived "very little pleasure" from the article and the attention that followed: "She just wished that Mother had been alive to see it."

After her mother's death, Mina devoted even more time and energy to her work—although she was now worried about her father being alone. A little more than a year after Ruby died, Albert remarried. Mina welcomed his new wife, Eliza, into their family; she was genuinely fond of her and relieved that Albert would have someone to take care of him.

By the middle of 1975, Mina had completed what she considered to be a first draft of *Errors and Expectations;* however, when she showed the manuscript to Bob Lyons, he thought it was so brilliant that he encouraged her to submit it immediately for publication. Lyons recalls, though, that she needed convincing:

> Mina was not sure that it was good enough—as hard as that is to believe—she was very nervous about it. She and my wife, Bridget, were very good friends, and Bridget taught at Rutgers with Janet Emig, so Mina asked both Bridget and me to read it. We were so convinced that the book was of the highest quality, of such importance, that we encouraged Mina to submit it to Oxford [University Press], since we held John Wright, who was an editor there, in such high regard.

Mina had already submitted the manuscript to friends at Prentice-Hall, Jossey-Bass, and Winthrop Press (in Cambridge, Massachusetts), but she had made no commitments. Convinced that the book needed more work, she wanted to know if her contacts at these publishing houses thought the book had any promise; she did not expect any offers of publication at that stage.

Later in 1975, Mina chaired a panel at the National Institute of Education on Studies in Reading in Washington, D.C. Janet Emig also participated, and she remembers that Mina was "as intelligent, effective, and persuasive as usual." Mina edited the report of the panel, entitled "Reading Comprehension and the High School Graduate," earning even more national recognition and prominence.

In addition, during 1974 and 1975 Mina completed a thirty-page bibliographic essay entitled "Basic Writing." It was to be included in a 1976 publication entitled *Teaching Composition: Ten Bibliographical Essays,* edited by Gary Tate and published by Texas Christian University Press, a collection that was being produced in recognition of the new importance that composition had taken in the college curriculum. Tate explained the purpose of the book in his introduction: "My approach was to find the best people I knew and turn them loose, asking only that they write bibliographical *essays* rather than mere listings of important works" (viii).

Mina explained the purpose of her essay in this way:

> Without an accumulation of published information across a range of experiences with the new [basic writing] students, we are left with a highly circumscribed literature, essentially the bits and pieces of information that make their way back from a frontier, tempting us to premature judgments about the students and how or what they are learning. The literature consists largely of articles and dissertations which concentrate on two subjects: the students, how they write and what they appear to need; and programs and methods, what they are and how well they are working. I will describe each of these categories briefly, suggesting articles or studies that a basic writing teacher might find useful. (142)

Mina then cited the contents of thirty-four books, forty five articles, eleven dissertations, and eight reports or monographs, weaving descriptions of these readings together with comments, information, and suggestions about their usefulness to a basic writing teacher—erudite, engaging, and informed comments that reflect an understanding not only of the readings she cited, but of the complex issues involved in basic writing education. She referred several times in her essay to the "frontier" of basic writing, a metaphor she was using more and more often to describe the unexplored, "wide-open" field of basic writing:

> Despite some excellent individual studies of programs or methods, one is left after reviewing the literature with the sense that there is something premature, repetitive, and unavoidably reductive about

our attempts so far to evaluate instruction in writing. Few teachers have been trained for this kind of research. Few schools or programs are organized to generate or process information about their effectiveness, with the result that the individual researcher is overburdened by clerical and administrative duties that quickly discourage experimentation. Furthermore, writing is a slow-developing skill that should be measured over longer periods than a semester, but no system for collecting longitudinal data on writing performance exists to my knowledge in any program. We lack information and the habit of getting information about individual students that would enable us to isolate outside influences such as previous training or career commitments from methods of instruction. We lack adequate (i.e. precise and economical) instruments for measuring writing and then for controlling the unruly variables that swarm about the classroom situation. In the jargon of the systems analysts, we have difficulty measuring output (writing) and even greater difficulty relating output to input (teaching). Finally, we lack a tradition of collaborative research, within colleges as well as among them, that would enable us to combine resources and conduct more systematic experiments. Nowhere in the profession of teaching writing is the frontier more wide open. (146)

In her conclusion, Mina addressed those who were engaged in teaching basic writing at the college level:

I began by saying that the teaching of writing to unprepared college-age students is but the frontier of a profession. The readings I have cited in this essay must suggest that this is so. For basic writing teachers, the world is indeed all before them. The skill they have contracted to teach is itself among the most complex of human activities and the students who sit in their classrooms, young, intelligent, and miseducated men and women, depend as students have never depended before upon having good teachers. The "remediation" of their teachers may, in fact, be the most important education going on today. (167)

This reference to the "frontier" of basic education would appear again and again in Mina's writing, but it is particularly appropriate in the context of this essay, because she was offering the most accurate and complete road map that had yet been created as a guide to the "frontier of a profession," the place where teachers, as well as students, would begin their "remediation."

Bob Lyons believes that her use of the image of the frontier was particularly apt, given the time when Mina was writing. "The frontier is the place where everyone is a stranger," he explained in a conference address he delivered about her in 1979,

> and where nobody is fully at home or settled in. In this new terri-
> tory, everyone has to get their bearings, students and teachers alike,
> and everyone has to make adjustments in their habitual modes of
> thinking and acting. The frontier calls on everybody's resourceful-
> ness and ingenuity in adapting their particular kind of knowledge to
> new situations. It also calls for a special openness and trust—in a dif-
> ficult and sparsely populated land, people must cooperate for sur-
> vival. And the frontier is finally a place where the future is necessar-
> ily more important than the past. (16)

Lyons believes that Mina was particularly well suited to guide others because she recognized "the complexity of her subject and its constantly conflicting nature" (12). Mina, he recalls, did not believe that in order to arrive at a new idea or theory "it was necessary to debunk or dismiss other people or other theories." In fact, "Mina was interested in every-thing that people had to say about the issues of teaching reading and writing." Lyons recalled, in his conference address, the way her enthu-siasm for new ideas and discoveries affected her behavior at conferences:

> Mina had special expectations [of conferences]. In Scott
> Fitzgerald's stories, there are characters who gaze up at the lighted
> windows of Manhattan buildings in twilight and are filled with a sense
> of wonder at the variety of life they sense behind those windows.
> Mina has some of this anticipation, transferred to conference rooms
> and conference panels. She was always arranging to have friends and
> colleagues sit in on sessions running at the same time as one she was
> attending, always insisting that something interesting was likely to
> happen at every meeting. No matter how exotic the conference set-
> ting, no matter how tempting the sightseeing or the restaurants, Mina
> would always set her schedule by the conference schedule, listening
> to as many papers and discussions and workshops as she could. How
> often her hopes at these gatherings were realized I can't say, but it

was often enough to sustain her, for she never stopped poring over conference programs with an expression that belonged to someone reading the racing form at Aqueduct. (1)

Mina was being perceived by more and more people in the field of composition as the person best qualified to "guide" them through the new frontier (she once referred to it as a "new profession"), and the address she delivered at the Modern Language Association Conference in San Francisco in December 1975 further enhanced that perception. It was a turning point in Mina's career—and in her life. She had worked on the address for several months, entitling it "Diving In: An Introduction to Basic Writing." (See Appendix B.) In her address, she assigned four developmental scales to the teaching of basic writing:

> [S]ince it is common these days to "place" students on developmental scales, saying they are eighth-graders or fifth-graders when they read and even younger when they write or that they are stalled some place on Piaget's scale without formal propositions, I would further like to propose a developmental scale for teachers, admittedly an impressionistic one, but one that fits the observations I have made over the years as I have watched traditionally prepared English teachers, including myself, learning to teach in the open-admissions classroom.

Mina labeled (and capitalized in her text) the first "developmental" scale GUARDING THE TOWER, "because during this stage the teacher is in one way or another concentrating on protecting the academy (including himself) from the outsiders, those who do not seem to belong in the community of learners."

With the recognition by the teacher that "the class now appears to have at least some members who might, with hard work, eventually 'catch up,'" the teacher then moves into the second developmental stage, that of CONVERTING THE NATIVES, in which "learning is thought of not so much as a constant and often troubling reformulation of the world so as to encompass new knowledge but as a steady flow of truth into a void. . . . And so confident is [the teacher] of the reasonableness and allure of what he is presenting, it does not occur to him to consider the competing logics and values and habits that may be influencing his students, often in ways that they themselves are unaware of."

The third stage of development, SOUNDING THE DEPTHS, is reached, Mina explained, only when it finally occurs to the teacher that the things he or she is trying to teach the students are

> not in fact simple at all, that they only appear simple to those who already know them, that the grammar and rhetoric of formal written English have been shaped by the irrationalities of history and habit and by the peculiar restrictions and rituals that come from putting words on paper instead of into the air, that the sense and nonsense of written English must often collide with the spoken English that has been serving students in their negotiations with the world for many years.

Mina labeled her fourth and final stage DIVING IN, "in order to suggest that the teacher who has come this far must now make a decision that demands professional courage—the decision to remediate himself, to become a student of new disciplines and of his students themselves in order to perceive both their difficulties and their incipient excellence."

Mina concluded her address with a theme that she would repeat again and again to teachers of basic writing:

> The work is waiting for us. And so irrevocable now is the tide that brings the new students into the nation's college classrooms that it is no longer within our power, as perhaps it once was, to refuse to accept them into the community of the educable. They are here. DIVING IN is simply deciding that teaching them to write well is not only suitable but challenging work for those who would be teachers and scholars in a democracy.

Even before Mina delivered the address, she had already earned a reputation as one of the most brilliant, dedicated, and resourceful educators in the country (very few professors, after all, have four-column articles written about them in *The New York Times*). After the address, however, she was no longer merely an "expert"; her authority, her conviction, and her eloquence inspired those who heard her speak—and those who heard about her speech—in a manner that was simply unprecedented at the Modern Language Association, or anywhere else, for that matter. E. D. Hirsch, whom Mina met for the first time when she delivered her address, recalled the effect that she had on her audience that day:

> The audience was large—maybe 300 people. The occasion is deeply imprinted on my mind. For all my nervousness as the first speaker, I was powerfully struck by Mina's bearing and beauty, and I clearly remember how she made her way to the podium, moving deliberately and apparently calmly. She had been introduced with some self-consciously silly remarks, and when she arrived at the podium she did something that was quite startling, and as we later found out, quite characteristic. Without saying so outright, she indicated gently and with good humor that composition was too serious a matter to deserve such silliness. At her impromptu words, the audience burst into applause.
>
> Then, as she delivered her paper . . . she was interrupted with increasing frequency by more applause, and when she finished she got an ovation as long and enthusiastic as any I have heard at MLA. People who heard the talk have said that it changed their lives. They decided then and there to go into composition—to dive in. Wayne Booth came up afterwards to ask me who *was* that person, and said it was the most exciting MLA session he had ever attended. That was the electrifying effect that Mina always had on those who heard her speak. . . .
>
> Anyone who reads the text of her talk . . . will admire it as we did. But they will not be able to grasp quite why we responded on that occasion with such tremendous enthusiasm. Partly it was because Mina was a brilliantly accomplished public speaker. Partly it was because she radiated beauty and a devotion to something beyond herself. Mainly it was because she projected a moral authority that was unmistakable. (2)

The response to Mina's address was even more extraordinary, given the attitude that existed toward composition in general and to developmental writing students in particular. Ann Raimes, the coordinator of ESL at Hunter College at the time, recalls having chaired a session at the same MLA conference at which Mina spoke: "One must remember the way that ESL and basic writing were viewed at this time. When I began my presentation, someone raised his hand from the front row and asked me, 'What does ESL stand for?'"

David Bartholomae also heard Mina's address, and he recorded his impressions several years later in an essay entitled "Released into Language: Errors, Expectations, and the Legacy of Mina Shaughnessy":

> I have a vivid memory of attending the 1975 MLA Convention in San Francisco and hearing Mina Shaughnessy give a talk at the plenary session of the newly formed Division of Writing. It was a time when I was struggling to come to terms with the new direction in my professional life imposed by my first full-time appointment as a basic writing teacher and an administrator in charge of a basic writing curriculum. I had committed my career to the students she called Basic Writers and to the task of easing their precarious entry into the world of the university. At the same time, however, I was painfully aware that my ability to understand or alter their actual performance as writers was severely limited. It was a time of crisis, a crisis I found I shared with most everyone I met who was doing this kind of teaching and taking it seriously. The crisis had partly to do with the enormity of the task presented to us, having to make writers out of young adults who, many of them, had done almost no writing at all. But the crisis was due as well to the fact that we were so profoundly unprepared and that the existing models of instruction, what they were, so often ran against both our common sense and our sense of justice. . . .
>
> [Shaughnessy's] talk was given a resounding reception, and the reason for this reception, I think, was that she had given labels and order to the discouraging confusion of our professional lives, and she had done so in a way that made us believe that growth was possible (and occurring). Through her own tremendous warmth and dignity, she gave the work we were doing a dignity, a humanity, and complexity that made it seem the proper focus of a professional life. (67)

Mina was well aware of the effect her address had on her audience, and Marilyn Maiz recalls how pleased Mina was:

> When she returned to the office that Monday morning, she stood in the doorway and said, "They wouldn't stop applauding." Mina had received the academic equivalent of curtain calls. I also became aware of the extraordinary impact she had made at the conference when I started hearing about it from others, and when letters started

pouring in from all over the country, requesting copies of the address or asking her to make presentations at other conferences.

Mina answered each letter with extraordinary modesty. In response to a letter filled with high praise from the person who had invited her to deliver her address, she wrote, "I was delighted that the session went as well as it did and am grateful to have been invited to talk about basic writing."

Among the many other letters Mina received was one from Edward Corbett, an English professor at Ohio State University who had earned a prominent position in the field of composition studies as a result of his insistence to both the MLA and NCTE that composition be given greater recognition. He was also the editor of *College Composition and Communication* at the time Mina delivered her address. Corbett wrote what he describes as a "fan letter" to her two days after she delivered "Diving In":

I'm sorry that I didn't get to see you afterwards to tell you what an absolutely smashing talk you gave at MLA. But I don't have to tell you that: the prolonged applause of the audience said that much more eloquently than I could.

Now I'm going to switch from my role as an admiring friend to that of a designing editor. I'd love to have your talk for *CCC*—if you haven't already committed it.

And Corbett added a postscript: "I hope you won't be offended, but when I heard you talk on Sunday morning, I realized that you have one of the sexiest voices I have ever heard. But even that didn't distract me from the great good sense that you made in your talk."

Mina was not offended. She responded to Corbett on January 19, 1976, assuring him that he could publish the address, explaining why she had decided to give him permission to do so:

It was the postscript that did it. For an English teacher talking about remedial writing on Sunday morning at an MLA forum to evoke such thoughts suggests that there is really hope for the profession. I place my work in your hands with the utmost confidence! Should the voice so have distorted the reality as to flaw your editorial judgment, however, I'll understand.

Corbett was ebullient when he received Mina's reply. "Look what I got," he scribbled in a note to Andrea Lunsford, who was a graduate assistant at the time, "Mina Shaughnessy's great talk from the MLA meeting. The audience clapped for ten minutes after she sat down. Log it in and put it on top of the pile."

Mina's response to Ed Corbett was typical of the way she dealt with the constant references people made to her beauty, to her voice, to her demeanor. Marilyn Maiz remembers that Mina had grown accustomed to such responses; they occurred several times a day:

> Mina knew she was beautiful and she was well aware that others found her attractive. She had developed a manner of treating compliments and comments about her beauty and her features (her blond hair, her blue eyes, her height, her slim figure), lightly, knowing they were intended to please her, not to offend. It's also important to realize that people, particularly men, responded to her in this way *all the time,* so of course she became somewhat inured of it.
>
> Mina was vain in a wonderful, healthy way. During the mid-seventies, she decided to take ballet lessons twice a week, determined to get rid of her "awkwardness." None of us ever saw the slightest bit of awkwardness in her, but she insisted that she was gawky and wanted to be more graceful. Needless to say, the ballet lessons made her even thinner and more beautiful.
>
> And of course she loved clothes, but again, she wasn't obsessed with her wardrobe—she simply liked to shop and happened to look stunning in the clothes she purchased. Irving Howe used to tell a wonderful story about Mina. When she met him one day at the graduate center having come directly from teaching a class, he commented upon her beautiful outfit; she was wearing an exquisite cape that her friend Maggie Lane had brought her from Africa. When Howe asked if Mina's students were put off by her fancy clothes, she replied: "But Irving, my students know I dress up for them."

Mina had met Irving Howe late in 1973. He was one of the most prominent faculty members of the CUNY Graduate Center (his actual title was distinguished professor of English); he was the editor of

Dissent, a left-leaning journal that published the works of intellectuals and social reformers, and although his *World of Our Fathers* had not yet been published, he was viewed as larger than life by most people with whom he came into contact. Howe recalled their first meeting in a eulogy he delivered shortly after Mina's death:

> Some five years ago, a lady whom I had never met before, named Mina Shaughnessy, stormed into my office at the Graduate Center barely saying hello, racing to tell me that as executive officer of the English program I ought to do something about an injustice that had crossed her jurisdiction. Her eyes were blazing. It would be cowardly she pointed out, to evade the issue, though entirely understandable. I stared at her with wonderment and admiration, half wishing she would keep talking, half afraid she would not stop.
>
> The injustice she had in mind was indeed remediable; all it required for remedy was that we overturn the entire political structure of the city. When I remarked that this was not quite in my power, she dismissed my excuses impatiently. She said I was not supposed to be the kind of man who paid attention to such things, and then at the peak of her indignation, she suddenly broke into a lovely peal of laughter and said, "Okay, let's go out and have a drink." And so began a friendship.

It was a friendship that was a source of great pleasure for both Mina and Howe. They loved and respected each other and spent much time together.

Mina was meeting other prominent people as well, particularly when she began her new position at the CUNY Instructional Resource Center: Timothy Healy, the Jesuit priest who would later become president of Georgetown University and of the New York Public Library, had become vice chancellor of CUNY, and he and Mina developed a deep respect and liking for each other. He once told a CUNY colleague, Richard Donovan, that she was "guiding him" in the area of basic writing. "Don't worry," he said, "I may be a conservative Jesuit from Fordham, but Mina is bringing me up to speed." Benjamin DeMott, who at the time was a professor at Amherst, met her about this time and became acquainted with her work. He would later pay great homage to her not only in his review of *Errors and Expectations,* but in other references and essays about her as well. In addition, Mina had met—and instantly earned the respect and admiration of—several college presidents and the chairs and directors of major foundations. She developed close friendships with Alison Bernstein, who would later hold one of the highest positions at the Ford Foundation; K. Patricia Cross, professor of higher education at the University of California, Berkeley; and Virginia Smith, who would later become president of Vassar College.

Mina was highly effective in her interactions with these people, many of whom had enormous influence and impact on the direction of education in the United States. In 1975, she was invited to join the Advisory Committee for Alternatives to the Revolving Door, a project of the Fund for the Improvement of Post-Secondary Education (FIPSE), and later the FIPSE board itself. Dick Donovan, who chaired the FIPSE committee, remembers how pleased he and the other committee members were that she had agreed to join the panel:

> She was the first distinguished national figure in basic writing in the country; there was no one who was her equal. Mina knew everything there was to know about the politics of remediation, of course, but she never left the students out—everything was about them and for them, even when we talked about our personal lives. She described her ballet lessons to us one day, saying that she was the oldest, tallest, least coordinated person in the class. "I stand there," she told us, "trying to master the most elementary steps while the other students execute them mindlessly. It helps me realize what my writing students must be experiencing. Just because I didn't take ballet lessons when I was young, and just because they didn't learn how to write when they were young, we've got to learn the basics now."

Virginia Smith remembers observing Mina at one of the first FIPSE board meetings Mina attended:

> It's hard to describe the power that she had in her interactions with people and the way she used that power. Mina approached things not only analytically but with a great deal of optimism. She had the analytical qualities that made it possible for her to think things through, but she also had that desire to use her ability to analyze to make the educational system more useful and more productive for students who were marginalized.

I remember finding myself watching her on occasion, particularly in small meetings, and wondering if she was conscious of the effect she was having on all of us. She seemed to be utterly unaware of the impact of her beauty, her charisma, her conviction, her warmth and intelligence. She seemed to think her personal success was less important than using her talents to help others succeed. I was not the only one who held Mina in such esteem. All of us were, I think, a bit in awe of her. We liked to be with her and work through problems with her; she made things better.

Mina did not seem to have the same control in her personal life, however. She and Donald Shaughnessy remained married, and seemed to get along well when he was home on visits, but while she was still at Hunter, she had begun a long-term relationship with a CUNY professor. They were often seen in each other's company; Mina was discreet but not secretive about the relationship, and they celebrated her fiftieth birthday together on March 13, 1974. However, as the relationship grew more serious, Marilyn Maiz remembers that Mina began to question what would happen when her husband returned from Zaire.

Betty Fosdick recalls that Mina was troubled over her personal life. The death of Ruby had reawakened her interest in religion, and she would talk about "her moral obligations, her guilt, and her confusion" with Betty. John Updike once said, "As Protestant denominations go, Lutherans were rather soft on transgressions." Not Mina, however. Betty remembers that she talked about the commission of sin. "I was thirty years older than Mina, and I remember wanting to say to her: 'Child, you don't want to be alone. Just be happy.' But that would have offended her. She was very serious about her 'obligations.' I think she was suffering a terrible spiritual crisis."

Les Berger believes that although Mina had forged a highly successful professional career as a result of her brilliance and hard work, her personal life was, in contrast, becoming less satisfying to her, more troubling. "Perhaps that's one of the reasons why she worked so hard," Berger speculates, "to keep from having to come to terms with the growing dissatisfaction she was feeling about herself. She was never able to regain her balance entirely after her mother's death; it is almost as if she was freer to explore her own needs and nature, but she didn't like what she was finding."

Adrienne Rich has described Mina's tendency to "compartmentalize" her life as one of her "subtle defenses," but one which did not prevent her from experiencing much pain:

> I learned so much from Mina, came quickly to love her, and I believe that she loved and felt she learned from me. Yet our friendship was never really intimate, not as I have known intimate friendship, a fact I recognized and pondered for a long time. I felt I had to respect her defenses, her need to keep parts of her life separated, though I deplored this. We talked often of the mother-daughter relationship, and of her own mother, whose death I believe left her not free but unspeakably bereft. Her relationships with many women were, I think, founded on a mother-daughter model, in which she herself could or would, only rarely or momentarily, become a daughter. Many younger women saw in Mina a mother, extremely beautiful and effective and charismatic, as perhaps their own mothers did not seem to be.
>
> Rereading Virginia Woolf's *To the Lighthouse* several years ago, I thought of Mina, when the young woman, Lily Briscoe, says of Mrs. Ramsay, "Fifty pairs of eyes were not enough to get round that one woman with; among them must be one that was stone blind to her beauty." In the last years of her life, even before cancer had moved in so violently, I began to see her as partly imprisoned both in her beauty, to which it was so hard to be stone blind, and in the subtle defenses of a lifetime, which compartmentalized her being, causing her, I believe, much pain, for which she herself saw no possible remedy or relief.

Nor was Mina's professional life proceeding entirely without difficulty. Although Edward Corbett recalls that she was, with the publication of "Diving In," officially considered one of the "big names" in composition studies ("Diving In" appeared in the same issue with essays by Richard Graves, Janet Emig, Ann Berthoff, and Donald Murray), and although the publication early in 1977 of *Errors and Expectations* would earn Mina even more respect and acclaim, it was at about this time that she officially assumed her duties as an associate dean and director of the Instructional Resource Center of The City University of New York. (Although she had been awarded the position as an associate dean for CUNY, she was still officially a faculty member of the

English department at City College; she would continue to be eligible for promotion and salary raises based on the college's schedule.) Within months, a budget crisis that left New York City near bankruptcy resulted in drastic cuts in the CUNY operating budget. (When the federal government refused New York City's request for help, an infamous headline in *The New York Post* read, "Ford to City: Drop Dead.")

In *City on a Hill*, James Traub described the effects that the cuts had on City College:

> In 1976, with New York City having come within a whisker of bankruptcy, CUNY's budget was slashed by a third. The system actually shut down for the first two weeks in June. [Newspapers carried photographs of CUNY professors lined up outside unemployment offices throughout New York City.] City fired fifty-nine nontenured faculty members, including virtually the entire cadre of dedicated teachers whom Shaughnessy had assembled. And it wasn't only the remedial commitment that was circumscribed. To reduce the flow of students to the senior colleges, and to raise their level, admissions standards were changed to admit the top third, rather than the top half, of graduating classes. And in a decision that was no less shocking for being inevitable, CUNY ended its tradition of free tuition. That tradition, at City College, was over 125 years old. (77)

Ed Quinn remembers this period as the most painful in his long career at City College. As chair of the English department, it was his responsibility to lay off nontenured and part-time faculty members in order to protect the job of every tenured professor at City. As a result, entire departments were eliminated; foreign language departments were particularly hard hit, and their faculty members were assigned to teach basic writing courses. Mina and Quinn would meet or talk over the phone every day, but there was little they could do to save jobs. She wrote to a former colleague, Bella Halsted, and her deep sorrow over the events that were occurring is evident in the brief mention she made of the effects the cuts were having: "If you are in touch with anyone at City, you know about our hard times. Most of the basic writing teachers have by now been dropped and with them have gone much of the energy and will of the department, or so, at least, it seems to me."

Not only was Mina witnessing the dismantling of a program she had painstakingly assembled over a period of eight years, given her new position she was now expected to "facilitate, organize, and coordinate the resources of the University." Mina responded with her usual forthrightness and energy, despite the fact that the budget cuts resulted in a drastic reduction of the staff she had been promised. From a staff of seven, including four full-time experts—one each in math, reading, ESL, and writing—a secretary, a librarian, and an administrative assistant, the staff was cut to only four people: Mina, an administrative assistant, one skills expert, and a part-time assistant funded by CETA (Comprehensive Employment Training Act). Mina counted her blessings, however. She had been able to arrange for Marilyn Maiz to become her administrative assistant (on loan from City College), and Alice Trillin agreed to function as the "skills expert" on an hourly basis. Mina would work harder than ever, but at least she would be working with the most competent people available, people whom she could also trust. There was no room at the CUNY central offices for the new department, however, so she and her staff were forced to begin their work in three small rooms provided for them at CUNY's midtown offices. They would not move into their permanent office on East 80th Street until September 1976.

Mina kept a log of her early activities, and her struggle to continue to work on *Errors and Expectations* is evident:"February 26: Morning—worked on manuscript; Afternoon—correspondence from City College; visit to new office—furniture needed—3 desks, 3 desk chairs, files, paper, three phones; Call to Celia. My check probably not available until next month; submitted travel voucher; discussion with Les Berger about staffing."

Mina still found time for her friends, however, particularly when they needed her. In the middle of this period, one of the most tumultuous of her professional career, Priscilla Brandt became ill and was ordered by her doctor to remain in bed indefinitely. Mina wrote to Priscilla asking her "to think of ways in which I can help you. And I want no protests and arguments. I'm a very good ironer and I like to iron. I can come on Saturday afternoons and we can visit while I iron and I can come on one day during the week after work [and] prepare dinner for us all."

Priscilla recovered quickly, but soon after Mina, Marilyn Maiz, and Alice Trillin began to work together, Alice was diagnosed with lung cancer and was hospitalized for surgery to remove a lung. Alice and her husband, Calvin, were devastated: the cure rate for lung cancer at the time was not promising. Alice could think of little else but her two young daughters. She still remembers how Mina came to the hospital every morning, bringing with her a thermos filled with freshly squeezed orange juice, and how she would visit again in the late afternoon on her way home from work. "Mina knew how afraid I was," Alice recalls.

> She not only brought orange juice, she brought herself and her revelations about how she had felt fourteen years earlier when she had had a hysterectomy performed. She had been exactly my age—thirty-eight—and she had been terrified (and also unable to have children afterwards).
> She shared all of this with me, and also the assurance that the terror gradually goes away. Mina never tried to underestimate or ignore my illness or engage in platitudes as so many people do with cancer. And as I began to recover, and we became more hopeful that the cancer hadn't metastasized, she celebrated with me.

Mina came to appreciate Alice and Marilyn more than ever in her new position, particularly their friendship and loyalty. Not only were the budget cuts affecting her ability to succeed in her new position, but a professor at the Graduate Center who had wanted her position was making her life as difficult as possible—duplicating her efforts, accusing her of performing functions that were not her responsibility, sending memos to CUNY administrators and trustees of the Board of Higher Education questioning her competency and actions. Mina's work spoke for itself; she was so effective that the true cause of the problem became apparent rather quickly, but she was nonplussed enough to bring the problem to the attention of Les Berger, asking him to clarify her role and to make certain that "all interested parties" were duly informed.

Mina wanted to offer a graduate-level course at the CUNY Graduate Center to teachers from throughout the CUNY system. Her qualifications to offer such a course were impeccable: her teaching and administrative experience; her presentations, participation on national panels, and publications; and the fact that she had already designed and taught such a course when she was at City College made her the perfect candidate. But the same man who had so opposed her appointment as director of the Instructional Resource Center pointed out that she did not meet the qualifications to teach at the CUNY Graduate

Center because she did not have a Ph.D. Perhaps, he suggested, he should teach the course instead. Bob Lyons remembers that "Mina more or less stayed out of the fray," while he "got involved in the discussions":

> It's interesting, but Mina was not as offended as I was over their behavior. I think this stemmed from the fact that she always had this enormous respect for the "academy" and for higher education. Despite the fact that there were professors who foolishly tried to prevent her from doing meaningful work, she was one of the few people who did not turn away from the tradition of academics and the canon, while at the same time she was fighting for the rights of people who were supposed to be kept out—it was quite amazing really—the idea, for her, was to get them inside. That's one of the great puzzles of Mina: she never trashed the world of academics, and she never trashed the Graduate Center for all the foot dragging they engaged in
>
> As a result of the resistance we encountered, when Mina and I wrote the description for the course, we called it "Colloquium on the Teaching of Writing," we made it overly academic, knowing that we would have to meet with a review committee to have it approved. Mina and I worked closely on that course, and then we team-taught it. We decided to have a guest speaker at every meeting but the last, and we decided that the course should meet for a year rather than a semester. It was a very impressive course outline, but in the end, although the course was successful, many of the students noted in the course evaluation that they would have liked more time listening to what Mina had to tell us.

Mina would never have consented to such an arrangement, however. She was determined to use the same techniques in her involvement at the Instructional Resource Center that she had used at City College, only this time, she would draw on the expertise and experience of faculty from throughout the CUNY system, involving as many people as possible, convinced that the exploration of a field as new and challenging as basic writing should not be done alone. She never perceived herself as an expert, much less as *the* expert. Although she was, as Ed Corbett has said, one of the "big names" in composition, she was still most comfortable and secure (and successful) in the role of disseminator. The guest list for the seminar reads like a "Who's Who" of basic writing experts: in addition to Edmond Volpe's "official" visit as the president of The College of Staten Island, Tom Farrell discussed linguistics and his interpretation of Walter Ong's work in the field; Sarah D'Eloia of City College discussed "grammar and grammars in the teaching of writing"; Marie Ponsot from Queens College gave a presentation entitled "Teaching Forms of Non-Analytical Writing"; Carol Reed of Brooklyn College spoke about "Dialect and Second Language Characteristics in Writing"; Harvey Weiner of LaGuardia College and John Wright from Oxford University Press gave a presentation entitled "Examining Textbooks"; Don McQuade of Queens College gave a presentation entitled "Redefining the Literature of the Writing Course"; and Kenneth Bruffee discussed the work he was doing on collaboration at Brooklyn College in a presentation entitled "Teacher and Student in the Classroom." Bob Lyons and Mina gave a joint presentation entitled "Teacher and Student outside the Classroom: Conferences and Paper Grading." Janet Emig's presentation was entitled "Writing as a Process: The Stages of Composition," in which she discussed her ongoing studies of the writing process—looking at other age groups in much the same way she had first observed twelfth graders.

The responsibilities of being associate dean and director of the CUNY-wide Instructional Resource Center were staggering, and Mina was working even harder at her new position than she had at City. The problems of staffing and morale being caused by the budget cuts made the need for an academic resource center at CUNY even greater, and she was determined not to let anything interfere with her work. She had received grants totaling $25,000 from the Field and New York Foundations for research and development in the new resource center, but this money would have to be returned if CUNY was unable to make a firm commitment to support the center.

Adrienne Rich remembers that "throughout these struggles, Mina was there, armed with facts, with carefully worked out statistics, most of all with concrete examples of student potential and achievement. She presented her case over and over, never wearying, never defensive." Mina was determined to keep her focus on the needs of the students at CUNY, but more and more often, her new position forced her to balance the needs of the students with political and economic forces that were beyond her control. Irving Howe's description of Mina bolting into his office demanding justice and equality was piquant, but she was a highly skilled negotiator when she had to be.

Although she was officially on sabbatical during the 1975 academic year, her files from this period contain communications with some of the highest ranking members not only of CUNY but of the Board of Higher Education, and they include scores of reports and memos, each of which must have taken days or weeks to prepare. Mina was being asked to develop, evaluate, or implement policy and procedures on such matters as the CUNY admissions policy, the development of skills centers at individual campuses, a position paper on skills training, and personnel and budget decisions. The Board of Higher Education was determined to reduce the size of entering classes, and one method that was being considered was the implementation of admissions tests; this would, in effect, be an abandonment of the promise of Open Admissions—that anyone who possessed a New York City high school diploma was entitled to admission to one of CUNY's divisions. Mina responded to Alfred Giardino, the chair of the board, with a three-page memo in which she articulated her belief that economics should not be the determining factor in who is entitled to an education. The proposed plan, she argued, "reflects an unwarranted confidence in reading tests as accurate predictors both of reading competence and college performance." In terms which seem especially poignant today, she argued that:

The replacement of the diploma by a test is in essence the end of the University's Open Admissions policy, if by that term one includes the admission into higher education of students whose cycle of disadvantage has included not only poverty but an education so inferior to that of others as to blight their lives and rob the larger community of their best energies and talents. We have by now established that it *is* possible to change the lives of such young men and women through education at the post-secondary level. Indeed, the boldness of the University only six years ago in undertaking the task encouraged other colleges throughout the country to follow its lead with the result that the nation is now more deeply engaged in mass education at the college level than it might otherwise have been.

Should we now begin to exclude from our campuses the very students who most severely *tested* the possibilities of Open Admissions, it can only appear that the educational integration of our society and of our City must wait upon affluent times and that, under the crunch of hard times, we single out the disadvantaged first. For however strong our faith in meritocratic methods of selection, the correlations among race, class, and success in academia make it difficult to believe that the distribution of advantages in our City is by merit alone. Open Admissions was an acknowledgment of this problem. It would be a great shame if, in the name of "adjusting" to the financial crisis of the University, Open Admissions were in reality abandoned.

Forced to suggest alternatives, Mina suggested that other methods could be used to reduce the student population, including "a rigorous enforcement of the existing criteria for retention," including an evaluation of the use of the *WF* (withdraw failing) and *WU* (withdraw unofficially) grades, indicating "a possible lack of commitment to college work." "Certainly such possibilities ought to be fully accounted for," she urged, "before we capitulate to the reading test."

Mina also mentioned in this memo a concept that she and Ted Gross had been considering for several years—the belief that "the single most important factor in student success is the nature and quality of the instruction received at earlier levels. In this connection we believe that CUNY, in its relationship with New York City high schools . . . should require as a pre-requisite for entrance the successful completion of specific high school courses." During 1976 and 1977, Mina would devote more and more of her time to this proposition. She and Ted Gross would try to secure financial backing for a project that would begin to explore methods of improving the quality of education that students were receiving in high school. She would have liked nothing better than to eliminate Open Admissions at CUNY, but only by eliminating the *need* for such a program, and she saw the best hope for this in making changes at the high school level.

Mina was not at all certain that the resource center would continue to be funded. In the middle of 1975, she had made an agreement with the publisher, Scott Foresman, to write a handbook of grammar for basic writers. In July 1976, however, she wrote to one of the editors to explain why she could not complete the project. Mina had serious pedagogical concerns over whether or not she could write such a handbook, but she also explained in the letter some of the problems she was encountering as a result of the budget crisis: "The collapse of CUNY, most particularly of the programs I have been involved with here" would make it impossible for her to give the project the attention it deserved. The situation was so dire that she might have "to go back to a full teaching load at City (which is now heavier than it ever was), so I see myself overworked even without the handbook."

Although Mina was not sure that her new position would last, she immediately inaugurated a newsletter entitled *Resource,* which would be distributed to all CUNY faculty members who were involved in teaching basic skills. In the May 1976 issue, she explained the tenuous situation that existed as a result of the budget cuts, but she also described the work that she and her "staff" were already involved in:

> As I write this, we are still uncertain about the kind of University the budget cutters will finally allow us, and the survey of CUNY skills programs which we began this year runs the risk of being more historical than we originally planned. Nonetheless, it has seemed to us increasingly important to describe what has been evolving at CUNY in skills instruction if only to record where we were going before the skies fell.
>
> In carrying out this task, we have begun to get a sense of the remarkably various ways in which colleges and teachers have responded to the skills needs of Open Admissions students, and we hope that our descriptions of the programs will reflect that variety. By the end of the semester we will have completed our descriptions of the reading, writing, and math programs at [ten of the CUNY divisions]. Should you want to see any of these reports or browse through some of the materials we have gathered from the programs, we hope you will stop by.

By the end of 1975, Mina had not taught basic writing for more than two years because of the Carnegie Foundation grant and her subsequent yearlong sabbatical. She began to fear that she would lose her sense of the capabilities the students possessed and the challenges they faced; in short, she was afraid that she would become a typical administrator. As a result, she arranged with Ann Raimes, who had become the director of the Writing Program at Hunter, to tutor basic writing students once a week, since the Hunter campus was relatively close to the CUNY administrative offices. Mina did not identify herself as a dean when she worked with these students, and Marilyn Maiz remembers that Mina would arrive back at the office after these tutoring sessions "refreshed and reinvigorated." Mina, she recalls, "never lost the joy of teaching, and those sessions may have kept her sane and on course as she dealt with an environment increasingly hostile to basic education."

Mina described that hostile environment to her colleagues in an address, delivered in April 1976 to the Conference of the CUNY Association of Writing Supervisors, entitled "The Miserable Truth." (See Appendix C.) She was among friends at this gathering: the association itself was the official extension of those Friday afternoon meetings Mina had attended with Ken Bruffee, Bob Lyons, Harvey Weiner, Don McQuade, Janet Emig, Richard Sterling, Sondra Perl, and the many others who had subsequently joined. She began her address by stating that "these are discouraging times for all of us," equating any attempt at beginning the conference "with a note of encouragement" with "something like trying to give a pep talk on the *Titanic*." "I can think of only one encouraging thought in the midst of this disaster," Mina told her colleagues. "It is best expressed in an old Jewish saying: The truth never dies; it simply leads a miserable life." She detailed the crisis each of them was experiencing daily:

> Our staffs are shrinking and our class sizes increasing.
>
> Talented young teachers who were ready to concentrate their scholarly energies on the sort of research and teaching we need in basic writing are looking for jobs.
>
> Each day brings not a new decision but rumors of new decisions, placing us in the predicament of those mice in psychological experiments who must keep shifting their expectations until they are too rattled to function.
>
> Our campuses buzz like an Elizabethan court with talk of who is in favor and who is out. And we meet our colleagues from other campuses with relief: "Ah, good, we say," (or think to ourselves)—"you're still here!"
>
> We struggle each day to extract from the Orwellian language that announces new plans and policies some clear sense of what finally is going to become of the students whom the University in more affluent times committed itself to educate.

Mina then returned to the problem she and Ted Gross were trying to address: "that it is possible to get a high school diploma in New York City without reaching minimal competence in reading, writing, and arithmetic."

Doubtless we suspected this before, but now we know the real taste of that failure. What Open Admissions writing teacher does not remember the shock of those first student essays, the stunning evidence of failure woven into the very syntax of sentences and the letters of words. For most of us it was a traumatic moment. We asked, "What went wrong? What were they doing for twelve years? How can I possibly teach them to write now? Where do I begin?" And behind those questions lay the troubling, forbidden thought—perhaps they are ineducable.

For the first time in the history of the city, we created, through Open Admissions, a massive feedback system which revealed an unconscionable failure to meet the educational needs of the poor and dark-skinned. To be sure, the roots of that failure are tangled, and now that college teachers have begun to talk and meet with high school teachers (largely as a result of Open Admissions), they are more sensitive to the many institutional conditions that have made teaching almost impossible in our schools.

But whatever the causes, Open Admissions documented the fact of failure. And until that happened, it was possible for thousands of students to drift quietly into the labor force of the city, taking up the jobs that others rejected, convinced somehow that something in *them* had caused the failure.

Mina also discussed the advantages that Open Admissions had brought not only for students but for teachers, and as always she was at her best. Bob Lyons remembers this address in particular, because "conditions were so unfavorable for all of us, but she made us feel that it was a privilege to be in the trenches at that time. She could convince us that we were capable of anything." Mina said:

> Open Admissions has taught us about learning, that is, about the importance of perceiving where students are in relation to what we teach them, about sequential and paced instruction, about being clear and realistic, about going below the surface of our subjects, not in order to become simpler but to become more profound, for it is at that level of principle as well as practice that young adults learn more efficiently. . . .
>
> If we imagine a continuum of competence, with at one end the exceptionally competent and at the other the barely competent, we could say that colleges have traditionally felt it their responsibility to

identify the students at the upper end of this scale and give them four more years of education. The Open Admissions college, on the other hand, makes a commitment to involve itself in the education of young men and women *all along* the continuum on the assumption, first, that people are not consigned to their places on that continuum forever but are capable of remarkable growth and development when given the opportunity; second, that the social benefits of advancing as many as possible along that continuum are inestimable; and third, that this broadening of the base of higher education, if properly planned and supported, can further the education of *all* students on the continuum.

But the decision to open a college to a more diverse population commits that college to becoming a *teaching* college, a college where everyone, not just the remedial teachers, accepts the responsibility of *teaching* rather than merely *presenting* a subject. Certainly this message about teaching has reached the skills teachers of CUNY. Working this year at the Instructional Resource Center, I have had a chance to do what few of you have perhaps had the time or occasion to do, that is, to take a close look at the work going on in skills instruction. We are all aware, of course, that many of our colleagues have gained national recognition in our field—have published articles, read papers at conferences, served on various professional organizations, produced textbooks. (It is no accident, I'm sure, that when five major publishers decided over the past year or so to produce new writing handbooks—a major publishing decision—they chose CUNY English teachers to write them.)

What I had not been so aware of, however, was the number of teachers who, without fanfare or remissions and with heavy class loads, have been at work developing imaginative new materials for our students. Probably at no school in the country is there such an accumulation of wisdom and know-how in the field of compensatory education as there is within this university at this moment. I cannot imagine a group of teachers who have ever had more to say to one another. It is a special fraternity joined not only by our common problems as teachers but by our having come to know, through our students, what it means to be an outsider in academia. Whatever our individual political persuasions, we have been pedagogically radicalized by our experience. We reject in our bones the traditional meritocratic model of a college. We reject it not only on principle; we would simply be bored teaching in such a college.

Such changes, I would say, are indestructible, wherever we go from here. And indestructible, too, are the ideas that have awakened our students. It is puzzling how long people can go on—for generations—tolerating the inequalities that restrict and even shorten their lives. But once the possibility of change touches their imaginations, once a right has been extended to them and they have felt its power to open and enrich their lives, they cannot go back. They may have setbacks. But they cannot go back. CUNY extended a right, six years ago, that has been revoked, and we appear to be back where we started in 1970, only much poorer. But no one can revoke what has gone on in us and in our students.

So the lion got out of the cage before the gates were shut. And we had better keep learning how to teach writing because the brothers and sisters and cousins and children of our students will be back. If we can transcend for a moment the personal disappointments and uncertainties that surround us now, we can perhaps agree that this is a fairly strong truth for a miserable time. And it is a truth we helped to make.

Mina was too modest to say so, of course, but everyone in the audience knew that no one had gained more national attention than she. In fact, she would earn even greater recognition as a result of her speech to the CUNY Association of Writing Supervisors. Someone who had attended the conference brought her address to the attention of Andrew Young, one of the few African American members of Congress at the time, representing Georgia's fifth district, and the first black man elected to Congress from the South since 1901. In September 1976, five months after Mina delivered her address, he wrote to her, explaining that he had found the speech "to be so impressive and important, I inserted it in *The Congressional Record* for my colleagues in Congress to read." Young enclosed a copy of *The Congressional Record,* dated September 9, 1976, page E4955, hoping, he wrote, "that comments and efforts such as yours may arouse a greater interest throughout this nation in the concept of open admissions at public institutions of higher learning." So it was that Mina's complete address was reprinted in *The Congressional Record,* preceded by Andrew Young's explanation:

Mr. Speaker: In 1970 the City University of New York established a bold and innovative educational policy by providing tuition-free admission to its vast network of city colleges for all recent graduates of New York City's high schools. In the wake of New York City's recent financial crisis, this policy was abandoned. Sizeable tuitions were instituted, and admission to CUNY's colleges ceased to be automatic.

In a recent speech to the Conference of the CUNY Association of Writing Supervisors, Mina P. Shaughnessy, director of CUNY's Instructional Resources Center, discussed the value of and need for open admissions at CUNY. This is an important speech which raises many issues regarding the quality of education in this Nation.

I recommend this speech to my colleagues with hope that it may contribute to further reexamination of and interest in the concept of open admissions to public institutions of higher learning throughout the Nation.

Mina was pleased, of course, but she was not sure that such attention would make very much difference. The budget cuts were having an impact on so many of the programs and projects that she had worked so hard to establish that it was difficult, if not impossible, for her to enjoy, even momentarily, such honors. And matters were not made any better, Marilyn Maiz recalls, by the fact that in the second reference to Mina's name it was spelled "Mira." "Mina just groaned and made a small circle in pencil around the error," Marilyn recalls.

One of Mina's proudest accomplishments was the founding, with her City College colleagues, of the *Journal of Basic Writing.* However, given the severe budget cuts being imposed throughout the CUNY campuses, it was not even certain if funds would be available to publish the second issue. Despite this uncertainty, Mina was determined to do everything possible to keep the journal going. She wrote to the other editors on August 27, 1975, explaining "our problems and plans":

While the Instructional Resource Center has not yet been cut out of the new budget it may well have lost its allotment of release time. I will not know until the middle of September. Meanwhile, this means that there is no provision for Pat [Laurence] to serve as editor. The only solution I can see at this point is for this office to handle the administrative duties that Pat has been managing since spring and for all of us to share in the editorial work of reviewing manuscripts.

Early in 1976, Mina made a final decision to publish *Errors and Expectations* with Oxford University Press. She had begun a dialogue with John Wright, an editor at Oxford, based on the recommendation of her colleagues, Bob Lyons and Harvey Weiner. Wright was an excellent editor, having worked with such authors as Lionel Trilling, Harold Bloom, and Peter Elbow, and he would prove to be an equally effective salesman. He had heard Mina speak at the MLA Convention in San Francisco at the end of 1975, and it was at that time he discovered that Mina had written a book. "I simply assumed she was already under contract," Wright recalls, "particularly after hearing her address at the convention. I realized how brilliant and dynamic she was. I remember thinking that whoever had signed that book was one very lucky publisher." In addition, Wright knew that Mina had been having discussions with Scott Foresman about writing a grammar handbook for basic writing students, so he assumed that she had probably already made a commitment to them.

Mina was not under contract, however. Although she had sent copies of her manuscript to friends at other publishing houses simply for their opinion of its "readiness" for publication, readers for two publishers—Prentice-Hall and Winthrop—recommended immediate publication. "The manuscript is every bit as important as I thought it would be, and considerably more practical," Bill Oliver, a highly respected composition editor, reported to Prentice-Hall. The unidentified reader for Winthrop Press reported that Winthrop "would be smart to snap up the Shaughnessy book. I find it to be a superb combination of grassroots knowledge of the real problems and balanced, intelligent analysis stemming from solid research." After almost two pages of such observations, the reader (who was obviously a basic writing instructor) concluded by saying: "Please let me know if and when you will publish it because I need it yesterday."

John Wright wrote to Mina on January 23, 1976, informing her that he had only recently discovered that she was not under contract and asking her to "allow Oxford to consider your work." He assured Mina that he would be available at her convenience and that he looked forward to hearing from her. Wright referred to his friendship with Bob Lyons to further his cause: "Bob Lyons has invited me to participate in your colloquium at the graduate center, so failing other opportunities at least I know we will meet in the near future."

Mina sent part of the manuscript to Wright about two weeks later, along with a letter in which she described the genesis and purpose of the book. (The opening paragraph of the letter is strikingly similar to the book's preface.) Mina's letter reflects the same seriousness of purpose that she had exhibited at the MLA Conference in San Francisco:

The first day I met my first "remedial" writing class at City College some nine years ago, I asked the class to write something about themselves. And after the class was over I began eagerly to read over what they had written in order to take the measure of their difficulties with writing. After no more than five minutes of reading, I realized that I had run into a problem I hadn't the slightest idea how to solve, although I had been teaching composition for a number of years. I think, in fact, I suspected at some unconscious level that the papers reflected problems *no one* could solve.

Needless to say, I have changed my mind about that, but I am often troubled by the thought of the numbers of students who passed through my classes (or didn't pass through them) while I was trying to figure out what on earth to do with young adults who *really* didn't know how to write. I haven't, by the way, found an answer that I can "lay on" the profession, but this manuscript represents an attempt to sort out the problems a teacher can expect to find in the papers of basic writing (BW) students, to suggest wherever possible the causes that underlie them, and to point toward teaching solutions. I would expect the work to be suitable as a text in teacher education classes and as a resource book for teachers already in (or about to go into) the classroom, or for administrators who are trying to understand why it takes so long or seems so complicated to teach unprepared freshmen to write for college assignments. It is the first book-size attempt to describe remedial-level writing and to do so with what seems to be a wealth of examples. Anyone who reads it should be able afterwards to look at a remedial-level paper and not faint. I would even hope that they would be prepared to set about planning a course or program for such writers that would avoid many of the pitfalls the rest of us have discovered in harder and more expensive ways.

The manuscript has seven parts, two of which are not done (the introduction and conclusion), but these should be done by the end of March. I enclose three chapters and that part of the introduction (not in its final draft) that explains where I "stand" on the controversial matter of error.

After naming each part, Introduction, Handwriting and Punctuation, Syntax, Common Errors, Spelling and Vocabulary (these two topics were treated in two separate chapters in the book), Beyond the Sentence, and Expectations, Mina wrote: "I will be eager to know what you think of it."

Within a week, Wright wrote to Mina offering her a contract: "You have addressed yourself to what is undoubtedly going to be a concern of all teachers for a very long time, but I am most impressed with your ability to do so without a hint of apology or patronization." She had told Wright that she had sent the manuscript to other publishers, and he responded: "I hope you will understand my lack of modesty when I say that I doubt if anyone can offer you the same things that we will."

Wright made arrangements to meet Mina for dinner at Le Toque Blanc, a rather upscale restaurant for a university press, but Wright remembers that he was convinced of the quality of *Errors and Expectations* and intended to do whatever he could to convince Mina to sign a contract with them. She was utterly unaware of the quality and value of her manuscript, however. "She couldn't believe I wanted to offer her a contract," he recalls. "She kept asking me why I wasn't having it reviewed. I told her that the only people in the country who were qualified to review such a book were the people whom she had trained." (Wright did eventually have the manuscript reviewed by Susan Miller and Andrea Lunsford at Ohio State University.) Mina then protested that the book was not complete, but when Wright pressed her, she admitted that only the introduction and conclusion needed "some work." It took three more months, but he finally convinced her to sign a contract with Oxford University Press. She did so, but only with the agreement that he would show the manuscript to a linguist, Mina "didn't feel comfortable with the sections in the book concerning linguistics." Wright sent the manuscript to a good friend, Marilyn Rosenthal, who held a Ph.D. in linguistics. Rosenthal saw no major problems, but did note that "if a linguist should happen to be caught reading the book, she might bump in certain places." Rosenthal then suggested that changes be made in six sentences—in a manuscript that ran well over five hundred typed pages.

Mina was not as sanguine about *Errors and Expectations* as Wright was for another reason. During this period, she told Len Kriegel that when the book was published, she "would be attacked both from the left and from the right." She was concerned, in particular, with the chapter entitled "Common Errors"; at seventy pages, it was by far the longest chapter in the book. She had already confronted resistance to such attention to the concept of errors after she and the editorial staff of the *Journal of Basic Writing* had decided to devote the entire first issue to errors made by basic writing students. In that publication, Mina had addressed the issue in her introduction:

> Error may seem to be an old place to begin a new discussion about teaching writing. It is, after all, a subject English teachers already know about. Some people would claim that it is the English teacher's obsession with error that has killed writing for generations of students. Yet error—the unintentional deviation from expected patterns—dominates the writing of many of the new students, inhibiting them and their readers from concentrating on what is being said. And while no English teacher seems to have difficulty counting up and naming errors, few have been in the habit of observing them fruitfully, with the intent, that is, of understanding why intelligent young adults who want to be right seem to go on, persistently and even predictably, being wrong. (3)

Mina's concern with criticism from "the left" centered around the (very legitimate) fear of many basic writing instructors about the potential result of "exposing" the errors of basic writing students to the public by publishing samples of their writing. In an address he delivered in 1979, Bob Lyons explained the concern that all basic writing instructors shared in reproducing for public viewing the writing of their students:

> It represented the dirty little secret of basic skills courses, classified information, because if it leaked out it was sure to appear as part of some professor's demonstration that such students were on the face of it uneducable. This was not a matter of paranoia. It was clear from several essays on Open Admissions and from several letters to the *Times* that examples of unskillful writing by non-traditional students were considered a powerful weapon by those opposed to the broadening of public higher education. From this point of view, Mina had great courage in choosing to examine publicly such quantities of error-laden student writing. (4)

Furthermore, in the many references to "dialect interference" that were made about basic writing samples, very often the "dialect" being discussed was that used by black students—again providing critics of Open Admissions students with "evidence" of the poor skills that "certain" students being admitted to college possessed.

Mina was also concerned that people on "the left" would criticize her seeming obsession with error; as she explained in *Errors and Expectations,* she was not advocating "trying to clear them completely before moving on to other things." Rather, she was suggesting a method of codifying the errors, "suggesting wherever possible the logic behind them," so that teachers could "recommend ways of helping a student recognize and correct them" (93). She was not immune to the surprisingly graceful and sharp prose that basic writing students often produced: "I am surely not the first to have sensed, in working with the new students on their writing," she wrote, "a directness and freshness of response that will strengthen the public language even as it represents them in the larger world" (126).

In fact, Mina cited in *Errors and Expectations* what she once described as "by far my favorite sentence" from one student's essay, a sentence written in response to a request "in an exam at the end of the semester to add adverbial modifiers to the base 'The problem will be solved'":

> The problem will be solved with the help of the Almighty, who, except for an occasional thunderstorm, reigns unmolested, high in the heavens above, when all of us, regardless of race or religious difference, can come together and study this severe problem inside out, all day and night if necessary, and are able to come to you on that great gettin' up morning and say, "Mrs. Shaughnessy, we do know our verbs and adverbs." (132)

Mina was not convinced that such prose would result simply by providing a student with more frequent opportunities to write, and she explained her position in the middle of the error chapter:

> The alternative course of ignoring error for fear of inhibiting the writer even more or of assuming that errors will wear off as the student writes more is finally giving error more power than it is due.

The "mystery" of error is what most intimidates students—the worry that errors just "happen" without a person's knowing how or when— and while we have already noted that some errors can be expected to persist even after instruction, most of them finally come under the control of the writer once he has learned to look at them analytically during the proofreading stage of composition. Freedom from error is finally a matter of understanding error, not of getting special dispensations to err simply because writing formal English is thought to be beyond the capabilities or interests of certain students. (128)

Mina expected the same criticism from "the right" that she and her colleagues in Open Admissions had experienced from their earliest days of teaching. These students couldn't write, and as long as they couldn't write they didn't belong in college, particularly a college being funded with taxpayers' money. Furthermore, why would anyone waste her time writing a book about such students, particularly someone who was on the payroll of the college being funded with taxpayers' money?

Mina's fears were actually unfounded not simply because so many people agreed with, recognized the brilliance of, and learned from the material contained in *Errors and Expectations,* but because of the way she presented the material; again she had assumed the role of disseminator rather than expert, and David Bartholomae described the effect this had on his response to the book:

Besides the traditional placement of thank you's at the beginning of the volume, Shaughnessy's acknowledgments spill out beyond the preface to the notes at the bottom of many pages. There, she does more than document scholarly quotations. She thanks teachers who have shared with her a lesson or provided a significant example: "I am indebted to Sarah D'Eloia for this and the preceding example"; "I am indebted to Kenneth Bruffee of Brooklyn College for this example," etc. Besides this evocation of her own colleagues in the City University, Shaughnessy invites all readers into the ongoing conversation. She immerses us in examples, making us colleagues who are free to disagree with the inferences she draws. In these ways, Shaughnessy helps us to create an interpretive community: she takes seriously a subject which some previously thought trivial; she connects that subject with the world of traditional scholarship; she joins with others who are seeking new ways to address seemingly insoluble problems; and she involves the reader actively in making interpretations. (92)

Mina signed the contract with Oxford University Press on March 26, 1976. Fittingly, Marilyn Maiz witnessed the signing. According to the contract, Mina would receive an advance of thirty-five hundred dollars, half on signing and half on completion of the manuscript. The royalty rates were the usual for a university press: 10 percent on the first five thousand copies sold, with the rate rising to 12.5 percent and then to 15 percent for subsequent sales. John Wright had told her that he was a "lucky" editor to work with, explaining the successes other authors he had worked with enjoyed. Thus, when Mina returned the signed contracts to him, she enclosed a note that read: "John, Here are the contracts. Now your luck is my luck!"

Luck had very little to do with it. Mina had worked on the writing of *Errors and Expectations* for more than three years, engaging in painstaking research, analysis, writing, and rewriting. In actuality, however, she had been gathering ideas and material for the book from the moment she began teaching. As far as the philosophy of equality and opportunity manifested in the book, it can be argued that she had been harboring those beliefs for her entire life, perhaps from the moment she read the note her father had written to her mother before Mina was born—containing misspellings and grammatical errors, to be sure, but also reflecting wit, wisdom, and intelligence.

The editor who was assigned to Mina's book, Stephanie Golden, was as much of a perfectionist as Mina herself. (Only two typos escaped their notice: "somethng" and "repersenting" on page 291.) They communicated almost daily during the months of preparation, and as was usual with anyone who came into contact with Mina, Golden soon developed a fondness for and friendship with Mina that would continue even after the book was published.

By 1976, feminists were beginning to demand that the male pronoun be used only when referring specifically or exclusively to males, but much of Mina's manuscript had been written earlier. She decided to address the issue in a footnote in the introduction to *Errors and Expectations*. "After having tried various ways of circumventing the use of the masculine pronoun in situations where women teachers and students might easily outnumber men," Mina explained, "I have settled for the convention, but I regret that the language resists my meaning in this important respect. When the reader sees *he,* I can only hope *she* will also be there" (4). In the Fall/Winter 1976 issue of the *Journal of Basic Writing,* Mina further acknowledged the problem (and the irony) of male references; in describing programs for basic writers, she noted that some "remedial fix-it" stations were "manned (usually 'womanned' in fact) by one overworked paraprofessional" (1).

There was so little time between the signing of the contract with Oxford and Mina's submission of the final manuscript that on June 11, 1976, she received the entire advance of thirty-five hundred dollars rather than two separate installments. She knew immediately what she would do with part of the money: she bought herself a full-length mink coat, "a full, shiny, dark brown fur coat" Marilyn Maiz recalls. Marilyn could not resist chiding Mina, asking her if she didn't worry about the animals that had been sacrificed to make the coat. Mina was not the least bit offended. "You eat the critters," she replied to Marilyn, "I wear them."

A few days after signing the contract, Mina delivered an address entitled "Speaking and Doublespeaking of Standards" at the California State University and Colleges Conference on Improvement of Student Writing Skills, in Los Angeles. (See Appendix D.) Again, she pointed out that it was in Open Admissions colleges where teachers had made a commitment "to involve themselves in the education of men and women all along the continuum," rather than "identify the students at the upper end of this scale and extend *their* education by four more years." Standards had to be set, of course, but Mina argued that "if we are serious about standards, we must set them for ourselves as teachers and administrators as well as for our students." Only then would we move deeper "into the realizations of a democracy." The audience was quiet for just a moment when she finished her address, then they gave her a five-minute standing ovation—a repeat of the reception she had received at the MLA Convention in 1975.

In November 1976, Mina completed a working paper for the CUNY Task Force on Writing entitled "Statement on Criteria for Writing Proficiency" (see Appendix E), in which she advocated the use of holistic grading and argued against the use of quantitative measures. "Although instruction in writing usually focuses systematically on specific sub-skills of writing such as grammatical inflections and paragraph design," Mina argued, writing competence is more than the sum of these discrete competencies. Rather, it is the successful integration of a number of linguistic skills which interact and combine in ways so difficult to delineate and measure that the holistic judgment of an experienced reader remains the most accurate form of assessment in writing. (1)

As a result of her argument, CUNY adopted the six-level placement scale for holistic evaluation; it is still in use today.

The next month, December 1976, Mina delivered a paper entitled "Some Needed Research in Writing" (see Appendix F) as a member of the Research in Writing Panel at the 1976 MLA Conference; it was published a year later in *College Composition and Communication*. In this essay, she posed four questions (similar to the four stages presented in "Diving In") "that have concerned me lately and that might in turn generate specific research plans that would move us toward the pedagogy I speak of" (317). That pedagogy was, of course, one that "respects, in its goals and methods, the maturity of the adult, beginning writer and at the same time admits to the need to begin where the beginning is, even if that falls outside the traditional territory of college composition" (318). Mina apologized if her four questions seemed "embarrassingly rudimentary"; however, she explained that what she was suggesting through these questions, and others,

is that we have as yet no sociology nor psychology (not even an adequate history) of teaching the advanced skills of literacy to young adults who have not already acquired them. Yet many such students are now in college classrooms. We cannot hope to solve the problems that arise out of vast inequities in public education by arguing that when those problems were *not* being solved, or even thought about, higher education was in excellent shape. (320)

As always, the response to Mina's eloquent defense of basic writing students was overwhelmingly positive. Letters, invitations, and requests for information poured into her office, and as always, she responded to every one of them.

John Wright was true to his promise that he would market *Errors and Expectations* aggressively. Throughout the editing process, he planned an elaborate direct-mail campaign for *Errors and Expectations,* requesting that Oxford's sales people send him the name of every freshman English director in their major schools. "I know this is a bit extraordinary," he wrote, "but so is the book. One last word. You should know that there were other publishers trying to get this book, so it's not a big secret that we're publishing it. In fact, we'd like you to start telling people right away."

Wright wanted to have the book ready for the December 1976 MLA Convention, but it simply was not possible. Despite his best attempts, the official publication date was January 1, 1977. One of the last sections Mina submitted was the conclusion, but even at that time, in June 1976, she had not yet decided on a title for the book. "The only title I have been able to come up with is *Baselines: A Guide for the Teacher of Basic Writing.*" Mina explained what she wanted in a title in a letter to Wright: "Somehow, the title should suggest that the book is concerned with describing where remedial-level students are when they start out. I want to avoid the impression that this is a detailed guide on how to set up a program, evaluate, etc." Wright was unhappy with Mina's title, particularly the word "baselines." He suggested instead three other choices: *New Priorities: A Guide for the Teacher of Basic Writing; New Realities: A Guide for the Teacher of Basic Writing;* and *Errors and Expectations: A Guide for the Teacher of Basic Writing.* Mina liked the balance suggested by the last title, and Wright remembers that he would often joke with her over the fact that he had made such "a major contribution to the book."

There was no question about the dedication page. Less than a year after Mina's mother died, Mina wrote a three-line inscription:

In Memory of My Mother
Ruby Johnson Pendo
1896–1975

By the time Mina finished the conclusion, a chapter she entitled "Expectations," the budget cuts that had been imposed on CUNY had taken a devastating toll not only on the number of students being admitted, but on the quality of the programs that remained to serve them. In fact, many of the instructors whose work Mina had cited in *Errors and Expectations* had lost their jobs. Furthermore, her work at the CUNY Instructional Resource Center had given her an even broader exposure to the cynical attitudes held by so many educational administrators and politicians. Many of the passages in her conclusion reflect a fear that whatever idealism had factored into the decision to implement Open Admissions at CUNY was losing to political practicalities and shortsightedness. Mina expressed her fears, and her hopes, for the future of basic writing students:

> Most of what has been written in this book has been intended for teachers, particularly for teachers who are only beginning, or are about to begin, their work with BW students. But BW teachers are far from autonomous beings in their departments and divisions and colleges. It is not usually they who set limits on class size or teaching load or the number of semesters granted to writing instruction. They do not control the extent to which writing permeates a college curriculum and therefore reinforces their work, nor can they rearrange the reward system in such a way as to encourage teachers to concentrate their scholarly energies in the sorts of questions that arise in basic writing. Such matters are in the hands of administrators, whose perceptions of the so-called remedial problem largely determine whether basic writing is to be viewed as a college contagion ward staffed by teachers who are brought in for the emergency and expected to perform miracles (even though they are at the same time restricted from having a professional future there) or whether it is to be viewed as a frontier in higher education which, while it may send some hurrying back to the safety and familiarity of the past, ought to draw many others of talent into its challenge. (290–91)

The prose that Mina employed throughout *Errors and Expectations* was clear, thoughtful, and precise. However, she saved her best for last. The final paragraphs of her conclusion have the same effect on her readers as her words had on her listeners at the MLA Conference. She reminds her readers of the vulnerability of their students, noting that

> College both beckons and threatens them, offering to teach them useful ways of thinking and talking about the world, promising even to improve the quality of their lives, but threatening at the same time to take from them their distinctive ways of interpreting the world, to assimilate them into the culture of academia without acknowledging their experience as outsiders. (292)

She reminds her readers that there is much that students can accomplish:

> Far from being eleventh-hour learners, these students appear in many ways to be beginning their lives anew. And while the skills and priorities of studenthood are not easily acquired at the age of eighteen or over, students are demonstrating that competency *can* be acquired at that age. And much of the energy they mobilize for the effort seems to come from the opportunity college gives them to redefine themselves as young adults who might accomplish something in the world. To encourage this emerging view they have of themselves while at the same time representing honestly to them the amount of work that lies ahead is the teacher's most delicate and essential task. (291)

Mina had written in "Open Admissions and the Disadvantaged Teacher" that "Open Admissions is forcing the real question—not how many people society is willing to salvage, but how much this society is willing to pay to salvage itself." In the final paragraphs of *Errors and Expectations,* she repeated this challenge:

> Just how we are finally going to reconcile the entitlement and capacities of these new students with our traditional ways of doing things in higher education is still not clear. As we move closer to this goal, however, we will be improving the quality of college education for all students and moving deeper into the realizations of a new democracy.
>
> Meanwhile, we must hope that our enterprising new students will somehow weather *our* deficiencies and transcend our yet cautious expectations of what they can accomplish in college. (293–94)

Early in January 1977, Wright called Mina at her office to inform her that the first shipment of *Errors and Expectations* had arrived. He told her that he would have a messenger bring a copy to her office. "No, don't do that," Mina replied. "I'll come over to pick it up." She took a cab from her office on 80th Street to the Oxford University Press offices on 35th Street and Madison Avenue, wearing her mink coat, of course. It was a wonderful moment for Mina, and John Wright remembers that she was deeply satisfied and pleased with the book, happy finally to be holding it in her hands.

CHAPTER SEVEN

A Grand Experiment

The response to *Errors and Expectations* was extraordinarily favorable—and quick. Within months of its official publication date, lengthy reviews and articles appeared in scores of popular and educational publications, including *The New York Times, The Chronicle of Higher Education, The Atlantic Monthly, Change,* the *Harvard Educational Review, College English, College Composition and Communication, School Review, Teachers College Record, Choice Magazine,* and the *TESOL Newsletter.* Reviews would continue to appear throughout 1977 and 1978 in magazines, newspapers, and journals not only in the United States but in England and New Zealand as well. The reviewers described Mina's brilliance and tenacity, referring to the hundreds of hours she had spent analyzing thousands of student essays and the precision with which she was able to identify the nature and sources of the errors she found. However, it was her representation of basic writing students as intelligent, interesting, serious, and motivated men and women that so impressed them. As Benjamin DeMott noted in his review in *The Nation,* Mina's "intense concentration" was not on errors, but "on what it is like to be the new academic learner." She was presenting basic writers in much the same way Robert Coles and Jonathan Kozol describe their subjects, and the result was, as DeMott concluded, "personal at its core, individual: a reflection of a sensibility at once acute, loving, and brave" (645).

Mina asked Marilyn Maiz to start a file to hold the letters she was receiving in praise of *Errors and Expectations;* within a month, Marilyn had to begin another file, and then another. Many of the letters were requests for more information or requests for Mina to deliver an address or conduct a workshop, but many more letters were written by high school and college English instructors simply to thank her for what she had done. "We responded to every letter," Marilyn recalls, "and in many cases, Mina asked the writer for more information about his or her program." Ed Corbett spoke for the entire profession when he wrote to her on February 18, 1977: "You have put us all in your debt." Oxford University Press was receiving a similar number of letters. "I've honestly never had a book like this one," John Wright wrote to Mina on March 9, 1978. "The praise doesn't stop, and the inquiries about other projects don't stop either."

The comments in *The Chronicle of Higher Education* were representative of many of the reviews, praising Mina for bringing to the field of basic writing the same "first-rate scholarship" and "all the critical and creative intelligence that literary scholars have traditionally been trained to lavish on T. S. Eliot, James Joyce, and Ezra Pound." *Errors and Expectations* is more than a guide, the reviewer (Maurice Hungiville) noted, it is a "force that can redirect the energies of an entire profession" (18). *The Atlantic Monthly*'s reviewer (C. Michael Curtis) described "the particular beauty" of *Errors and Expectations:* "It is a book about the *spirit* as well as the mechanics of teaching, and its clarity, commonsense humanity, commend it to anyone interested in the quality of writing in American classrooms" (72). Edward B. Fiske, the education editor of *The New York Times,* wrote a lengthy front-page article about the book and described Mina as "rapidly establishing the City University of New York as a major national force in the growing field of remedial writing." Mina's research, Fiske explained, "also served to demonstrate that most remedial writing students were not stupid but simply inexperienced" (1). The reviewer (Sandra Stotsky) who praised the book in the *Harvard Educational Review* noted that Mina was not providing teachers with a "highly structured writing program"; rather, she was explaining "in a profound and moving way, the difficulties with formal written English evidenced by Basic Writing students and the approaches developed by their teachers to help these students write readable expository prose" (594). Mina's good friend, Kenneth Bruffee, wrote a full-page essay in *The Chronicle of Higher Education* describing the way that teaching Open Admissions students had become a transforming experience for him and his colleagues, forcing them to ask new and important questions not only about their students, but about themselves: "And to some of the questions that baffled us, some of us did succeed in finding answers." The most successful among them, he wrote, was Mina Shaughnessy, whose book

> is the best evidence I can give of the potential for theoretically imaginative, intellectually exciting, professionally rewarding work that can emerge from this field of basic studies. The book serves its intended purpose admirably: to help those of us who teach basic writing do our job. But it also shows how basic studies teachers . . . have the potential even to transform their discipline. Shaughnessy devotes to the work of basic writing students all the care and respect that other scholars in English reserve exclusively for conventional problems in literary criticism. In doing so, she not only raises the level of discourse among people concerned with the subject she addresses . . . but she also puts much conventional academic research in English to shame (40)

Mina must have been particularly satisfied at the glowing review *Errors and Expectations* received in the May 1977 issue of *Change,* a prestigious, liberal educational journal, particularly since it appeared directly after a scathing review of *The End of Education* by Geoffrey Wagner, the same professor who had lamented that it was Mina and her "minions" who were destroying City College. Alison Bernstein, Mina's good friend and fellow board member on the Fund for the Improvement of Post-Secondary Education, wrote a review that appeared in *School Review,* describing *Errors and Expectations* as "perhaps the first book to emerge from the crucible of the Open Admissions classroom which doesn't minimize the challenge and yet reaffirms the possibilities of genuine progress toward a more literate student body" (294) Bernstein sent a copy of the review to Mina along with a note hoping that "a thousand copies" of the book would sell, the usual number for a scholarly book whose topic was limited to a specific field or discipline. In fact, more than twelve thousand hardcover copies were sold during the first six months after publication, and more than forty thousand copies of the soft cover edition, released early in 1979, were sold.

Mina was famous—and happy. John Wright recalls that she was surprised over the favorable response to the book:

> I don't know what she expected; perhaps she thought it would receive a little notice from basic writing instructors and then fade into

obscurity, but she was ebullient over the response. She was as close to a celebrity as we have in our field—*Errors and Expectations* was even outselling Peter Elbow's *Writing Without Teachers,* but what pleased Mina, I think, was the fact that the letters that people were writing indicated that the book was of real value to them as teachers and administrators. One of her concerns was that people would look to her book as a "how to" manual, but the responses indicated that readers had understood her intentions.

But Wright also remembers that Mina began to experience serious health problems at this time, and her pleasure over the response to the book was tempered by her inability to obtain an accurate diagnosis or relief from the stomach pains she was experiencing. "A doctor had told her that she probably had an ulcer," Wright recalls, "and given the stress of her work at CUNY, particularly since the budget cuts, that did not seem unreasonable. However, she was getting no relief from the medicine the doctor had prescribed."

Leonard Kriegel remembers that Mina was in such discomfort during this period that she had begun to carry a bottle of Pepto-Bismol in her purse. "We'd be in the middle of a conversation and she would take the bottle out of her handbag and take a swig. We laughed about it at the time; little did we realize how ill she actually was."

In March 1977, less than two months after the release of *Errors and Expectations,* Mina was diagnosed with kidney cancer. Doctors admitted her to Memorial Sloan-Kettering Cancer Center, where a kidney was removed. After she was released from the hospital, she spent three weeks recuperating at Betty Fosdick's home in Connecticut. Marilyn Maiz remembers that Mina recovered quickly. "She was optimistic and positive, buoyed in large part by the response that *Errors and Expectations* was receiving. Whenever I visited her, I usually had a folder bulging with congratulatory letters and invitations to address conferences or write articles." Mina's co-op apartment, on East End Avenue and 81st Street, was just across the street from the Instructional Resource Center, so after she returned home, she was able to walk to the office and spend a few hours there each day.

In April, although she was feeling better, Mina was not well enough to attend the taping of a debate between Geoffrey Wagner and Ed Quinn on William Buckley's *Firing Line.* The program, which aired on April 25, 1977, attracted little public attention: by 1977, most people had already made up their minds about Open Admissions. Buckley's cynicism, coupled with his arch conservatism, did little to further the debate—he spent ten minutes trying to get Quinn to admit that Open Admissions students couldn't read Shakespeare. Quinn was honest and eloquent, describing the problems and issues confronting both the students and the teachers, and wondering if excluding these students would in fact solve any of the problems cited by Buckley, Wagner, and other conservatives. Mina watched the debate on television, and Quinn's performance must have pleased her, in contrast to Wagner's inflammatory denouncements of the students as illiterates and thugs. The debate was simply one more indication of the polarization that existed at City College, at CUNY, in New York, and in the country over Open Admissions. Things had not changed very much at all from the time Mina began her work at City College in 1967. (In addition to the "discussion" between Quinn and Wagner, three City College students were asked to speak as well. One of them—an honors student—was Peter Rondinone; today he is a professor at LaGuardia Community College, CUNY, and an eloquent spokesperson and defender of the field of basic writing.)

Despite Mina's illness, she continued to work with Ted Gross on their plan to establish an institute for the training of writing teachers. Gross and Mina, realizing that CUNY and the Board of Higher Education would not fund their project, given not only the budget crisis but the increasingly conservative climate that existed, had begun to write to corporate and foundation executives explaining their vision and requesting funding for a National Center for Literacy that would be affiliated with, but not funded by, CUNY. They put together a twenty-five-page proposal that examined the problems of literacy and possible solutions. They suggested the formation of a teacher fellowship program to train elementary and high school teachers, an intensive summer program to hone the writing skills of high school students preparing for college, and the organization of conferences around the nation to disseminate findings and results. Although the proposal was written in 1976, it could still serve today as a model for an enlightened and practical guide for eliminating the need for remediation at the college level.

Ted Gross was providing much of the administrative and organizational support for the project; given Mina's illness and her workload at the Instructional Resource Center, this was essential. However, she was, as always, providing the vision and inspiration. "Even after all those years," Gross recalls, "Mina was still educating me." In several drafts and memos that she wrote at the time, she listed and explained the problems she had become so familiar with as a result of her work with the students at City College. Mina was convinced that high schools and universities had to work together, *without* pointing fingers or laying blame. "We need to begin," she wrote to Timothy Healy in the CUNY Chancellor's Office,

in systematic and serious ways to work for what I would call the vertical integration of the City's educational system, and we need to begin doing this by introducing a number of integrating strategies that would extend our understanding of the learning problems of the poorly educated into the upper divisions of the college and university and into the high schools.

Mina decided to illustrate her point with the field she "knew best, basic writing":

The other day I came upon the papers of my first class of SEEK students, written nine years ago. I recall how stunned I was by the papers, how discouraged I was at the thought of teaching my students when I hadn't any idea of where to start or what to single out from the mass of problems I found there. (And I was then an experienced teacher and editor.) Today, when I look at those same papers, I quickly classify the problems I find there and know approximately which ones will take a long time, which will respond quickly to intervention, and which will have simply to rub off by more exposure to books and academic talk. More important, I know more about the logic that undergirds those problems and am neither alarmed nor discouraged by the work ahead.

Yet I constantly encounter my earlier self in the comments of other teachers who have no background in this kind of teaching and no understanding of how to teach writing but who will nonetheless be getting students in their classes who arrive with but a fragile competence as writers and are yet in need of practice and criticism and whose understanding of any subject is certain to be tested and extended by having to write about it.

Such teachers would benefit, it seems to me, by being able to consult with skilled teachers about the reading and writing in their classes and by taking some measure of the difficulties that inhere in their subjects. Similarly, there is a great need in the high schools for skills experts who might help in a variety of ways to improve the quality of instruction—an advance that will only happen, I am certain, if the high school curriculum is a skills-saturated curriculum, where reading and writing permeate the instructional process and where the word and sad concept of the isolated "remedial" class is finally put to rest.

Mina's reputation was growing, fueled in large part by the success of *Errors and Expectations.* She was invited to become a member of a recently formed ad hoc CCCC Committee on Teaching and Its Evaluation in Composition; John Brereton, one of the original members of the National Writing Project, invited her to speak to the Bay Area Writing Project group, and in the same letter, he mentioned to her that the director of the National Humanities Faculty wanted to know if she was interested in working as a consultant for the organization. Mina was asked to participate in a conference, to be held in California during the summer of 1977, sponsored by the National Institute of Education, a division of the Department of Health, Education, and Welfare. Here, she would be joining some of the leading educators, sociologists, and anthropologists in the country: Edward Corbett, Janet Emig, Linda Flower, John Gumperz, Mary Healy, Shirley Brice Heath, E. D. Hirsch, Alan Hollingsworth, Richard Lloyd-Jones, David Olson, Robert Scholes, Roger Shuy, Ross Winterowd, and Edward White. Joseph Gibaldi of the MLA invited Mina to join the Committee on Teaching and Related Professional Activities, and Joseph A. Califano invited her to serve on the Board of Advisors of the Fund for the Improvement of Post-Secondary Education. (She had already served as a member of one of FIPSE's subcommittees.)

Mina hoped that the favorable publicity she was receiving as a result of *Errors and Expectations* would enable her to reach an even wider audience with her concerns over the inequality that existed in public education. As a result, she wrote an editorial entitled "The Other Side of Literacy" and sent it to *The New York Times.* In it she repeated many of the same concerns she had been expressing to her colleagues all along. (In fact, Mina ended her essay with the same words she would use in a speech entitled "The English Professor's Malady," which she would deliver later in the year.)

Of the two skills of literacy, reading has ever been judged the more important skill for ordinary citizens to acquire. Some people—English teachers among them—have even insisted that writing is a skill not everyone *can* acquire or needs to acquire, especially in an age when television and tapes have liberated speech from transiency and telephones have reduced the burden of ritual and routine correspondence.

To be sure, learning to write is hard work. And few, even among those who become highly skilled at it, ever seem to do it for fun, as they might watch television or read a book. Still, there is a special advantage to learning how to get one's thoughts down on a page, one that is related to the very functioning of a democracy. For one can imagine the advantages to *any* state of having a population of readers: reading remains the cheapest and most efficient technology for passing out directions and information and propaganda. But it is in the nature of writing to encourage individuals to discover and explore their *own* hunches, to ponder their *own* words, to respect their *own* thoughts enough to entrust them to the written page. Writing even teaches about reading. It is the other side of literacy, without which the reader too often reads uncritically.

Despite these benefits, or possibly because of them, the skill of writing is essentially a class-distributed skill. Unless they are exceptionally talented, the children of the poor learn even less about writing than about reading. They learn handwriting, perhaps, in the early grades, but most of them leave school without having learned to compose and perfect their thoughts in the medium that allows for the greatest independence of mind and exacts the greatest effort of articulation. What is worse, they leave school believing that they were in some way natively unqualified to learn to write and must now find ways of evading the various writing tasks that are certain to be posed for them in their work and in their lives as parents and citizens.

The experience of open admissions both at City University and in other universities and colleges throughout the country has not only revealed the plight of such students but demonstrated that there are no pedagogical reasons why writing should be an exclusive skill rather than a common skill among our citizens. It simply needs to be taught. And the fact that it is not taught to the students who need it most constitutes a true crisis of literacy in this country, where being able to *initiate* messages is as important as being able to receive them and where the most fruitful and necessary activity is arguing rather than agreeing.

Today, people are, for the most part, alarmed over the declining levels of literacy among the privileged, not over the traditional sub-literacy of the poor. But until this traditional illiteracy is as alarming to the American people as the declining literacy of the affluent, our schools will continue to cultivate literacy as a privilege rather than an entitlement.

To prepare only some people to flourish in a democracy and then to argue that they are the only people with the native ability to do so is to consent to the existence, within the boundaries of what we call public education, of the most exclusive country club of all.

Less than a week after sending the editorial, Mina received a rejection letter from *The New York Times*, signed by Charlotte Curtis, who wrote: "Your article is charming, but our space crunch continues and there's just no way we can accommodate the piece. I'm so sorry." Marilyn Maiz remembers that she and Mina "had a good laugh, particularly over the word 'charming,'" when they read Curtis's response, but they both knew it was simply another indication of the lack of knowledge and interest that existed, even among many intellectuals, about the problem to which Mina and many of her colleagues had devoted their lives.

In June 1977, Mina delivered an address at the Association of Departments of English Conference in Albany entitled "The English Professor's Malady." (See Appendix G.) This "malady," Mina explained, was a "territory of general ill-preparedness" that could be divided into three parts: professors' unfamiliarity with the psychology of writing, "that is, with the behavior of writing itself"; their lack of knowledge of the history of writing, "the record of what has gone on in the name of freshman composition over the past hundred years or so"; and third, the "anthropological or cultural part of writing," which she defined as "the study of the functions as well as the forms of academic writing, the attempt to construct the social realities that give rise to specific kinds of behavior." The English professor's malady was caused, Mina explained, "by provincialism—by too 'local' a conception of the subject he teaches." In addition, she described another "condition that helps explain the

malady": "a tendency to underestimate the capabilities and the difficulties of students whose backgrounds and states of preparation are very
different from his." The "remedy," she suggested, was for the English
professor to discover that "literateness is not to be confused with intelligence, and that young adults who by all traditional measures don't
belong in college do in fact have the capability of surviving and even
flourishing there." Even that would not be enough, however. "The
teacher who wishes to give his best energies to the instruction of ill-
prepared freshmen must be ready to forgo many of the rewards and
privileges of his profession. He must be resigned to being an altruistic
teacher." Mina concluded:

> To this, we must add another rude fact—that despite the opening of
> many educational doors since the late sixties, there is little evidence
> that much has changed behind those doors. If anything, the lines
> that divide the privileged from the unprivileged in this society have
> simply been extended into the terrain of higher education. And
> nowhere is that gap between the two groups more sharply drawn
> than in the area of writing. . . .
>
> To prepare only some people to flourish in a democracy and then
> to argue that they are the only people with the native ability to do
> so is to consent to the existence, within the boundaries of what we
> call public education, of the most exclusive country club of all.

Mina's address was well received—fan mail arrived back in New
York before she did, inviting her to deliver even more addresses, attend
even more conferences, join even more committees. A representative
of the Los Angeles division of California State University wrote to her
asking her to consider spending a year at the college as a distinguished
visiting professor, where she would teach two courses and "provide
consultation in curriculum development."

But shortly after she arrived home from Albany, Mina was readmitted to Memorial Sloan-Kettering. Her cancer had metastasized,
and doctors removed a tumor from her right lung. Again, she recovered relatively quickly, but this time she was not as sanguine. Marilyn
Maiz remembers that Mina began to talk about the possibility that she
would die of cancer. "Her moods would change from one day to the
next," Marilyn recalls. "I remember during one of my visits to the hospital, I reminded Mina that we had to prepare her promotion folder,

since she would soon be eligible for a full professorship at City. She replied, 'It's just not very important to me anymore.' But then, a few days later, when she began to feel better, she asked me if I had done any work on her promotion application."

Mina felt well enough to begin planning another book. Her proposed title was *The State of Literacy in America.* In writing *Errors and Expectations,* she had drawn on the expertise, experience, and knowledge she had gained during the five years she had spent teaching and directing the basic writing program at City College. Now, she was ready to expand her topic. As a result of her research and planning for a national literacy center, her work at the Instructional Resource Center, her voracious reading, her visits to campuses, her lectures and workshops, and her communication with so many other teachers and scholars throughout the country, Mina had come to realize that the problems exhibited by her basic writing students were simply part of a far larger problem affecting the entire nation. At about the same time, E. D. Hirsch consulted with her about his plans to write a book on a similar topic; the result was *Cultural Literacy: What Every American Needs to Know.* It is easy to imagine how different—and how much more useful—Mina's book would have been.

In June 1977, Mina's father, Albert Pendo, collapsed while working on the ranch, and he was rushed to the hospital. Mina was distraught, calling her brother, George, repeatedly until she was assured that her father would be all right. She wrote him a letter begging him to take better care of himself and describing her love for him—never once mentioning her own illness. "I love you deeply," she wrote,

with all those years we have shared, the sorrows and the joys—and I will be waiting each day for good news. And soon I will be there, and we can sit on the porch and do those tape recordings I've been going to do for years. While you're recuperating, jot down some reminders of the things we should describe. Be sensible and patient and obedient and remember how much you are loved.

In the same letter, Mina thanked Eliza, her father's new wife, for taking care of him.

Mina traveled to California that June to attend a conference on writing sponsored by the National Institute of Education. (She had been asked to deliver a paper at this conference, but because of her illness, she had had her name removed from the program.) She visited her father on her way home from the conference. George remembers that she seemed tired during her visit and did not have the time—or the energy—to record her father's stories and anecdotes about his years working in the mines. In fact, she seemed so weak during the last days of her visit that her father did not believe she could make the trip back to New York alone. Mina, who would do anything to assuage her father, pretended to call the man whom she had been seeing for the past several years and "arranged" for him to meet her at the Denver airport for her connecting flight home. "I didn't realize at the time that she was simply staging the phone call for Father's benefit," George recalls. "But I did realize that she was very ill. She knew it, too, but believed—or wanted to believe—that they had gotten all the cancer." It was the last time that George would see his sister.

Ed Corbett remembers seeing Mina at the conference in California. "After each speaking session," he recalls,

> the audience was given a fifteen-minute break. During at least two of those breaks, I saw Mina sitting alone in a courtyard, soaking up the bright California sunshine. I did not disturb her on either of those occasions. I had heard that she was ill, and I did not want to distract her from the healthful rays of the sun. That may very well have been the last time I saw Mina Shaughnessy alive.

In July 1977, Mina was readmitted to Memorial Sloan-Kettering, where doctors removed a small malignant tumor from her other lung. Marilyn Maiz remembers that the doctors were able to reach the tumor through an incision under the arm; therefore, Mina healed relatively quickly. "We were all very hopeful and positive at that time," Marilyn recalls. "Mina was strong and confident. She often said that she liked the idea of being treated at Sloan-Kettering because the staff there was so familiar with cancer that they didn't 'give you the death looks' every time you walked in there."

During this particular stay at Sloan-Kettering, Mina met Kathleen O'Hare, an oncology nurse specialist from Belfast, Northern Ireland, who would play a large role in providing her with understanding, comfort, and support. She liked O'Hare immediately, partly because of her appearance and demeanor: O'Hare was one of the few women around who was as tall as Mina; she exhibited a no-nonsense strength and beauty, and she spoke with a lilting, soothing brogue. O'Hare remembers that Mina exhibited an interest in Catholicism at that time, but concluded that this was simply a result of her curiosity. "She talked quite a bit about religion, and she knew quite a bit about Catholicism," O'Hare recalls, "but she talked about many other things as well. She was curious and interested in everything and everyone; she asked a lot of questions and truly seemed to enjoy hearing the answers."

By October 1977, Mina was well enough to travel to Michigan State University to deliver an address entitled "Basic Writing" at the Modern Literature Conference. (See Appendix H.) She referred again to the "malady" of English professors, a malady manifested in their "moans, laments, and ultimatums" over the errors of basic writing students. These teachers, who were "accustomed to learners who, like themselves, had over the years been slowly, silently acculturated to the ways of literacy in academia," were "reluctant in spirit to begin from scratch, and ill-equipped by education to determine where, in fact, scratch was." To those teachers, she declared:

> I can only say that the Open Admissions experiment, wherever it has been seriously undertaken, has yielded a few truths that I, and I suspect many other teachers, would walk the plank for—and one of them is that the young men and women we call remedial have the capacity (by now the proven capacity) to become competent writers and to do so, if everyone works very hard, even within the harsh time limits imposed by the college timetable.

But Mina addressed a "second group of teachers" as well, those who "now insist that the arbitrariness of the formal written code relieves students of the need for mastering that code." She declared that the arbitrariness of conventions was not enough reason to ignore those conventions. To both groups of teachers, she suggested instead that the

> errors and shortcomings we as teachers have become fleet at seeing and naming deserve a different quality of attention than we have customarily given them, something closer to the sort of careful and imaginative observations we have been trained to make of literary

texts, except that instead of focusing on how a successful text succeeds or what it means, our task is to note how and why unsuccessful student texts fail and what it might have meant.

Mina repeated again her belief that basic writing students were educable, and it was society's obligation to provide them with that education:

> The experience of Open Admissions both at City University and in other universities and colleges throughout the country has not only revealed the plight of such students but demonstrated that there are no pedagogical reasons why writing should be an exclusive skill rather than a common skill among our citizenry. It simply needs to be taught. And the fact that it is not taught to the students who need it most constitutes a true crisis of literacy in this country, where being able to initiate messages is as important as being able to receive them, and where the most fruitful and necessary activity is arguing rather than agreeing.

After the conference, a question-and-answer session was held with the audience, and a doctoral student from the University of Michigan taped the interview. It is obvious that the questions were being asked by graduate students who would soon find themselves in classrooms: "Do you lecture to a class or do you tutor?" "Do the students discuss each other's papers in class?" (The audience laughed when Mina observed that the students *do* discuss each other's papers, but their reaction at first is "terrible," she noted, because they model their responses after "all the teachers they've had. I find these *dictatorial* students saying, 'What's this? This is illiterate.'")

As always, Mina responded thoughtfully and carefully, offering anecdotes about her students' behavior and her own, to help her listeners realize that basic writing students are *writers*. She realized almost immediately that the future teachers in the audience were more interested in "how-to" rather than why, so she described the process that she had followed in her basic writing classes. The "process" was, however, similar to the one being espoused by the National Writing Project. (In fact, Mina had recently been asked by Jim Gray, the national director, if she were interested in directing a writing project in the New York City area.)

We would have about fifteen students in the class. Then you need a couple of in-class tutors. We get those by having a seminar that gives credit to English majors for the teaching of composition, and those tutors are in the class two days a week and meet with the teacher outside the class. Now once the assignment has been made, it's divided into first draft, and then a second draft, then a final draft. During this time, the students are constantly conferring with one of us, the tutors or the teacher. When the papers are final—this means that some tutor has worked with the student until the paper is in good shape, that it does not need to be corrected—we have the student put the final paper on a ditto master. Then we run off the ditto sheets of each of the assignments as a separate booklet. And the assignment for the class then becomes reading their finished papers as texts. In this way, we create a reading audience for the writers at the point where they're willing to go public instead of at the point where just the teacher sees it, looking for errors.

Mina responded to the students' questions with her usual eloquence and precision, but her humor and charm were particularly evident on this occasion. The transcript indicates several occasions when the audience interrupted her responses with laughter or applause. But she was also pragmatic in her answers; she no longer believed that writing instructors could perform miracles, and they had to begin to realize as much:

> The problem is that we've worked ourselves into a kind of corner, you with your five classes and more students than you can possibly teach. We've sort of put it upon ourselves that somehow we *have* to. I think you have to say you *can't*. I mean, you do what you can. Maybe you can get fragments solved, or something like that. I don't think you can do much in a semester; I think it takes three semesters to be able to make a dent in these sorts of problems. And programs that are trying to do everything in one semester . . . . [transcriber's ellipsis] After all, either this sort of neglect and betrayal happened, in which case it's costly if you're going to remedy it at this point, or it didn't. Now if it did, it's not going to be solved by a cheap course. It just can't be. The institutions that want it both ways finally can't have it both ways; they either have to decide that they can or they can't. And I know it's putting on teachers more than they can even safely bear to say, "Look, I can't do this because . . . " and then they'll say, "Well, there's plenty of unemployed teachers out there who can."

So you're almost always in a difficult situation. I hate to end on that note.

Rather than ending "on that note," Mina decided instead to describe for her audience the conditions that existed in 1968 when she first arrived at City College. There was a touch of nostalgia in her recollections—a result, perhaps, of her illness—but one senses also that she was not recalling the early days of her City career to show how far the field of basic writing had evolved, but rather to show how far it had to go. For Mina, it was still very much a frontier:

When I first went to City [College], I remember, we were so little that nobody cared. We were just three hundred, a queer program of three hundred kids out there somewhere on North Campus. We never went to the English Department meetings. I didn't even have a desk. I finally got a part-time woman to help me type. I said, "Look, I don't care whether you type, but sit at this desk and make a sign that says, 'The Basic Writing Desk.' We've got to get some place where we can hang our hats." Our first class was assigned in the men's room by some mistake. The whole thing was just a little thing, and we were teachers struggling, almost privately, not even being able to admit how difficult what we were trying to do was.

We had to put makeshift rooms in a great big auditorium, so you could hear what was going on in other teachers' cubicles. And I used to drift by some of those cubicles, and I'd hear students laughing, and I'd say, "My students never laugh." And then teachers would say, "Oh, we had a great class today. We did this and that." And then when I sat in classes, I found that "we" was one student and one teacher. It was such a vulnerable occupation, high one day, and absolutely down in the dumps the next. And slowly, as we began to trust one another as teachers. . . . [transcriber's ellipsis]

I remember once saying to one of my trusted teachers as we were walking to North Campus, that this program doesn't have a center. And he said, . . . "Rent a center!" And I said, "Oh, I mean I've got to act like a center." Then I realized that we somehow had to trust one another to tell each other, not defensively, what was really going on, because there were no answers. There wasn't a book, and there wasn't a specialist, and there wasn't a college that knew much more about this than anyone else. And what happened? Our journal started this way; we started doing papers for one another. And we said, "We haven't seen that paper anywhere. Why don't we try to start a journal?" Then we went to other conferences, and we began reading. We talked at lunch hours. We were a group, and when we met people like us at other campuses, we had immediate rapport. We just knew the same things. We were talking about the same things. That's still very much where this field is. It's all open in a way; it's a frontier. We really still don't . . . even know if we're doing anything like what we can do for these students.

Toward the end of the question-and-answer session, one of the students asked Mina,

What in your life or experience caused you to decide to collect the four thousand papers on which you based your book and try to make some sense out of them? Also, I'm wondering what role the analysis of a series of papers by one student can play as opposed to grouping great numbers of papers that have similar themes.

Mina responded with a fuller explanation than any she had provided before:

That's a very good question. I think both of these are ways to discover what it is we want to know, what the research boundaries ought to be, what the research questions ought to be. During some five years of working with students, my own students, with all of these problems, and keeping their folders, I tried to get some sense of longitudinal change. I would stop them, like the Ancient Mariner, whenever I saw them in the hall and say, "What are you doing with your writing? Do you have a sample?" At some point I realized that being responsible for the program, we really should be accountable for whether students improved or not.

It dawned on me one day that we turn back the data—the papers—and keep the grade books, and it was such a strange, unscientific thing to do. So I decided to collect the papers, because I realized that while you can't generalize about case histories, except about the individual student involved, you could say, with a large batch of papers, that these errors or those errors are common. My great interest then was in trying to produce handbooks, to get publishers interested in handbooks, that dealt with these basic writing problems. The traditional handbook says, "Students will not have any difficulty with the regular inflections," and there you are with a whole batch of papers that prove the opposite.

As to why I did it, I don't know. I've often wondered. You know, my grandparents all came from one part or another of Europe and got on wagons and went out West. I often thought, after going back to [visit] where they were born, "Why did they leave? It's such a beautiful place; it's such a lovely setting." I'm sure they did it because they hadn't the slightest idea of what they were getting into.

Again, fan letters followed Mina home, but this time they contained references to her health; it was obvious to everyone who saw and heard her that she was ill, and they were worried about her. In November 1977, doctors removed another tumor from the lining of her lung. Again, she healed quickly. Marilyn Maiz remembers that doctors told Mina she had the healing capacity of a teenager. "I bet they say that to everyone," Mina joked.

In the fall of 1977, the Carnegie Foundation asked Margo Viscusi, a freelance writer, to conduct an interview with Mina. The foundation had given Mina the original grant for her work on *Errors and Expectations,* and in response to the enormous success of the book, they wanted to feature her in an article in one of their publications. Although the foundation never published the article, Viscusi saved the tapes. As one listens to Mina's voice, it is difficult to believe she had less than a year to live. It is strong and confident; her commitment to Open Admissions students was as deep as ever; and she expressed her ideas with grace and precision. Marilyn Maiz remembers that although Mina was still recovering from surgery, she welcomed the opportunity to talk with Viscusi. "Mina did not want us to treat her as an invalid. She was determined to recover. She was one of the leading authorities in the country on basic writing and that is what interested her and drove her, not her illness." Mina could not ignore her illness completely, however. She was still weak from surgery, and Viscusi had to conduct the interview in two sessions, one in September and one in October 1977.

Alice Trillin once described Mina's talent as a speaker and a thinker by declaring, "Mina spoke in perfect paragraphs." Nowhere is this more evident than in the interview she gave to Viscusi. Although the questions were sometimes disconnected, Mina was able to articulate those beliefs, theories, and practices that had guided her throughout her career and that were inspiring so many other teachers as a result of the publication of *Errors and Expectations*. This interview also reflects her growing interest in the role teachers play in their students' lives, and frequently it seems as if she were describing the kind of teachers she had known as a child, particularly her mother. "Teachers are society's bridge between the family world and the indifferent world," Mina explained.

> They are responsible for making us grow, for making us learn, for shaping us, for changing us. . . . It's almost unfashionable to view teaching in this way. Yet there is something about it that is more like a calling of the sort that you get with doctors or nurses or people who tend in the most personal ways to the development of other people. I don't think we have that perception of a teacher at all anymore. I don't think teachers have that perception of themselves, and nothing in our certifying procedure even attempts to acknowledge this as an important feature. Yet when I think of the important teachers I've observed in this work, they are all teachers who have had this sense, not only the sense of the seriousness of the work they are doing, but of almost the sacredness of the subject they teach. So many English teachers have lately been rather apologetic for putting students through all of the problems they have to go through in learning to write, in learning correct grammar, and all of that. There is a kind of uneasiness, a feeling of "I'm sorry you have to do this but this is the way it works." The best teachers in this subject haven't that attitude at all. It's almost as if they are saying, "You have the privilege of entering into this world of the written language. If you work hard, if you dedicate yourself, you may be able to do this." That's a rare attitude.

Mina explained that students need a "safe place" before they can communicate with a teacher, recalling: "I had a student once write, 'I'm sorry I wrote about this experience because it was important.'" And Mina described the effect her teaching had had on her own writing style:

> [You] write better in a way because you've added a new consciousness to your own repertoire. . . . You keep thinking, "how would this look to them?" I recently attended a very scholarly conference where there were some quite brilliant papers on literary criticism,

and I kept thinking as I was listening to it how arcane the whole experience was. It was very pleasurable, it wasn't that. . . . They were battles: they were destroying some concept that a particular writer had used or a Freudian view of something. It's really a battle of different ideas being put up against other ideas. In the first place, the language was so full of allusions that the student would be lost, but he also wouldn't understand what the contest was. It gives you a kind of cultural perspective on your own society. This, it seemed to me, has been one of the things we needed, all of us, in interpreting the academic world, because we always thought it was a universal, what we were leading students into were universal truths and universal ways of pursuing those truths and so on. Therefore, a person would just sort of fall into it once they reach a certain level of sophistication. But it's a culture, a very special highly ritualized world with a special language. I think maybe academicians are the ones who can't focus; I think they probably are among the most provincial people in this way of assuming that people understand their ways.

Mina articulated her conviction that basic writing students were perfectly capable of learning to "do all of the analytical work of a society or culture," just as long as that society or culture does not prevent them from learning:

Unless we revolutionize our colleges, where we are producing only a few people who master the skills and do all the analytical work of the society, we are really betraying the students. The task of a writing teacher in a basic course is to prepare students to write close, organized, reasoned prose and to encourage students to make judgments and to work with larger and larger collections of data. I would consider this a bit like some of the basic skills you need in a society, driving a car, knowing how to penetrate the rhetoric of politicians.

It's hard for me to imagine anyone entering into any job or any particular civic responsibility where they don't have a chance to control things instead of being controlled by them. The people who are so ready to dismiss the need for this skill are generally the people who have already acquired it to a great degree themselves and are using it to make an argument against it.

Viscusi assumed that the students about whom Mina was speaking were unable to write because of the "dialect they use in their own homes." Mina immediately sensed that Viscusi had gained her impressions about dialect from the recent spate of publicity, tinged with racism, claiming that black children in the inner city were being raised unable to speak or understand "standard" English. Mina responded:

> I don't think that the problem of dialect, in the sense of certain grammatical forms, is at all as important an issue as it has been made out to seem. That is, my own experience was that those grammatical errors that arose out of dialect collisions were limited to two or three types and were already residual. I mean after all, the students that we work with have come through a whole twelve-year process; they had heard a lot of standard English and recognized it and could often speak it at will and then move back into their dialect which is in English.
>
> I don't think that's really the problem. I don't think that it is so much a matter of abandoning a dialect or exchanging it. It is more the problem of a spoken as opposed to a written culture. . . .
>
> I've always felt that the issue of dialect and all the political activity that it has inspired has somehow put us on the wrong track in terms of what students need, and has also made it more difficult for students. I've never known a student who didn't want to learn to write. I've never known a student who didn't want to be able to manage the work in his classes as long as he opted to go to college. We certainly have many, many students coming from disadvantaged areas; certainly they rightly resented being treated like people who had not learned anything, and who didn't have their own bridges and their own advantages linguistically. That was of course one of the things that teachers had to learn and are still having to learn.
>
> It just never seemed to me the big issue. The big issue was that they weren't writers; they had never done any writing. Their hands didn't move; they couldn't spell; they couldn't do all of these things. One would have settled to teach them to do all of these things even in whatever dialect people say they spoke. It was more you wanted facility, you wanted ease, you wanted habit with this medium, and not that they had some grammatical forms that were different from other students. I think anyone who learned all of the other things could survive with those few grammatical features. That wasn't the issue.

Mina's interview with Margo Viscusi lasted more than four hours, and although she began to sound tired toward the end of the second session, she continued to argue for the rights of Open Admissions students to be instructed by teachers who possessed "pedagogical imagination":

> Sure, there are some people who will have to be born again to be good teachers, but there is also a large group that simply has to have their imagination trained the way it is trained to read poetry. This is a form of imagination that involves intuiting what has been going on in the mind of another person. Teaching is not only the mastery of the content, but it's the sharpening of that ability to see and imagine what is going on in somebody else's mind. I would encourage teachers to become students in some very difficult subject. I once took a course in Mandarin Chinese, because I had a lot of students coming from Chinese backgrounds. I did it just to feel what it was like to be a potential dropout all semester. To see that suddenly things just go swimming by your head, and you know you're in deep water, and you get annoyed with the teacher for not backing up, but you also feel utterly incapable of saying "I didn't understand that." It's like a vast emperor's clothing story with the teachers and the students all carrying on their own sort of deceptions.
>
> But I have seen the seasoning of imagination in teachers as they work with their students, particularly English teachers because they have to talk to students. I used to walk past teachers' offices. I would see the teacher leaned over, straining to understand the student, and the student leaned over straining to explain himself. Then every once in a while there would be an "Oh, I see what you mean." Suddenly two people found a word. . . . It begins to give you a sense of the geography of that kind of student's mind. It's not a mysterious thing; it's not a mystique; it's knowledge.

In December 1977, Mina had a seizure in the hall of her apartment building, and she was again taken to Memorial Sloan-Kettering. X-rays revealed a brain tumor. Until this point, her friends had either believed, or at least pretended to believe for her sake, that she would survive. Now, however, many of them were convinced that her determination to continue to undergo further surgery was futile. "We didn't know what to say or do," Leonard Kriegel recalls. "It was obvious to us that Mina was dying, but she was absolutely determined to fight the cancer, convinced that each operation would be successful. It was so painful to visit her, to see her wasting away." Marilyn Maiz remembers

Mina's determination as the only weapon she had left:

> I remember visiting Mina one day shortly after the doctor had examined her following one of her many operations. When I asked her what the doctor said, she replied: "He said I'm healing well. They say that to everybody." But then she explained that she couldn't give up, no matter what. "I have to believe that I can make it," she said. "Because if I don't, then I truly *won't* make it."

It was a dreadful time. Doctors decided that Mina should not endure the ordeal of brain surgery unless they could establish that the cancer had not spread to other vital organs. As a result, she had to undergo a full week of tests—and the suspense of waiting for the result of each test—before the brain surgery could be performed. When doctors finally operated, they were unable to locate the tumor. As a result, less than a week later Mina had to undergo surgery a second time. This time, they found and removed the tumor. Again, her optimism astounded her friends. She told Marilyn that she had had headaches that were worse than the pain she was feeling as a result of the surgery, but the subsequent radiation treatments, ten of them, left Mina weak and ill.

Invitations continued to arrive for Mina to speak at conferences, present workshops, deliver addresses. In fact, she was in such demand that organizers were often willing to plan their conferences around the time that she would be available. Several days after the brain surgery, she received an invitation from James Hammond, the chancellor of the Massachusetts State College System, dated December 20, 1977. A conference was being planned for the faculty and staff of the ten four-year institutions in the state, and Hammond asked Mina to participate—in any way she wished. "This invitation is about as vague as any you will see," he wrote, "but it is so deliberately, out of respect for you and the significant contribution you are making to education. Please be assured that we will make every accommodation so that you can be part of the conference and that we would be prepared to meet any cost that you suggest."

Mina was not able to respond to Hammond until January 10, 1978, and she described in great detail, and with great dignity, what she had been enduring:

Unfortunately, I must refuse your invitation. I have been caught up during the past year in a battle against cancer. There's a good chance I may win, but the cost so far has been six operations in eight months, the last of which was in December. I am now convalescing and expect to take up my duties at the University in March, but I have had to eliminate all "extras" for the spring. Should all go well and you have a similar conference in the fall, I hope you will think of me again.

I go into this perhaps unnecessarily detailed explanation only to assure you that were it within my power I would be at your conference.

Mina's illness was preventing her from reaping the rewards and accolades she so rightly deserved not only as a result of *Errors and Expectations,* but in recognition of her tireless efforts to improve the quality of education being offered to the students at the City University of New York and throughout the country as well.

During each of Mina's stays in Memorial Sloan-Kettering, she spent time talking with Kathleen O'Hare, the nurse whom she had met in July 1977. On one occasion, O'Hare recalls,

> Mina brought up the conversation of death. I believe she knew she was dying, and realizing death was no stranger to me, given my occupation, I shared my belief in an afterlife with her but admitted the process of dying was a concern to me. She kept a Bible with her in the hospital, and she had several favorite passages that she read frequently.

Marilyn Maiz and Alice Trillin did everything they could to make Mina comfortable, and Priscilla and Alan Brandt, with whom Mina had remained extremely close, visited her every day, either in the hospital or at home. Although she recovered quickly from the brain surgery, she was devastated over her appearance: her head had been shaved for the surgery, and the radiation treatments were preventing her hair from growing back.

In addition, Mina began to fear that she would lose her mental capacities. "She could deal with the loss of physical capacities," Alan recalls, "but she didn't want to lose her ability to reason and think." As a result, she asked several of her friends to consider helping her in the

Mina shortly before her death; sketch by her friend Maggie Lane. Courtesy of Marilyn Maiz.

event that she became unable to function. In addition, she asked them to procure drugs for her to take in the event that she decided she no longer wanted to live. Alan remembers that he was finally able to help her. "I can't even remember what I got for Mina or where I got it. I do remember that it was very difficult for me to get the pills, and I remember being very afraid of the possible legal consequences of my action. But I could not bear to think that she would not have access to something so important to her. She was grateful to me; it helped her realize, I think, that I would do anything for her."

Several days later, however, one of the nurses found the medication in Mina's jewelry box and confiscated it. "We never talked about it again," Alan recalls. "But I remember thinking that I might not be able to replace the drugs. It was a terrible time for all of us, especially Mina."

Mina's friends did whatever they could for her. "We had a wig made for her," Priscilla recalls, "and Mina's good friend, Maggie Lane, hand-sewed an exquisite nightgown that Mina loved and wore all the time in the hospital." Kathleen O'Hare remembers that Mina continued to wear make-up—her appearance was still very important to her. Marilyn

and Alice were visiting her in the hospital one day when a male orderly walked into the room and noticed Mina's beauty, accentuated by
the nightgown with its delicate needlework. "Wow," he said to her, "Are
you a movie star or something?" She smiled graciously, but after the
orderly left she told Marilyn and Alice that she really wanted to reply,
referring to the nickname that had been bestowed on her by her colleagues at CUNY: "A movie star? Baby, I'm the Queen!"

Marilyn recalls another example of Mina's ability to keep her sense
of humor during this period:

> We did not know that the cancer had spread to Mina's brain until
> she collapsed one Saturday morning on her way out of her apart-
> ment house. She was taken to the hospital, and I was contacted. When
> I arrived, she was extremely ill and frightened, so much so that she
> wondered if she was dying. When she stabilized a bit and was finally
> settled and comfortable in a hospital room, she told me that we had
> to talk about what would happen in the event of her death. We dis-
> cussed a few things, then the issue of a memorial service came up.
> Mina had given this some thought, because she already knew that
> she wanted Len Kriegel, Ed Quinn, Adrienne Rich, Lottie Wilkins,
> and Irving Howe to speak.
>
> This may sound macabre, but Mina and I had worked together
> for so long that we immediately got down to specifics. "How long
> should each person speak?" I asked her. She replied, "About twenty
> minutes each." I responded, "Mina, think of the survivors! That's
> almost two hours." "Okay," she said, "then how long do *you* think
> they should speak?" I replied, "Five minutes each." Mina thought
> about that for a few seconds, started laughing, and said, "Nope, there's
> no way they can do me justice in five minutes. Give 'em ten."

But Marilyn also remembers those times when Mina began to
consider the world after she was gone. She wondered what direction
her career would have taken had she not become ill. "Mina would have
become a college president," Marilyn recalls. "There actually had been
an offer from a college in Pennsylvania, and we joked about her taking
that position when she got better, but she said that simply wouldn't do,
she loved New York too much to leave it."

Ed Quinn remembers talking to Mina over the phone during this
period:

We had often met for drinks at the Algonquin Hotel, particularly after Mina left City and went to the Instructional Resource Center, and we joked about going there again—both of us knowing how unlikely it was. I would hang up after these phone conversations so disconsolate that I was barely able to speak; it was so evident that she did not want to die.

Ironically, as a result of her illness, Mina finally had time to write poetry again. Early in 1978, she wrote a poem entitled "The Invalid." It was a depiction of her view of the world from her hospital room high above midtown Manhattan as she recovered from her sixth operation in less than a year:

> I watch from my window
> The people doing the work of the world
> Floor upon floor of them
> Too busy to note that the winter afternoon has lit
> Them up like film strips.
> They are busy in the world I lately lived in.

Donald Shaughnessy had returned from Zaire by this time and realized almost immediately that Mina would probably not recover. He, too, was amazed at her optimism. His return complicated Mina's life even further, however. She was now unable to spend time with the man with whom she had been intimate for almost ten years. Don took an active role in ensuring that she received the best care available, and she was greatly amused by his mock indignation in response to the fact that *Errors and Expectations* had not been dedicated to him. Marilyn Maiz remembers that he told Mina she should have written, "To my husband, Donald Shaughnessy, without whose absence this book would not have been written."

After the brain surgery, Mina remained in the hospital for the duration of her radiation treatments. However, she had herself officially checked out for one afternoon in order to travel to Harlem to attend the wedding ceremony of her former student, Lottie Wilkins. "We all knew how sick Mina was," Lottie recalls. "She could barely stand up. Of course, she didn't stay for the reception. But she told me that she wouldn't miss my wedding for anything in the world."

Marilyn Maiz continued to visit Mina every day, informing her of everything going on in the office, getting her input and approval. Marilyn had completed Mina's application for promotion to full professor, and occasionally, she would ask if Marilyn had heard anything. "Her interest in her promotion vacillated; it was an indication of the way she was feeling about her chances of survival," Marilyn recalls. Mina's application had been approved in November 1977, effective January 1, 1978; however, neither Marilyn, Leonard Kriegel, nor Ed Quinn told her that some members of the English department had still resisted her promotion. "By this time," Quinn recalls,

> Mina's book had been heralded in every publication; the president of City College had distributed memos about it; it was the best thing to come out of our department in years. People were well aware that Mina was battling cancer, but, as hard as this is to believe, the same guys who had resisted her all along came up with the same arguments: she had no Ph.D., her work wasn't "literary" or "scholarly." Both Len and I argued on her behalf of course, but it was more painful for us than it had been in the past, knowing it was one of the last times she would need our help.

On December 31, 1977, Alice and Calvin Trillin had dinner delivered to the hospital from the Cafe des Artistes and the Trillins, Marilyn, Mina, and Don celebrated New Year's Eve in her hospital room. Kriegel and Quinn visited her in the hospital regularly, and Quinn remembers that Mina speculated over the cause of her cancer. "She believed that her mother's death had left a deep void. But she also theorized that the summer before Open Admissions was the most stressful period of her life. Preparing for thousands of incoming students had been such a burden that she actually felt that the stress had made her vulnerable to the disease."

Mina tried to hide the fear and loneliness she was feeling from her friends, but in another poem she wrote at this time, she described the "subtraction" of herself being caused by the cancer:

> The subtraction of me came violently first,
> and then there were the days
> when my vast minuend

kept shining quietly
in ways I never learned to compute.
I counted awesome things from my window,
waited on friends to carry over my history,
And lay still in the eye of the terror
Breeding a new mathematics.

Mina's condition continued to deteriorate. She felt weak and tired, was running a persistent low-grade fever, and a loss of appetite caused her to lose even more weight. In April 1978, doctors diagnosed a tumor on her liver. She had to receive several blood transfusions before she was strong enough to undergo yet another operation to remove the tumor.

Shortly after this operation, Mina attended what was to be her last professional conference, sponsored by the Rockefeller Foundation. It was being held in New York City, and she and Ted Gross had looked forward to attending the conference in order to interest the foundation in their idea for a literacy center. Mina's appearance at the conference shocked everyone: thin and pale, she walked and spoke slowly and with great difficulty.

The guest speaker at the conference was Benjamin DeMott, who was at the time an English professor at Amherst College. The title of his address was "As Yet We Lack . . . Notes on Open Admissions as 'A New York Tragedy,'" a reference to a series of articles that had recently appeared in *The Chronicle of Higher Education* that was critical of Open Admissions and had defined it as a tragedy. Ed Quinn had been asked to write a review of Mina's book for *The Nation,* but he suggested that DeMott be asked to do it instead, since his opinion of the book would be more "objective." As a result, DeMott had just finished reading *Errors and Expectations,* and the book had an extraordinary impact on him. As long as such books were being written, he contended, and as long as there were teachers writing such books, the word "tragedy" would remain in quotation marks. It was highly unusual for someone of DeMott's stature to devote the subject of a major address to the description and praise of someone else's work and ideas rather than to espouse his own. This, however, is precisely what he did. DeMott did not know Mina well; he had met her briefly only once or twice before. He was, he recalls, simply struck by the way that Mina perceived literacy. I realized that her work was the kind of work you would do if you were really going to take democracy seriously. Instead of giving inflated speeches about what a democratic society was all about (as so many people were doing at the time), she was doing the grainy, difficult work that would help those of us who were already "privileged" realize there are people in the world who are just beginning to take the steps toward developing an educated mind.

The address that DeMott delivered at the conference was reprinted in *The Nation* less than two weeks later. He began his praise of *Errors and Expectations* by noting:

> Not for some years has comment on open access to higher education been other than disheartening. When chic literary minds allude to the subject, the tone taken is invariably cynical. . . . The implication is that teachers made no commitment to the Open Admissions experiment, but simply used it as further justification of personal laziness and absorption. . . . Among educational journalists, on the other hand, it is understood that the right line on these matters isn't cynically dismissive but piously mournful. The series of articles on the history of Open Admissions at City University published in the *Chronicle of Higher Education* appeared under the title "The New York Tragedy," and the pieces were unremittingly insistent that a whole academic world had been utterly destroyed. Radicals adopt more serious postures but aren't less critical, fundamentally; they challenge open access to higher education on the ground that it's primarily vocational in focus, and has never risked an effort to make liberal arts education relevant to the life needs of the new student constituencies. And the etiologists, for their part, are frozen in the conviction that "explanation" in this area can't have another focus except breakdown and calamity.
>
> In a word, the experiment that began in high optimism longer than a decade ago is now dealt with by most commentators as a downer.
>
> By most, but not all. The exception—and in my opinion the product of the CUNY open admissions experiment that blazes our best path toward the future—is Mina Shaughnessy's *Errors and Expectations*. (646)

DeMott proceeded to describe and discuss the book in great detail, citing passages from it, commenting on its "precision," "reason," "sense of inquiry," and "firm understanding of the ambiguities of progress in her field, and of the need for developmental models of progress."

Mina thanked DeMott for his comments. Of all the praise of her work and her writing that she had received in her career, this was quite possibly the most extraordinary, and its effect on her was extraordinary as well. John Wright would write to Benjamin DeMott less than a month after her death: "I was never able to convince Mina that she had written a revolutionary book, but I think you did, or at least Mina intimated to me shortly before she died that you and others had succeeded in letting her know that her work would last. I know that she died more easily knowing that her accomplishment had been understood and appreciated."

There was great irony, however, in DeMott's address—although he could not have known it at the time. One month before, in February 1978, Ted Gross, Mina's good friend, the man who had been chair of the English department at City College during the most difficult period of Open Admissions, and the man with whom she was collaborating to raise funds for a national literacy center, had published an article in the *Saturday Review* that was perceived by everyone who read it as the worst possible publicity City College, CUNY, or Open Admissions could have received, particularly given the budget cuts and the lack of administrative and political support for Open Admissions that existed at the time. Gross's article could have been perceived, had it been issued as an internal memo, as the soul-searching of an exhausted administrator who had been involved in the planning, administration, and then dismantling of a program affecting thousands of underprepared students. In fact, he never blamed the students for the problems—he did confess, however (among many other things), to a "nagging doubt that we might not be able to take an eighteen-year-old who suffered deep linguistic shortcomings and bring him to college level verbal competence" (16). The fact that he went public with his observations and, even worse, the fact that the magazine entitled the article (without his approval) "How to Kill a College" and featured it on the cover—with a picture of a huge dagger being thrust into one of the City College buildings—did nothing to bolster Gross's popularity with administrators, particularly the president of City College, Robert Marshak. In fact, at the time of the conference, Gross was being forced out of the college as a result of his article, and was therefore being perceived as something of a pariah.

Gross remembers that Mina was one of the few people who greeted him warmly, sat with him, and talked with him. There is no doubt that she had read the article; in fact, she and every other administrator in the CUNY system had received a copy from President Marshak himself, together with a memo explaining why Marshak believed Gross's article was an affront to City College and CUNY. The article garnered extraordinary attention among CUNY faculty and students: there were those who supported Gross's right to publish anything he wanted, but students stormed his office, calling him a racist and a traitor. He insisted that his views were, in fact, reasoned and justifiable, and he later defended them in a book entitled *Academic Turmoil*. He had no idea that the magazine would give the article such an inflammatory title and feature it on the cover—dagger and all.

Whatever Mina thought of the article, she knew that Ted Gross had supported her in everything she did at City College and that as chair he had borne the brunt of criticism and attacks from the faculty as a result of the basic writing program. Mina was a loyal friend, and she was a pragmatist—she knew that the real enemy of Open Admissions was not Ted Gross.

In May 1978, Alice Trillin celebrated her fortieth birthday. She and Mina had been best friends for more than ten years, and Mina knew that Alice understood her fear, perhaps more than anyone else, as a result of Alice's own battle with cancer. Mina wrote a poem entitled "For Alice on her Fortieth Birthday, May 8, 1978":

> Having been through rough territory
> where thistles really pierce
> and cliffs loom insurmountable at times,
> shading whole days,
> You know that the journey into forty is just a fiction,
> a line chalked across our lives because the digits change,
> even though we are still stalking adventure,
> still longing for our mothers,
> still believing that the world is only as old as we are.
> So please beautiful girl, become forty as if

you have just skipped over a hopscotch line
and all the fun is just beginning
and ornery Time has not even thought yet
about calling you home to supper.

Time was running out for Mina, however. In August, a pelvic tumor was discovered during a routine gynecological exam, and she had to endure yet another operation. Then in October, she underwent surgery to remove a tumor that was causing intestinal blockage. Her friends and colleagues could barely keep up with the most recent news of her health; there were so many operations, and they were occurring so frequently, that friends would often call Marilyn Maiz or Alice Trillin to find out the results of one surgical procedure only to learn that another one had been performed.

Marilyn remembers that at the same time that Mina had begun to come to terms with the fact that she would probably die, she had also begun to realize that most of her friends and colleagues were unwilling and unable to acknowledge this fact. "We didn't want to let go of her," Marilyn recalls. "Everyone wanted to visit her—every day—and so it became more and more difficult for Mina to have the peace and quiet she needed. It was terrible for her. We wanted something from her that she couldn't give us." Len Kriegel described the frustration and need he and Mina's other friends felt; in a eulogy he delivered shortly after her death, he described a visit he and Ed Quinn made to Mina in the hospital:

> I think of a Sunday afternoon—Ed Quinn and I sat with her in a hospital room. And I remember Mina laughing, and trying to reassure two of her friends who would be left with their terrible sense of loss. When Ed and I left that room several hours later, it was still with the sense of impending loss, but with a sense of privilege, too, to be her friend—that was a privilege.

But Mina had still not lost her ability to become interested in the world around her. Ed Quinn was a devoted Yankee's fan, and the October 1978 World Series, pitting the Yankees against the Dodgers, was the most exciting in years. He remembers that Mina, watching the games from her hospital bed, "fell in love with Thurman Munson" (as did the rest of the population of New York City) because he scored to save a game, enabling the Yankees to travel back to Los Angeles, where they won the series.

Nor had Mina lost the ability to attract people to her and to enjoy their company. Lewis Thomas, the author of *Lives of the Cell* and several other books that Mina had read and admired, was on the staff of the hospital, and he, along with several other doctors, got in the habit of visiting with her regularly. "Even when she was gravely ill," Kathleen O'Hare recalls, "Mina was a delightful person to be with. She still loved life and wanted to know everything that was going on."

Priscilla Brandt recalls that Mina felt "abandoned" by a Lutheran minister whom she had come to consider her spiritual adviser. "Mina attended Lutheran services regularly during her battle with cancer, but when she became seriously ill, she never heard from him. She suspected that he was unwilling or unable to be there for her when things got most difficult. She actually called him and told him that he had abandoned her."

Mina continued to talk with Kathleen O'Hare, and she had begun to talk regularly with a Catholic priest, one of the chaplains at the hospital, about converting to Catholicism. John Wright remembers receiving a phone call from Mina one afternoon in which she asked him what he thought of the idea. Although Wright was no longer a practicing Catholic, he did not want to deprive her of the potential for comfort— no matter what its source. Many of her friends could not understand her actions, however. Janet Emig had heard about her interest in converting to Catholicism. "I remember hearing from one of Mina's friends about 'a roving band of Irish Catholic nurses.' I didn't take it very seriously; knowing of her strong Lutheran roots, I was sure she would resist such pressure." In fact, Mina did convert to Catholicism during one of her last stays in the hospital. Until the day she died, she received communion regularly. She had finally, it seems, found the spiritual comfort she had been seeking for her entire life.

In October 1978, a month before Mina's death, she was informed that she was going to be honored by a proclamation, signed by President Jimmy Carter, in recognition of her work on behalf of literacy. The award would be presented by Joseph Duffey, chairman of the National Endowment for the Humanities. Marilyn Maiz helped to coordinate a reception in Mina's honor, to be held at her office in the Instructional Resource Center on October 23rd. Irving Howe, Les Berger, Len Kriegel, Ed Quinn, Lottie Wilkins, Alice Trillin, and scores of other close friends, colleagues, and administrators with whom Mina had worked at City and at CUNY for the past ten years were there.

While Joseph Duffey was aware that Mina had cancer, he probably did not realize how gravely ill she was or what she had endured for the past year. As a result, he was nonplused and confused when each of her friends, upon arriving at the office, embraced her and kissed her, making no attempt to hide their love for her. Duffey simply assumed that this was some sort of New York custom. He began his address by saying: "I'm Joe Duffey. I don't expect a kiss until next year." What he could not realize, and what everyone in the room was too kind to point out to him, was that the extraordinary display of affection for Mina was in large part because everyone realized there would be no next year. In all probability, most of the people in the room would never see Mina alive again. Marilyn Maiz has saved the pictures taken at this ceremony; Mina's face was thin and gaunt, and she was clearly exhausted and weak. In fact, she remained sitting throughout the ceremony and reception.

Marilyn made an audio tape of Duffey's presentation and of Mina's response. Duffey praised Mina's work as "testimony to our concern not only for scholarship in the humanities but for humanistic scholarship. I wanted personally to bring one of the original proclamations that President Carter signed. I think it expresses—beyond the walls of this great university—the appreciation of teachers and students for the work you have done." Mina replied in a voice that was raspy and breathless, but it still resonated with the same dignity and grace that she had displayed for the past ten years—despite the constant attacks on her and her work. As always, she took the high road. "I am deeply honored," she said,

> not only because of a recognition of my work, but because the Endowment has recognized this area [of literacy] as a very serious problem in our country and in our culture. I don't know why it is that after two hundred or so years of mass literacy and after thousands of years of literacy among the privileged, we still don't know how to teach it. I suspect it's because we haven't really had to examine the problem until we began to face the implications to a democracy seriously.

In an attempt to close the circle, Mina declared: "I'm very sorry that I couldn't make it up to City College because that is where I did all my work, and that is where I learned all that I learned from my students. It was, I would say, a grand experiment, one that I hope will continue in some form."

The New Yorker described the ceremony in its "Talk of the Town" section on November 6, 1978. The article, entitled "Literacy," gave a brief account of Mina's background at City and her introduction to the field of basic writing, praised *Errors and Expectations,* and described her as "a tall, blond woman who moves with a dancer's grace." It also described her office on the fourth floor at the Board of Higher Education, on East 80th Street: "A blackboard hangs on the wall outside the doorway; a window in the opposite wall overlooks the East River. Around the room there are Japanese prints, African carvings, a woodcut, a watercolor, a map of New York City."

After quoting from Duffey's speech, the article, in typical *New Yorker* fashion, offered an "intimate" glance at some of the proceedings:

> The people in the office applauded, Mrs. Shaughnessy thanked Mr. Duffey, there was more applause, and the gathering broke up into small groups. We joined one of these. Robert Marshak, the president of City College, was talking to Irving Howe, Distinguished Professor of English at the Graduate School of the City University. When we asked Mr. Howe to describe the importance of Mrs. Shaughnessy's work, he had no trouble finding the words. "The challenge is to teach people to read and then to write," he said. "Mina approached this with absolute faith in her ability to do the job. With her students, it's not as if you were starting from scratch. You're starting way beyond scratch. She assumes that there's a kind of coherence behind the jumble. She finds the coherence of idea and then enables students to see the way in which sentence structure enables coherence—to see that syntax isn't a notion handed down arbitrarily but a means of creating order through language. She's free of condescension. There's something absolutely straight about her." Mr. Howe glanced across the room to where Mrs. Shaughnessy was still seated. The Presidential proclamation lay on the table in front of her. "With the exception of Camp David," he said, "that proclamation is the best thing Carter has signed." (36–37)

The article in *The New Yorker,* Marilyn Maiz recalls, brought Mina much pleasure. The magazine was one of the most prestigious in the country at the time, and Mina loved to read it. Her illness was not mentioned and that, too, pleased her; the article focused on her work—not on her cancer. The reference that gave her most pleasure, however, Marilyn recalls, was the description of Mina, particularly the reference to her moving with "a dancer's grace." "Her healthy vanity was still very much intact," Marilyn recalls. "She was absolutely delighted when she saw that passage."

Mina spent the last month of her life at home in the apartment in which she had lived for more than twenty years. She insisted that she did not want to return to the hospital under any circumstances, so Kathleen O'Hare helped Donald Shaughnessy find nurses to care for her; two of Mina's favorite nurses were from the Little Sisters of the Sick Poor convent nearby. In addition, O'Hare spent as much time as she could spare from her full-time job at the hospital visiting Mina and tending to her needs.

Albert Pendo and his wife, Eliza, traveled to New York for a weekend to say goodbye to Mina, and Priscilla Brandt remembers that the prospect of Albert and Eliza being in New York on their own upset and worried Mina; she feared for their comfort and safety. Priscilla made arrangements for Mina's father and step-mother to stay with her and Alan—"of all the things I did for Mina," Priscilla recalls, "I think she was most grateful for that." Priscilla also remembers Albert's helplessness—and Eliza's extraordinary efficiency—in the face of Mina's grave condition. "Albert could barely function, but Eliza baked Mina a wonderful apple pie. Mina declared it the best she ever tasted."

Priscilla and Alan remained at her bedside during the last few days of her life, and Priscilla remembers that Mina tried to say goodbye to her. "Look at us, Priscilla," she said. "We've known each other since we were teenagers. We're closer than sisters. How are we supposed to do this?"

One of the last things Mina wrote was an acceptance speech. Soon after *Errors and Expectations* was published, her good friend, Ken Bruffee, who directed the basic writing program at Brooklyn College, nominated *Errors and Expectations* for the David H. Russell Award for Distinguished Research, a prestigious NCTE honor. Mina's book won, and she was scheduled to accept the award at the annual NCTE convention. Marilyn Maiz remembers that Mina struggled to write the speech; she was weak and ill and found it difficult to concentrate, but she had been deeply moved by the honor, and she wanted people to know that. In addition, she knew that this would probably be her last opportunity to address her colleagues about a topic that had consumed most of her professional life.

I am honored—even intimidated—by the award of the David H. Russell prize for work on the writing of unpracticed adults. I must confess that during the years when my research associates and I were trying to make our way through thousands of blue books, simply noting as precisely as we could the various types of errors and problems that showed up in them, we were simply in a mess, not in research. Since that time, for me research will always bring to mind that dusty, dark room jammed with bulging boxes of blue books, waiting to be classified according to a system that we had not yet even devised.

But I have come to respect that process as an essential part of beginning to look at language in a fresh way. We didn't know at first just what questions we should be asking. This allowed us to let the questions emerge from the evidence in the essays themselves, and from our hunches as teachers about the students who had written those essays.

Some of the questions that this process produced, and some of the answers we suggested, may have seemed to be new ones. The response to my book—a response that truly surprised me—made me realize that we had touched upon questions and answers that had, in fact, long been in the minds of a great many teachers across the country—the intuitions that had guided them late at night as they struggled to find order in the piles of papers that lay on their desks. When the letters came in, not just from big cities but from towns like Missoula, Montana, El Dorado, Arkansas, and Antigonish, Nova Scotia, I felt enormously reassured and much less isolated than I had felt in that room on 138th Street and Convent Avenue. And I found, reading those letters, that just as the problems of our students were widespread, so was the desire of teachers to help solve them.

Teachers have responded to the book because they recognized the problems it pointed out, but they also responded, I think, to the book's almost unconscious assumption: that the work we are doing is not only important but inevitable. Much more waits to be done. The Russell Award which I so proudly accept tonight is prestigious recognition of the fact that English teachers and researchers must continue this important work. I am more confident than ever that what we began in that dusty room will be continued.

Mina would not live long enough to deliver that speech. By mid-November, she was confined to her bed, still relatively comfortable and free from pain, but growing steadily weaker. One of the last phone calls she made was to her brother, George, in South Dakota.

Mina had asked Eliza to say goodbye to me, so when Mina called, we both knew that had been taken care of already. Instead, she told me that each evening, as she went to sleep, she would try to think about the cabin in Hannah where we went each summer when we were children. She told me that she thought of the smells there—the clean strong earth, the pine needles, her pony. On another night, she said, she concentrated on the smell of the small yellow roses that bloomed along the side of Granddad Johnson's house in Oregon, a place we had visited more than forty years ago. Mina said that just in case she died during the night, she wanted those thoughts, those impressions to be her last.

Mina died peacefully, at home, on Thursday, November 16, 1978. She was fifty-four years old. Marilyn Maiz and Alice Trillin had visited her earlier in the day. Alan and Priscilla Brandt, Kathleen O'Hare, and Donald Shaughnessy were with her when she died. Mina's friends gathered at Alice's house the next day simply to be together in their grief. Len Kriegel remembers realizing as he looked at the people gathered there that everyone in the room had been in love with her. "We would have done anything for her. We talked about how we had called Mina the 'Queen' because of her power to help her students, and it slowly began to dawn on us that we, too, had lost our 'Queen,' that she had done so much for us as well, and we were inconsolable. The only one who could have consoled us was Mina."

On Friday, November 17, 1978, a two-column obituary written by Eric Pace was printed in *The New York Times*. In the obituary, Mina was described as

an expert on remedial writing instruction for underprepared college students. . . . Dean Shaughnessy was instrumental in changing attitudes, notably in the academic community, toward underprepared students. This she did largely by demonstrating, through skilled and persuasive analysis, that rational patterns existed in underprepared students' work—mistakes and all.

Mina's body was returned to Spearfish, South Dakota, where a Catholic funeral mass was held, attended by Mina's father, Albert; her step-mother, Eliza; her brother, George; his wife, Norma; their children; and more than one hundred friends from Lead, Spearfish, Rapid City, and Deadwood who had known Mina and her family for many years. She was buried on a small plot of land just a few yards from the ranch house, next to her mother—as Mina had requested.

Mina's friends and colleagues gathered at the City College campus to mourn, to pay homage to her, and to remember her. They knew that Mina had wanted such a ceremony to take place; she had chosen the speakers and had discussed the details with Marilyn Maiz. On December 8, 1978, less than a month after Mina's death, more than two hundred people gathered in The Faculty Room, located in Shepard Hall, the same building in which she had done her painstaking research for *Errors and Expectations,* to pay tribute to her.

Although Alice Trillin was not one of the scheduled speakers, friends convinced her to read the poem that Mina had written for her. The speakers, Ed Quinn, Len Kriegel, Adrienne Rich, Irving Howe, and Lottie Wilkins, each described Mina's talent, brilliance, and dedication as a teacher and recalled eloquently her steadiness of purpose, her devotion to Open Admissions students, her refusal to abandon the ideals of Open Admissions for the practicality of budgets and politics. "In all the years I knew Mina," Len Kriegel noted, "I never heard her categorize, I never heard her speak in abstractions; dedication, integrity, compassion, a sense of reality, these were what she brought to this college, to the students, and to us." Irving Howe remembered that Mina "never condescended to students with pap about creative benefits of illiteracy nor patronized them with rant about maintaining standards. She knew her job was hard, and she went about it." Ed Quinn, like most of the people who worked with Mina, would forever associate her with "those blue books"; those "same blue books that the rest of us prayed to be delivered from or self-righteously cursed, she looked at with that western horizon vision, seeing more in those strangled semi-sentences than we ever imagined could be there."

Lottie Wilkins explained that there were two things that she could be sure of after having Mina (whom she referred to as Shaughn) as her instructor: "One, that I could be taught to write, and two, that the tall white lady with sparkling eyes really liked me and believed in my capabilities." Adrienne Rich remembered what Mina taught her—and so many others—about teaching:

> By personal example, Mina taught many of us that teaching is not charisma, or inspiration, but careful preparation and hard work. That impressionistic and histrionic methods were a waste of a student's time, that a romantic pedagogy cannot take the place of a truly accurate identification. She managed to convey all of this without preaching or admonishing, by the kinds of examples she brought to staff meetings, by her own presence which became, for me at least, a kind of personified intellectual conscience, and above all, by her respect, untinged by white liberal romanticism, for the minds of the young women and men with whom we were working.

But these speakers were also Mina's best friends, so they related as well anecdotes that reflected the special relationship they had shared with her. Len Kriegel remembered her generosity, and her love for the city:

> Here was a woman from a small town in South Dakota who responded to New York's frailties and beauties so fully, so completely, that for me at least, she came to embody the quintessential New Yorker. Her toughness was as good as this city had to offer. And she loved this city enough to forgive it anything, even its terrors. But it was a love rooted in her own solidity, her sense of place. Home for Mina remained South Dakota. I remember once when she returned from a trip home and gave me a small, white cardboard box for my son, who was then nine years old. Inside the box, carefully wrapped in cotton, was a Sioux arrow head. "I found it on our ranch," she said, "and I think Mark should have it."

Irving Howe also remembered Mina's love for New York, and her comfort in living there:

> Mina loved this city with its elbowing fraternity, its misplaced passions, its range of styles that might reveal some bond of values. It amused her to treat her friends as quintessential New Yorkers, parochial apologists for the city's discomforts, who would rise to hau-

teur in defense of its culture and its radicalism. She liked to take over a few of our words from Yiddish, once telling me that she had had a long schlep from Convent Avenue to 42nd Street. In an essay I wrote later, I brought her in anonymously as a cosmopolitan from South Dakota who did a lot of schlepping. She liked that, and she said in turn that she wanted me to visit her ranch back home. "What for?" I asked. "To see me," she said with a smile, "on a horse." What an imagination.

Ed Quinn made Mina's friends laugh when he recalled her infatuation with Thurman Munson:

> We who knew her know that the ability to reach behind the object to show what's really there and to have it come leaping to life, that ability was not reserved only for basic writing papers; it was an essential aspect of her life. I recall her talking to me on the phone not long ago about the World Series; this, remember, was October, when the pain must have already been beyond endurance. And there she was, teaching me as always, to learn to see what I thought I already knew. The face of Thurman Munson, certainly one of life's more ignoble spectacles, assumed in her description a kind of Homeric dignity, even a kind of beauty. And I thought to myself, my God, she's right. Thurman Munson is beautiful. It was the basic writing papers all over again. Whatever she saw was really there; you just had to look at it with joyful eyes.

Quinn also described Mina's greeting to him on the day she received the NEH award, offering his recollection as an example of her healthy, vibrant love of life:

> The gaiety even showed in her vanity, the vanity that all of us have but only she owned up to. At the NEH ceremony, I went up to congratulate her on the citation and she said: "Never mind that! How do I look?" I told her the simple truth of course, that she looked wonderful. And she did. Because even the ravages of that absolutely remorseless killer couldn't extinguish the gaiety that was her center.

Lottie Wilkins recalled something the priest had said at a memorial mass that had been held a few days before for Mina. "During the service," she recalled, "the priest mentioned how concerned Shaughn was that her life wasn't worthwhile. I was flabbergasted. How could a person who had lighted up so many lives have been in darkness about her worth, about her vast accomplishments?"

Of all the people who knew Mina, Adrienne Rich came closest to providing the answer to that question, and in doing so, she exposed that part of Mina—the spiritual and emotional insecurity—that had remained hidden to so many of her friends and colleagues:

> How difficult to do justice to Mina, meaning, to allow her the complexity of her existence, the several parts of her nature, the woman's life none of us could entirely know. . . .
>
> I learned so much from Mina, came quickly to love her, and I believe that she loved and felt she learned from me. Yet our friendship was never really intimate, not as I have known intimate friendship, a fact I recognized and pondered for a long time. I felt I had to respect her defenses, her need to keep parts of her life separated, though I deplored this. . . .
>
> In the last years of her life, even before cancer had moved in so violently, I began to see her as partly imprisoned both in her beauty, to which it was so hard to be stone blind, and in the subtle defenses of a lifetime, which compartmentalized her being, causing her, I believe, much pain, for which she herself saw no possible remedy or relief.

It was an extraordinary ceremony, and Leonard Kriegel remembers that after it was all over, everyone agreed that once again Mina had been right—twenty minutes would not have been too long for each speaker. "Mina was gone forever," he recalls, "so the next best thing would have been to stay there, together, for as long as possible, talking about her." He also remembers that Irving Howe's closing comments offered great comfort to Mina's friends and colleagues, in part because they acknowledged her tenacious battle to live, but also because Howe captured her essence when he referred to "the brightness of her." "She did not want to die," he concluded.

No, she wanted desperately to live. The last time I saw her, two days before her death, she still, I think, wanted to live. She was at

the peak of her gifts; she was vital and beautiful; she had work to
do; she was loved and human enough to enjoy being loved. The
decades of which she was cheated—one wants to rail against the
outrage of it. Some of us may find modes of reconciliation, and blessings to those who can; but for me, and perhaps for others, there is a
need to express the feelings that the death of this splendid woman
reveals an injustice at the very heart of things. Yet even in rebellion
against this unbearable waste, one wants also to fumble, if not to reconciliation, then at least to some terms of peace. The Hebrew prayer
asks "for perfect rest for the deceased in the exalted places among
the holy and the pure who shine as the brightness of the firmament."
Brightness. That is the word we want here. The brightness of her—
the memory that at least once in our lives there shone among us a
figure of model radiance.

Mina's colleagues across the country needed the same closure that
the City College ceremony had provided for her New York friends and
colleagues. The moment Ed Corbett learned of Mina's death, he asked
Janet Emig to write a eulogy for *College Composition and Communication.* Emig's work had influenced Mina's research and writing, and in
addition, they had become good friends. The quality and cogency of
her tribute is even more remarkable when one realizes that she had only
a few days to prepare it in order to make the deadline for the February
1979 issue. She described her friend with subtle precision, enabling
English teachers across the country to know and understand the essence of Mina's most extraordinary life:

> Like many of you, I first met Mina Shaughnessy at a CCCC con-
> vention—in 1972, at New Orleans. I had missed her splendid key-
> note address because of a late plane, but I did attend the afternoon
> session she chaired. Almost immediately, we both realized that we
> had begun an important friendship; and subsequently, we came to
> attend certain NCTE and CCCC conventions together. Like many
> of you, we ate our Thanksgiving dinners in some exotic, non-sea-
> sonal places—once, an oyster bar in the French Quarter. Then, like
> many of you, I learned of her death from cancer, at yet another con-
> vention, our most recent. Marilyn Maiz, her wholly devoted secre-
> tary and friend, had tried to reach me; but I had already left for Kansas
> City. Ed Corbett, a survivor, informed the Commission on Com-

position the Tuesday morning before the convention. The circle closes.

The mailing address is Spearfish, South Dakota. From Mount Rushmore, take the left fork, Alternate 14, past Lead, that astonishing perpendicular mining town, back toward the main highway, where 90 turns into 14 and 85. The Pendo ranch extends up those mountains and down that valley, one of the most contained and limpid in the entire West. Mina Pendo Shaughnessy lies buried there, next to her mother's grave.

In every way Mina is home. She had hoped to live there again: on napkins in Manhattan restaurants she would sketch for me the cabin she planned to build, halfway up a mountain, on land her family had given her, a cabin with windows and a front porch looking out over her cherished Black Hills.

Mina could not be understood without understanding that she came from the West. At the December 8th memorial service for Mina at City College, speaker after speaker spoke of Mina coming from the West; yet it was obvious that, for some of them, the West was a romantic blur. But the West, like the East of course, is highly specific. Mina's West was—a lush corner in a beige prairie state, near the moon surface of the Badlands; a corner in which a herd of 200 bison can still amble or rumble across the vision; where wild ponies block a car.

There were those eyes—in my experience only certain sailors and Westerners have those eyes, with a purity of vision, coolly undeceived, and a fatality that comes from looking out over indifferent expanses—of sea or mountains or prairie grass. Then, related, the clarity about what was central, bedrock, and what was peripheral, surface green; and an ability I think regional, never to reverse the two.

From Lead, Mina went East. Initially, East meant to her Chicago, as it often does for those in the Dakotas and Nebraska, although later, it came to mean, far more powerfully, New York itself. Specifically, she left to attend Northwestern. I can remember how she described disembarking from the train in Chicago, dressed, she claimed, like Greta Garbo. She helped earn her way through college by doing readings in the local Lutheran churches, selections she had arranged from *I Remember Mama. . . .*

Whenever I see Vanessa Redgrave, who so resembles Mina physically, as say, Guinevere or Julia, I always think Mina would have made a splendid actress. Indeed, she was a splendid actress in the forum, the theater of academe, that she chose over the absolute certain uncertainty of the actual theater, for which she knew she was temperamentally unprepared.

Eventually, she went instead to graduate school at Columbia, where her passion was Milton. Just two weeks ago, Paul Cubeta, the director of Bread Loaf, described a meeting with Mina last October in which she was attracted to teaching at Bread Loaf not only because she could teach a course in writing but also because she could teach a course in Milton as well.

For Mina came to her interest in writing the way most of our generation, especially women, came to it—through a back door. She stayed, as many of us did, for visceral, as well as ever-deepening intellectual, reasons. She once described this scene at City College. It was at the end of the sixties, and one of the first groups of SEEK students was taking the placement exam, the very exam Mina analyzed into clarity and importance in *Errors and Expectations.* It had been raining, and the hair on the bent heads caught the ceiling lights so that all seemed to Mina nimbused, angelic. . . .

Mina lived long enough to watch at CUNY, her university, what many of us are watching at our own—the quite systematic dismantlement of what she had so laboriously built, to which she may have quite literally given her life. She was even asked to participate in the demise and destruction; for the Savage Seventies are nothing if not thorough in trying to divest us of our most hard-won beliefs and actions.

There is, I believe, only one adequate and appropriate memorial to Mina: that we enact her courage; that we fight the current retreat—no, rout—into the elitist irresponsibility of earlier decades, where once again we agree to teach only those who can learn without our active and imaginative efforts; back to those mean responses to "What is knowledge" and "Who shall have access to that knowledge?" Mina truly believed without sentiment, in the republic as the shining city on the hill. And she would undoubtedly agree with many of us that unless, as a community, we reverse ourselves and the direction that our schools, colleges, and universities are currently taking, this country is truly no longer morally habitable. (37–38)

In April 1979, the staff of the Instructional Resource Center published the spring issue of the newsletter, *Resource,* the first one to appear after Mina's death. The staff explained what her death meant to the center and to them:

A Grand Experiment

This issue of our newsletter is the first we have published since the death of the Instructional Resource Center's founder and first director, Dean Mina Shaughnessy. Whatever materials may be stored in the Center's bookcases and files, we are all aware that the single greatest resource the Center offered to the University was Mina Shaughnessy herself. The word "resource" here needs to be redefined and enlarged, as would most terms when applied to Mina. She was, first of all, the best possible resource in the academic sense: widely read in many subjects, gifted as a teacher and writer, consulted and admired by leading figures in her field. Because her work was in what she often called the frontier of a profession, she was also a guide for people in a new territory, showing them its topography, convincing newcomers that they could live and work fruitfully there. She became a moral resource for basic skills teachers because she made them feel the worth of difficult and often unrewarded work. At the same time, she showed them how to enter imaginatively into the thinking processes of students whose skills, and often whose lives, seemed of such a different order from those of their teachers. Mina's book, *Errors and Expectations,* is cherished by teachers because it is both academically rigorous and morally exhilarating.

The Resource Center itself is the product of two of Mina's convictions. She believed basic skills learning is an area in which research must be encouraged and information must be made available to more teachers. She also believed that CUNY faculty have made significant progress in discovering ways of teaching underprepared students and she wanted such discoveries to be shared within CUNY as well as with teachers in other urban areas. The Center was the result of Mina's respect for the CUNY faculty engaged in skills instruction; she was determined that work of such importance being done in the University should get the recognition and support it deserved.

A friend of Samuel Johnson expressed his sense of loss at Jonhson's death by saying "Johnson is dead. Let us go to the next best: there is nobody; no man can be said to put you in mind of Johnson." We at the Center feel a similar sense of bereavement, undiminished as time passes. No one puts us in mind of Mina Shaughnessy. Her writing and the example of her life remain, however, to keep in our minds the pursuits she valued and the standards she upheld.

The Staff of the Instructional Resource Center
Robert Lyons, Director
Barry Kwalick
Marilyn Maiz
Virginia Slaughter (1–2)

In May 1979, less than six months after Mina's death, Bob Lyons delivered an address at the Conference of the CUNY Association of Writing Supervisors (CAWS), the organization that Mina had helped to found. The theme of the conference was "Errors and Expectations: Writing and Related Disciplines," in honor of her contributions to basic skills instruction. In his address, entitled "Mina Shaughnessy and the Teaching of Writing," Lyons presented a cogent and eloquent description of the work she had done, and the work that still remained to be done. It was in this speech that he recalled her enthusiasm for conferences, remembering how "she never stopped poring over conference programs with an expression that belonged to someone reading the racing form at Aqueduct." And he also noted that the CAWS conferences had always satisfied her: "I am sure," he observed, "that Mina's own choice of a privileged occasion would be a day like this one when concerned teachers gather to talk, to argue, to encourage one another, and to learn from one another" (2). Bob Lyons closed his address by predicting, ever so accurately, "Today at this conference, and for a long time to come, what Mina Shaughnessy has written will continue to give us a great deal to say to one another" (18).

At the Modern Language Association Conference, held in December 1979, E. D. Hirsch addressed a session that had been scheduled especially to honor Mina. It was during this address that he described her "unforgettable talk" at the 1975 MLA Conference, when she delivered her address entitled "Diving In." He praised her moral force and authority, quoting Irving Howe's eulogy, which described her "authority" as "without bluster, or prophecy, or ego, or system." Hirsch remembered Mina's "human influence," noting that it "radiated out beyond the sphere of ideas to inspire people and bring out their best instincts and efforts." He observed that she alone "seemed to give us a sense of community amid our conflicting ideologies" (4).

Hirsch remembers that there was an enormous sense of sorrow in the room on that day, and an enormous sense of loss. "We all knew that Mina was irreplaceable," he recalls, "and it frightened us. We knew it would never be the same without her."

In the early 1980s, when John Brereton decided to edit a volume of essays, entitled *Traditions of Inquiry,* about teachers who had had an enormous impact on their students and their fields of discipline, he asked Bob Lyons to contribute an essay about Mina. By 1985, when the volume was published, some teachers and researchers had begun to question Mina's attention "to the matter of error," isolating this issue from the many others that she had so carefully considered as she tried to transform public education to include all citizens. Lyons provided the historical and political framework necessary to better understand what was beginning to seem to some a "conservative pedagogy." In addition, he explained what Mina and so many other basic writing instructors were accomplishing when they intervened "to reduce the incidence of error":

> The surmounting of error stands as one part of Shaughnessy's larger concern with basic writing students' need to gain control of a language that would enable them to participate more fully in a wider society. She would not contest "the students' right to their own language" (the theme of a resolution adopted by CCCC in 1974), but she would insist that more than one language was necessary, and the second language should be the public discourse that the schools should assist us all to master. (184)

The tributes to Mina continued, but they began to take on a more professional tone: colloquiums and conferences held to discuss her work, awards presented in her name for outstanding articles and books, grants for individuals to conduct research. Don McQuade dedicated *The Territory of Language,* a collection of essays about college composition (most of which were written by her colleagues and friends), to Mina. Benjamin DeMott dedicated *Close Imagining,* a college-level anthology to her as well. In addition, in his foreword to a book about language, he referred to Mina as "the subtlest (because most loving) writing teacher of her time" (xiii). Her impact on teachers of composition and of basic writing in particular was permanent and profound: Patricia Bizzell described the change in attitude that Mina's work had on her:

> Shaughnessy's definition of a category called "basic writing" or "basic writers" came to me as a dramatic revelation. I had felt that my students had some kind of serious problem, expressed by the "remedial" or "developmental" name and approach attached to the course I was teaching. But at the same time I had felt that they did not deserve to bear the entire onus of this problem themselves. Now, under the model of basic writing, I could see them as beginners, newcomers to a complex discursive world with whose ways of us-

ing language they were relatively unfamiliar. Using this model, I could shape the masses of errors in their writing into patterns that made sense in terms of the newcomers' attempts to approximate what they thought academic writing was. . . . Shaughnessy's analysis seemed to diagnose exactly what I needed by way of pedagogy: some method of demystifying academic writing, laying bare its habitual patterns and mindsets so that students could imitate them more easily. (7)

Errors and Expectations continued to sell so well that for several years Donald Shaughnessy was able to use the royalties to fund a scholarship for female residents from South Dakota to attend the summer Bread Loaf conference in Vermont. (In fact, in the early eighties, he met one of the recipients of the scholarship, and they were married in 1986.)

Marilyn Maiz's devotion to Mina did not end after Mina's death. She answered the scores and scores of letters that continued to arrive, kept Mina's father and brother informed of the many testimonies and tributes that continued to be made in her honor, and continued to oversee the production of the *Journal of Basic Writing.*

Soon after Mina's death, Donald Shaughnessy asked Marilyn to help him dispose of Mina's personal belongings. One of the most painful tasks Marilyn ever had to perform was to deliver Mina's fur coat to the Memorial Sloan-Kettering Thrift Shop; proceeds from the sale of the coat would be used to help cancer patients.

Marilyn kept a few of Mina's possessions. One was a plaque that one of her first classes at City College had given to her, with the inscription: "To Mrs. M. Shaughnessy / As a token of our appreciation for your unselfish and dedicated service, Class of Spring 1968." Another was the photograph that Mina always kept on her desk, first at her office at City College, and then in her office at the Instructional Resource Center. It is a view of the South Dakota hills from the ranch house. Marilyn has preserved a mental image of Mina as well:

Unfortunately, many people remember Mina only when she was ill, or we've formed this romanticized version of the wide-eyed girl from the Midwest, on some sort of crusade or mission. When I think of her, I remember in particular, as if it just happened, one occasion that portrays the Mina whom I knew so well.

During the mid-seventies, when we were still in the 42nd Street offices, shortly before we moved to 80th Street, I would occasionally drive my car, a convertible, into the city, rather than take the subway. On these occasions, I would give Mina a ride home. I remember one particular Friday afternoon. It was a hot and humid summer day; cars were barely moving in the rush-hour traffic; half of the street was closed due to construction. Cabs and trucks were honking, and cars were coming perilously close to each other as they tried to merge. But none of this bothered Mina very much at all. As we approached Central Park, we were suddenly surprised by the magnificent view of trees and the wide expanse of lawn, and the Manhattan skyline loomed before us. She just looked at the view with a sense of wonder and happiness on her face—the hot afternoon sun shining on her magnificent hair and skin and eyes—and she declared, "I really love this city." That is the way I will always remember Mina.

But those who did not know Mina Shaughnessy will best remember her by the permanent legacy of her work and her accomplishments. "We would do well," Adrienne Rich noted in the conclusion of her tribute to Mina,

> to ponder her words—as writers, as teachers, as students, and as lovers both of language and justice. Her work illuminates the links between literacy and illiteracy, between student and teacher, writer and reader, grammar and literature, between the failures of our society and its vision. She is one of our major educational theorists, whose quality I believe will be recognized more and more as time goes on. I would place her among the greatest of those who have understood that intelligence is not determined by privilege.

Appendix A

Open Admissions and the Disadvantaged Teacher

Partisans of Open Admissions find it difficult to know these days whether they are in a rear- or a vanguard action. Viewed from the widest perspective, Open Admissions seems inevitable—part of a much vaster shift within and even beyond this society from a rural to an urban population, from an industrial to a service-oriented labor force, from a culture of conformity to one of diversity.

But viewed from a narrower perspective, the perspective of shrinking budgets and growing pessimism about the importance or effectiveness of schools in righting even the educational wrongs of the society, let alone the larger inequities they reflect, Open Admissions seems doomed.

For anyone who has witnessed the success of many young men and women who were taught to fail, has watched them lay claim to their talents, meet their commitments and set out with a plan in their minds, the widespread pessimism about whether Open Admissions can "work," as they put it, is baffling. Especially baffling is the fact that this pessimism was deep-rooted even before any of the new students had stepped on our campuses. By now, there is a literature of pessimism, a theology—more precisely, a social science—of despair that serves the purposes of those who have already rejected the social policy implicit in Open Admissions.

"Open Admissions and the Disadvantaged Teacher" was originally delivered as an address at the Conference on College Composition and Communication in 1973 in New Orleans. It was published in College Composition and Communication *in December 1973.*

Unfortunately, the debate about Open Admissions has been and is being carried on in the language of those who oppose it: the alphabet of numbers, the syntax of print-outs, the transformations of graphs and tables, the language, in particular, of a prestigious group of social scientists who perceive through their language truths that even they seem, at times, unwilling to hear, much as scientists of another kind in another era were led inexorably by the dictates of their language to an atomic arsenal. They are saying, in their language, that schools, when measured by the indicators they have selected, affect only marginally the quality of people's lives, and further, that programs designed to help the poor overcome their disadvantages do not succeed. These messages are proliferated through the media and made available to the policy makers, who dip into the reservoir for the numbers they need.

Meanwhile, the two groups who have experienced directly the importance of schools and compensatory education—the students and the teachers—grope for their answers, grapple with words and methodologies they don't understand, experiencing as they do all the frustrations and embarrassments of the person who must say something important in a strange language.

Let me comment upon the disadvantage an Open Admissions writing teacher feels in the face of this arsenal.

There is the feeling of disadvantage itself, the contamination from being perceived in some way inferior. Thus, too often, writing teachers, sensing that their students' growth as writers cannot be quantified, certainly not in semester segments, perhaps not at all, speak timidly of what is accomplished, or bow to the crude measures of attrition rates, grade-point averages, or objective tests. Unable to describe in the language of the scientists what went on, they often abandon the effort to do so in any language, even the one they have loved enough to study and teach. Or worse, they become easy converts to the new language, vesting it with more authority than the social scientists themselves would claim for it.

What teacher has not felt in those stark lists of behavioral objectives with their insistent parallels—the student will do this, the student will do that—a terrible flattening out of the language and the student in the service of numbers? In how many countless and unconscious ways do we capitulate to the demand for numbers? In how many ways has the mathematical tyranny of the "average" coerced us into moving faster through our lessons than we should in order to "cover the ground," "meet the standard," or play the losing game of "catching up"? In how many ways has the need for numbers driven us to violate the language itself, ripping it from the web of discourse in order to count those things that can be caught in the net of numbers? How many young men and women have turned from the wellsprings of their own experiences and ideas to fill in the blanks of our more modest expectations? All in the name of accountability!

But accountability to whom? Not to our students, who come to us so burdened with numbers—IQ's, SAT's, MAT's, etc.—that we can barely see them as individuals. Not to ourselves, who must teach for quick pay-offs that can be translated into numbers so that the ranking and winnowing of human talent can go on apace. Is this our task, then, to prepare productivity studies for management under the direction of social scientists who are evaluating what they have not studied nor understood? We cannot teach under such constraints; our students cannot learn.

Let me illustrate the insensitivity of numbers with the experience of one student. I'll call her Cora. She came to our college at a time when our writing placement test called for an essay on a person of public significance. (The list of suggestions included the names of some forty men—no women—from many walks and styles of life. Even Pogo was there.) Cora chose to write on George Washington, and this is what she said:

> George Washington has contributed much; in making of American History. A general in the army during the American Revolution. He commened many victories; that lead the thirteen colonies to an independent United States. Later became the First President of the United States. His picture is shown on the one dollar Bill and twenty-five cent picence (quart). Parks, Streets, Cities, People and plases are named after this great leader. Mr. Washington was an outdoorsman in the very sence of the word. He loved horse back riding and hunting. It has been said, "he cut down a cherry tree." Making his home in Virginia with his wife Martha.

Three years later, in another testing situation, she wrote this passage:

> Many Americans believe that Puerto Rico is fortunate to be exempted from paying taxes. What most Americans do not know is

that the tax exemption is not for Puerto Ricans but for the American investers. The Industrial Incentives Act of 1947, continued even after the commonwealth came into being. It authorized and incouraged private firms (American) to invest in Puerto Rico. This Act was enacted to supply jobs and hopefully raise the Island's economy. At first the idea was good; however, as time passed the Puerto Ricans received the short end of the stick.

Between those two passages lies a story, not a sum. To be sure, the reduction of her error count is impressive, but chances are an evaluator would not have taken the measure of her writing improvement, even on this surface level, from her writing but from an objective test, which she would probably have failed because of her allergy to blanks. At the end of four years, her grade-point average was not impressive because her first two years carried the record of her struggle to survive in academia. And finally, because she decided after four years of running between part-time jobs and classrooms, to get a full-time job and finish up her remaining requirements at night, she is probably entered now as an attrition number in the short memory of some computer. But where in the electronic labyrinth of that machine can I enter this bit: that one day, during her fourth year in college, Cora came into my office, sat down by my desk, and said, "You know something . . . I'm smart."

If, as I suggest, Open Admissions has reached out beyond traditional sources for its students, bringing into our campuses young men and women whose perceptions of themselves, whose needs and interests and styles of learning differ from those of the students we built our colleges around, and if the social scientists, ignoring these differences, continue to evaluate the performance of the new students with across-the-board statistics based on old criteria, then it falls upon us to formulate the new criteria ourselves. We must begin to keep our own books, recording in systematic ways our observations of our students' growth over significant developmental periods. We must organize our energies around important questions that bear upon the ways we teach, questions about the nature of error and its relationship to linguistic growth, about the schedules of institutions versus the imperatives of learning, about the costs and complexities of code shifting within the academy, about the very nature of the act of writing, with its power to intimidate or free.

As English teachers, we have fallen into prescriptive habits over the years that inhibit us as observers. My record of Cora's development as a student, for example, is sketchy—a list of her grades in English, a few class papers, some placement scores. Little more. No one who had her as a student kept a teaching log or thought to note the stations of her progress. Prescriptive and product-minded, we ignored the data that were generated by her development as a writer. Looking back, I recall that she went through many crises that are now blurred in my memory, as are the conferences we had where I was more the learner than she. We have been trained to notice what students learn, not how they learn it, to observe what they do to writing, not what writing does to them.

But until we can describe more precisely than we have the process whereby our students move toward maturity as readers and writers, we cannot challenge those critics who claim that the students do not move at all. The boundaries of our accountability thus lie far beyond the behavioral objectives we are now tacking onto old textbooks. They commit us to close systematic observations over extended periods, to a pooling of our research energies and resources, and finally, to a search within the social sciences themselves for techniques of observation and evaluation and for researchers who will help us see what our students are learning. For wherever numbers can become a measure that informs qualitative judgment without dominating it, we should welcome numbers. And wherever analytical modes such as the case history offer us an alternative to statistical averages or norms, we should welcome research. For we still know too little about the young men and women who are turning our colleges around.

When the first year of Open Admissions was over at City College, I wrote a short report in which I concluded that the presence of the new students challenged the entire college, much as, in Pascal's law, "pressure applied to a confined fluid at any point is transmitted through the fluid in all directions undiminished." Now, at the end of our third year of Open Admissions, we see the results of that pressure in the imaginative work of many of our teachers and administrators in the City University, in the new programs that are taking root in our colleges, despite our financial woes, in the beginning explorations, through research and study, of new territories that now appear related to the teaching of English, and, most important of all, in the questions we are trying to formulate about traditional conceptions of knowledge.

Open Admissions began as a remedial wing to a few departments on traditional college campuses, but it is now transforming the colleges themselves, exposing far more than the deficiencies of the new students. By probing into the nature of those deficiencies and resisting those who have tried to isolate the phenomenon of disadvantage from the society that caused it, Open Admissions is forcing the real question—not how many people society is willing to salvage, but how much this society is willing to pay to salvage itself.

The answer to that question is not yet in. Until it is, the issue of accountability is wide open.

Appendix B

Diving In: An Introduction to Basic Writing

Basic writing, alias remedial, developmental, pre-baccalaureate, or even handicapped English, is commonly thought of as a writing course for young men and women who have many things wrong with them. Not only do medical metaphors dominate the pedagogy (*remedial, clinic, lab, diagnosis,* and so on), but teachers and administrators tend to discuss basic-writing students much as doctors tend to discuss their patients, without being tinged by mortality themselves and with certainly no expectations that questions will be raised about the state of *their* health.

Yet such is the nature of instruction in writing that teachers and students cannot easily escape one another's maladies. Unlike other courses, where exchanges between teacher and student can be reduced to as little as one or two objective tests a semester, the writing course requires students to write things down regularly, usually once a week, and requires teachers to read what is written and then write things back and every so often even talk directly with individual students about the way they write.

This system of exchange between teacher and student has so far yielded much more information about what is wrong with students than about what is wrong with teachers, reinforcing the notion that students, not teachers, are the people in education who must do the changing. The phrase "catching up," so often used to describe the progress of BW students, is illuminating here, suggesting as it does that the only person

---

"Diving In" was originally delivered as an address at the Modern Language Association Convention in 1975 in San Francisco. It was published in College Composition and Communication *in October 1976.*

who must move in the teaching situation is the students. As a result of this view, we are much more likely in talking about teaching to talk about students, to theorize about *their* needs and attitudes or to chart *their* development and ignore the possibility that teachers also change in response to students, that there may in fact be important connections between the changes teachers undergo and the progress of their students.

I would like, at any rate, to suggest that this is so, and since it is common these days to "place" students on developmental scales, saying they are eighth-graders or fifth-graders when they read and even younger when they write or that they are stalled some place on Piaget's scale without formal propositions, I would further like to propose a developmental scale for teachers, admittedly an impressionistic one, but one that fits the observations I have made over the years as I have watched traditionally prepared English teachers, including myself, learning to teach in the Open-Admissions classroom.

My scale has four stages, each of which I will name with a familiar metaphor intended to suggest what lies at the center of the teacher's emotional energy during that stage. Thus I have chosen to name the first stage of my developmental scale GUARDING THE TOWER, because during this stage the teacher is in one way or another concentrating on protecting the academy (including himself) from the outsiders, those who do not seem to belong in the community of learners. The grounds for exclusion are various. The mores of the times inhibit anyone's openly ascribing the exclusion to genetic inferiority, but a few teachers doubtless still hold this view.

More often, however, the teacher comes to the basic-writing class with every intention of preparing his students to write for college courses, only to discover, with the first batch of essays, that the students are so alarmingly and incredibly behind any students he has taught before that the idea of their ever learning to write acceptably for college, let alone learning to do so in one or two semesters, seems utterly pretentious. Whatever the sources of their incompetence—whether rooted in the limits they were born with or those that were imposed upon them by the world they grew up in—the fact seems stunningly, depressingly obvious: they will never "make it" in college unless someone radically lowers the standards.

The first pedagogical question the teacher asks at this stage is therefore not "How do I teach these students?" but "What are the consequences of flunking the entire class?" It is a question that threatens to turn the class into a contest, a peculiar and demoralizing contest for both student and teacher, since neither expects to win. The student, already conditioned to the idea that there is something wrong with his English and that writing is a device for magnifying and exposing this deficiency, risks as little as possible on the page, often straining with what he does write to approximate the academic style and producing in the process what might better be called "written Anguish" rather than English—sentences whose subjects are crowded out by such phrases as "it is my conviction that" or "on the contrary to my opinion," inflections that belong to no variety of English, standard or non-standard, but grow out of the writer's attempt to be correct, or words whose idiosyncratic spellings reveal not simply an increase in the number of conventional misspellings but new orders of difficulty with the correspondences between spoken and written English. Meanwhile, the teacher assumes that he must not only hold out for the same product he held out for in the past but teach unflinchingly in the same way as before, as if any pedagogical adjustment to the needs of students were a kind of cheating. Obliged because of the exigencies brought on by Open Admissions to serve his time in the defense of the academy, he does if not his best, at least his duty, setting forth the material to be mastered, as if he expected students to learn it, but feeling grateful when a national holiday happens to fall on a basic-writing day and looking always for ways of evading conscription next semester.

But gradually, student and teacher are drawn into closer range. They are obliged, like emissaries from opposing camps, to send messages back and forth. They meet to consider each other's words and separate to study them in private. Slowly, the teacher's preconceptions of his students begin to give way here and there. It now appears that, in some instances at least, their writing, with its rudimentary errors and labored style has belied their intelligence and individuality. Examined at closer range, the class now appears to have at least some members in it who might, with hard work, eventually "catch up." And it is the intent of reaching these new students that moves the teacher into the second stage of development—which I will name CONVERTING THE NATIVES.

As the image suggests, the teacher has now admitted at least some to the community of the educable. These learners are perceived, however, as empty vessels, ready to be filled with new knowledge. Learning is thought of not so much as a constant and often troubling reformulation of the world so as to encompass new knowledge but as a steady flow of truth into a void. Whether the truth is delivered in lectures or modules, cassettes or computers, circles or squares, the teacher's purpose is the same: to carry the technology of advanced literacy to the inhabitants of an underdeveloped country. And so confident is he of the reasonableness and allure of what he is presenting, it does not occur to him to consider the competing logics and values and habits that may be influencing his students, often in ways that they themselves are unaware of.

Sensing no need to relate what he is teaching to what his students know, to stop to explore the contexts within which the conventions of academic discourse have developed, and to view these conventions in patterns large enough to encompass what students do know about language already, the teacher becomes a mechanic of the sentence, the paragraph, and the essay. Drawing usually upon the rules and formulas that were part of his training in composition, he conscientiously presents to his students flawless schemes for achieving order and grammaticality and anatomizes model passages of English prose to uncover, beneath brilliant, unique surfaces, the skeletons of ordinary paragraphs.

Yet too often the schemes, however well meant, do not seem to work. Like other simplistic prescriptions, they illuminate for the moment and then disappear in the melee of real situations, where paradigms frequently break down and thoughts will not be regimented. S's keep reappearing or disappearing in the wrong places; regular verbs shed their inflections and irregular verbs acquire them; tenses collide; sentences derail; and whole essays idle at one level of generalization.

Baffled, the teacher asks, "How is it that these young men and women whom I have personally admitted to the community of learners cannot learn these simple things?" Until one day, it occurs to him that perhaps these simple things—so transparent and compelling to him—are not in fact simple at all, that they only appear simple to those who already know them, that the grammar and rhetoric of formal written English have been shaped by the irrationalities of history and habit and by the peculiar restrictions and rituals that come from putting words on paper instead of into the air, that the sense and nonsense of written English must often collide with the spoken English that has been serving students in their negotiations with the world for many years. The insight leads our teacher to the third stage of his development, which I will name SOUNDING THE DEPTHS, for he turns now to the careful observation not only of his students and their writing but of himself as writer and teacher, seeking a deeper understanding of the behavior called writing and of the special difficulties his students have in mastering the skill. Let us imagine, for the sake of instruction, that the teacher now begins to look more carefully at two common problems among basic writers—the problem of grammatical errors and the problem of undeveloped paragraphs.

Should he begin in his exploration of error not only to count and name errors but to search for patterns and pose hypotheses that might explain them, he will begin to see that while his lessons in the past may have been "simple," the sources of the error he was trying to correct were often complex. The insight leads not inevitably or finally to a rejection of all rules and standards, but to a more careful look at error, to the formulation of what might be called a "logic" of errors that serves to mark a pedagogical path for teacher and student to follow.

Let us consider in this connection the "simple" *s* inflection of the verb, the source of a variety of grammatical errors in BW papers. It is, at first, an alien form to many students whose mother tongues inflect the verb differently or not at all. Uniformly called for, however, in all verbs and in the third person singular present indicative of standard English, it would seem to be a highly predictable or stable form and therefore one easily remembered. But note the grammatical concepts the student must grasp before he can apply the rule: the concepts of person, tense, number, and mood. Note that the *s* inflection is an atypical inflection within the modern English verb system. Note too how often it must seem to the student that he hears the stem form of the verb after third person singular subjects in what sounds like the present, as he does, for example whenever he hears questions like "Does *she want* to go?" or "Can the *subway stop*?" In such sentences, the standard language itself reinforces the student's own resistance to the inflection.

And then, beyond these apparent unpredictabilities within the standard system, there is the influence of the student's own language or dialect, which urges him to ignore a troublesome form that brings no commensurate increase in meaning. Indeed, the very *s* he struggles with here may shift in a moment to signify plurality simply by being attached to a noun instead of a verb. No wonder then that students of formal English throughout the world find this inflection difficult, not because they lack intelligence or care but because they think analogically and

are linguistically efficient. The issue is not the capacity of students finally to master this and the many other forms of written English that
go against the grain of their instincts and experience but the priority
this kind of problem ought to have in the larger scheme of learning to
write and the willingness of students to mobilize themselves to master
such forms at the initial stages of instruction.

Somewhere between the folly of pretending that errors don't matter
and the rigidity of insisting that they matter more than anything, the
teacher must find his answer, searching always under pressure for short
cuts that will not ultimately restrict the intellectual power of his students. But as yet, we lack models for the maturation of the writing skill
among young, native-born adults and can only theorize about the adapt-
ability of other models for these students. We cannot say with certainty
just what progress in writing ought to look like for basic-writing students, and more particularly how the elimination of error is related to
their over-all improvement.

Should the teacher then turn from the problems of error to his
students' difficulties with the paragraphs of academic essays, new complexities emerge. Why, he wonders, do they reach such instant closure
on their ideas, seldom moving into even one subordinate level of quali-
fication but either moving on to a new topic sentence or drifting off
into reverie and anecdote until the point of the essay has been dissolved?
Where is that attitude of "suspended conclusion" that Dewey called
thinking, and what can one infer about their intellectual competence
from such behavior?

Before consigning his students to some earlier stage of mental development, the teacher at this stage begins to look more closely at the
task he is asking students to perform. Are they aware, for example, after years of right/wrong testing, after the ACT's and the GED's and
the OAT's, after straining to memorize what they read but never learning
to doubt it, after "psyching out" answers rather than discovering them,
are they aware that the rules have changed and that the rewards now
go to those who can sustain a play of mind upon ideas—teasing out
the contradictions and ambiguities and frailties of statements?

Or again, are the students sensitive to the ways in which the conventions of talk differ from those of academic discourse? Committed
to extending the boundaries of what is known, the scholar proposes
generalizations that cover the greatest possible number of instances and

then sets about supporting his case according to the rules of evidence and sound reasoning that govern his subject. The spoken language, looping back and forth between speakers, offering chances for groping and backing up and even hiding, leaving room for the language of hands and faces, of pitch and pauses, is by comparison generous and inviting. The speaker is not responsible for the advancement of formal learning. He is free to assert opinions without a display of evidence or recount experiences without explaining what they "mean." His movements from one level of generality to another are more often brought on by shifts in the winds of conversation rather than by some decision of his to be more specific or to sum things up. For him the injunction to "be more specific" is difficult to carry out because the conditions that lead to specificity are usually missing. He may not have acquired the habit of questioning his propositions, as a listener might, in order to locate the points that require amplification or evidence. Or he may be marooned with a proposition he cannot defend for lack of information or for want of practice in retrieving the history of an idea as it developed in his own mind.

Similarly, the query "What is your point?" may be difficult to answer because the conditions under which the student is writing have not allowed for the slow generation of an orienting conviction, that underlying sense of the direction he wants his thinking to take. Yet without this conviction, he cannot judge the relevance of what comes to his mind, as one sentence branches out into another or one idea engenders another, gradually crowding from his memory the direction he initially set out for himself.

Or finally, the writer may lack the vocabulary that would enable him to move more easily up the ladder of abstraction and must instead forge out of a nonanalytical vocabulary a way of discussing thoughts about thoughts, a task so formidable as to discourage him, as travelers in a foreign land are discouraged, from venturing far beyond bread-and-butter matters.

From such soundings, our teacher begins to see that teaching at the remedial level is not a matter of being simpler but of being more profound, of not only starting from "scratch" but also determining where "scratch" is. The experience of studenthood is the experience of being just so far over one's head that it is both realistic and essential to work at surviving. But by underestimating the sophistication of our students and by ignoring the complexity of the tasks we set before them, we have failed to locate in precise ways where to begin and what follows what.

But I have created a fourth stage of my developmental scheme, which I am calling DIVING IN in order to suggest that the teacher who has come this far must now make a decision that demands professional courage—the decision to remediate himself, to become a student of new disciplines and of his students themselves in order to perceive both their difficulties and their incipient excellence. "Always assume," wrote Leo Strauss, to the teacher, "that there is one silent student in your class who is by far superior to you in head and in heart." This assumption, as I have been trying to suggest, does not come easily or naturally when the teacher is a college teacher and the young men and women in his class are labeled remedial. But as we come to know these students better, we begin to see that the greatest barrier to our work with them is our ignorance of them and of the very subject we have contracted to teach. We see that we must grope our ways into the turbulent disciplines of semantics and linguistics for fuller, more accurate data about words and sentences; we must pursue more rigorously the design of developmental models, basing our schemes less upon loose comparisons with children and more upon case studies and developmental research of the sort that produced William Perry's impressive study of the intellectual development of Harvard students; we need finally to examine more closely the nature of speaking and writing and divine the subtle ways in which these forms of language both support and undo each other.

The work is waiting for us. And so irrevocable now is the tide that brings the new students into the nation's college classrooms that it is no longer within our power, as perhaps it once was, to refuse to accept them into the community of the educable. They are here. DIVING IN is simply deciding that teaching them to write well is not only suitable but challenging work for those who would be teachers and scholars in a democracy.

APPENDIX C
The Miserable Truth

Conferences, I know, are times for saying encouraging things, for sharing successes with one another, and regaining a sense of being engaged with others in important work. But to begin this conference on a note of encouragement seems highly inappropriate today—something like trying to give a pep talk on the *Titanic*.

These are discouraging times for all of us, most particularly for the teachers who have been working with unprepared students on basic skills. Both students and teachers are already discovering that they are expendable, and the programs they have helped to build over the past five years to remedy the failure of the public schools (and the society of which those schools are an extension) now begin to shake and fracture under the blows of retrenchment.

We experience the crisis most directly on our individual campuses:

- ❖ Our staffs are shrinking and our class size increasing.
- ❖ Talented young teachers who were ready to concentrate their scholarly energies on the sort of research and teaching we need in basic writing are looking for jobs.
- ❖ Each day brings not a new decision but rumors of new decisions, placing us in the predicament of those mice in psychological experiments who must keep shifting their expectations until they are too rattled to function.

"The Miserable Truth" was originally delivered as an address at the Conference of the CUNY Association of Writing Supervisors in New York on April 26, 1976. It was published in The Congressional Record *on September 9, 1976.*

❖ Our campuses buzz like an Elizabethan court with talk of who is in favor and who is out. And we meet our colleagues from other campuses with relief: "Ah, good," we say (or think to ourselves)—"you're still here."

❖ We struggle each day to extract from the Orwellian language that announces new plans and policies some clear sense of what finally is going to become of the students whom the university in more affluent times committed itself to educate.

If we turn from our individual campuses to the university itself—this vast free university, the only one of its kind—we see it being pressed to retrench and retrench, treated as if it has been distributing handouts over the past six years rather than entitlements, fragmented now rather than federated as each college struggles for its survival and sees in the demise of sister colleges some advantage for itself.

And underlying all this turmoil we sense a growing national indifference to the goals of open admissions. Ironically, as the national press spreads alarm about the state of literacy in the country, funds (federal, state, and city) for teaching the educationally neglected and betrayed are disappearing. Somewhere, it has been decided that the experiment hasn't worked, that our hopes were overblown, that we are faced, in the words of *Time* magazine, with "continued failures to improve dramatically the lot of the disadvantaged" through compensatory education.

After no more than one generation of open admissions students have been allowed time to lay claim to a college education, and in the face of their achievements during our first faltering years of Open Admissions, the decision has come out against them. Not, one suspects, because anyone has taken a close look at the experience itself but because the times have shifted and allowed the society to settle back into its comfortable notions about merit, notions which have produced a meritocratic scheme that perpetuates the various brands of race and class prejudice that have pervaded this society since its creation.

Surely there is little in such a scene to generate encouragement. Wherever we look we find reason to feel discouraged, angry, and paralyzed. Open Admissions at CUNY is being trimmed and tracked to death and we cannot begin to count the cost of its collapse. I can think of only one encouraging thought in the midst of this disaster. It is best expressed in an old Jewish saying: The truth never dies; it simply leads a miserable life.

I have said enough, for now, about the misery. But I have not touched upon the truth—the truth, that is, of what we have learned during open admissions about our students, about ourselves as teachers, and about the art and science and craft of writing. Let me mention some of the truths we have uncovered or discovered because they seem to me indestructible, despite retrenchments and shifts in the winds of social doctrines.

First, we have learned—and documented—that it is possible to get a high school diploma in New York City without reaching minimal competence in reading, writing, and arithmetic. Doubtless we suspected this before, but now we know the real taste of that failure. What open admissions writing teacher does not remember the shock of those first student essays, the stunning evidence of failure woven into the very syntax of sentences and the letters of words. For most of us it was a traumatic moment. We asked, What went wrong? What were they doing for twelve years? How can I possibly teach them to write now? Where do I begin? And behind those questions lay the troubling, forbidden thought—perhaps they are ineducable.

For the first time in the history of the city, we created, through open admissions, a massive feedback system which revealed an unconscionable failure to meet the educational needs of the poor and the dark-skinned. To be sure, the roots of that failure are tangled, and now that college teachers have begun to talk with and meet with high school teachers (largely as a result of open admissions) they are more sensitive to the many institutional conditions that have made teaching almost impossible in many of our schools.

But whatever the causes, Open Admissions documented the fact of failure. And until that happened, it was possible for thousands of students to drift quietly into the labor force of the city, taking up the jobs that others rejected, convinced somehow that something in *them* had caused the failure.

Second, we have learned that late adolescence is a creative and critical juncture in life and that, far from being eleventh-hour learners, our students come to us ready to begin their lives anew. And while the skills and priorities of studenthood are not easily acquired at the age of eighteen or over, students have demonstrated that they *can* acquire them at that age. In fact, much of the energy they mobilize for the effort seems to come from the opportunity college gives them to redefine themselves as young adults who might accomplish something in the world. To encourage this emerging view they have of themselves while at the same time representing honestly to them the amount of work that lies ahead has proved to be one of the teacher's most delicate and essential tasks.

Neither like children nor the retarded—with whom they have been compared—they are a distinctive group: young adults who are capable because of their maturity of observing the processes they are going through as learners, of taking conceptual short-cuts that are not available to children, of alerting us easily and swiftly to the effects of our instruction, of committing themselves to routine and work and constant, often discouraging evaluation, in order to change the quality of their adult lives.

We have not unfortunately had the time nor the expertise to study our students as learners nor to document our sense of them as a unique group, ripe for learning and capable of both steady growth and dramatic leaps into new levels of competence. But we have, in a sense, discovered them.

Third, we learned that we didn't know much about teaching writing when we started out, even though many of us had been teaching the subject before, in traditional ways and with traditional students. There were many reasons for our deficiencies, but one of the chief ones was that most of us had not been formally trained to teach writing—only to read and analyze the outstanding belletristic literature of the centuries. Teaching writing was a kind of fringe penalty for teaching literature, and since students coming into college had generally been prepared for college writing by their schools and by the culture they grew up in, we got by. There was little motivation to give much thought to those features of the skill that now seem so central to our understanding of our task. Let me mention at least a few of those features.

We had not thought much about the writing process itself: how accomplished writers behave when they write; what sorts of stages they go through; what coordinations and perceptions are required of them; and how the behavior of our students as writers differs from that of accomplished writers—are they, for example, in the habit of re-scanning their sentences, can they objectify their own pages, looking at them at one moment for semantic sense and at another for formal correctness?

We had not given much thought to the relationship between oral and written language, a relationship that once seemed so simple (merely a matter of the writer's tending to his colloquialisms) but that suggests increasingly profound differences not simply in the ways we choose words but in the very ways we think under two modes.

Faced as we have been with students who have had very restricted and largely unpleasant encounters with written English, we have *had* to pay more respect to these differences, to observe them more carefully, for one thing, and to find ways of making the transition from one medium to the other more conscious. We have also had to turn our attention to the academic uses of written language, to that "dialect" of analysis that confronts our students not only with many new words and phrases, but with more heavily qualified sentences than they are used to producing in speech and with unfamiliar strategies for making their points or winning their arguments.

We had not thought much, until Open Admissions, about the fact of linguistic diversity, with which most of us collided from almost our first day of open admissions teaching when we found our classrooms filled with native Americans who had grown up with the sounds and melodies of other languages or dialects in their ears and on their tongues—Cantonese, Afro-American, Spanish, Yiddish, Greek, Polish, diverse language groups who nonetheless shared the experience of having had their language differences ignored or treated as a disadvantage, of having had the fun and pride of language drained out of their school lives.

How we have argued, and puzzled, and struggled over the issue of mother-tongue interference, over whether to change, how to change, when to change those nonstandard features of a student's language that distract the general reader. We have arrived by now, I think, at a rough and pragmatic consensus. But looking back, the important point seems to me that we grappled with both the phenomenon of diversity and the phenomenon of linguistic convention and in doing so developed greater respect for our students' linguistic aptitudes and for the subtle, stubborn, yet mercurial quality of language itself.

Such insights have had, of course, to be incorporated into our teaching. And here we can claim, I think, a major advance. Open Admissions has taught us about learning, that is, about the importance of perceiving where students are in relation to what we want to teach them, about sequential and paced instruction, about being clear and realistic, about going below the surface of our subjects, not in order to become simpler but to become more profound, for it is at the level of principle as well as practice that young adults learn more efficiently.

This was an inevitable consequence of Open Admissions. Traditionally, colleges have been able to guarantee success by *selecting* their students ahead of time rather than by *teaching* them after they arrived. Thus it has been argued that in the days when City College screened out all except the most highly prepared graduates from academic high schools in one of the largest cities in the world, the chances of the students succeeding in college were tremendous, whoever taught them.

If we imagine a continuum of competence, with at one end the exceptionally competent and at the other the barely competent, we could say that colleges have traditionally felt it their responsibility to identify the students at the upper end of this scale and give them four more years of education. The open admissions college, on the other hand, makes a commitment to involve itself in the education of young men and women *all along* the continuum on the assumption, first, that people are not consigned to their places on that continuum forever but are capable of remarkable growth and development when given the opportunity; second, that the social benefits of advancing as many as possible along that continuum are inestimable; and third, that this broadening of the base of higher education, if properly planned and supported, can further the education of *all* students on the continuum.

But the decision to open a college to a more diverse population commits that college to becoming a *teaching* college, a college where everyone, not just the remedial teachers, accepts the responsibility of *teaching* rather than merely *presenting* a subject. Certainly this message about teaching has reached the skills teachers of CUNY. Working this year in the Instructional Resource Center, I have had a chance to do what few of you have perhaps had the time or occasion to do, that is, to take a close look at the work going on in skills instruction. We are all aware, of course, that many of our colleagues have gained national recognition in our field—have published articles, read papers at conferences, served on various professional organizations, produced textbooks. (It is no accident, I'm sure, that when five major publishers decided over the past year or so to produce new writing handbooks—

a major publishing decision—they chose CUNY English teachers to write them.)

What I had not been so aware of, however, was the number of teachers who, without fanfare or remissions and with heavy class loads, have been at work developing imaginative new materials for our students. Probably at no school in the country is there such an accumulation of wisdom and know-how in the field of compensatory education as there is within this university at this moment. I cannot imagine a group of teachers who have ever had more to say to one another. It is a special fraternity joined not only by our common purposes and problems as teachers but by our having come to know, through our students, what it means to be an outsider in academia. Whatever our individual political persuasions, we have been pedagogically radicalized by our experience. We reject in our bones the traditional meritocratic model of a college. We reject it not only on principle; we would simply be bored teaching in such a college.

Such changes, I would say, are indestructible, wherever we go from here. And indestructible, too, are the ideas that have awakened our students. It is puzzling how long people can go on—for generations—tolerating the inequalities that restrict and even shorten their lives. But once the possibility of change touches their imaginations, once a right has been extended to them and they have felt its power to open and enrich their lives, they cannot go back. They may have setbacks. But they cannot go back. CUNY extended a right, six years ago, that has been revoked, and we appear to be back where we started in 1970, only much poorer. But no one can revoke what has gone on in us and in our students.

So the lion got out of the cage before the gates were shut. And we had better keep learning how to teach writing because the brothers and sisters and cousins and children of our students will be back. If we can transcend for a moment the personal disappointments and uncertainties that surround us now, we can perhaps agree that that is a fairly strong truth for a miserable time. And it is a truth we helped to make.

APPENDIX D

Speaking and Doublespeaking about Standards

I keep in my file a small folder of student papers that go back ten years in my teaching career. They are the first papers I ever read by severely unprepared freshman writers, and I remember clearly the day I received them. The students who wrote the papers were then enrolled in the SEEK Program at City College, a program for poverty-area youth which preceded Open Admissions and served in many ways as the model for the skills programs that were to be developed under that policy.

I remember sitting alone in the worn urban classroom where my students had just written their first essays and where I now began to read them, hoping to be able to assess quickly the sort of task that lay ahead of us that semester. But the writing was so stunningly unskilled that I could not begin to define the task nor even sort out the difficulties. I could only sit there, reading and re-reading the alien papers, wondering what had gone wrong and trying to understand what I at this eleventh hour of my students' academic lives could do about it.

Looking at these papers now, I have no difficulty assessing the work to be done nor believing that it *can* be done. Since that critical afternoon, I have seen many such students go through the long corridor of credits that begins with basic writing, and I have read and corrected and conferred over thousands of such papers. But at the time there were

"Speaking and Doublespeaking about Standards" was delivered as an address at the California State University and Colleges Conference on Improvement of Student Writing Skills on June 3, 1976, in Los Angeles. Mina Shaughnessy often revised her speeches up until the time she delivered them, making notations by hand directly on the typed manuscript. I have incorporated those changes into the text that appears here.

no precedents to raise my expectations, only those disturbing essays with their tangles of errors and puzzling incompetencies.

We now know much more about those incompetencies—about their roots and their logics; we have argued and conferred over them now for some years. We know something now about the pedagogical strategies and timetables that are involved in overcoming them. But *then* there were simply "the outsiders" with their baffling academic difficulties, their unpredictable gaps in preparation, their separate worlds which alternately frightened and fascinated their teachers, and their deep skepticism about ever learning anything important in school. How were such students to be brought into the academic fold? Could they be? Should they be? And what should we do with them until they were ready?

The word "standard" soon became one of these insidious labels that instantly *polarize* attitudes without *clarifying* issues. The Standard became everyone's private image of the good old days of college when by some unexamined principle of selection almost all the bright, lucky faces on campus were white and the cultural ties between students and teachers were strong enough to make their disagreements seem, in retrospect, like family squabbles. Those who supported open admissions or spoke optimistically about the prospects of the new students appeared, by this definition, to be *opposed* to maintaining standards. Those who resisted the policy and stressed the deficiencies of the students were seen to be defending standards.

Meanwhile the skills teachers, who were soon to be grouped among the enemies of standards because of their growing sensitivity to the rights and capabilities of the new students, were ironically enough coming to grips with the real issue, the central dilemma of standards in the remedial situation: namely, how does the initiate who has been *wronged* by the system internalize the linguistic norms of that system in ways that will enable him to turn them to creative use in his own life?

Perceived in this way, remediation has of course been permeated from the start by a concern with standards, with matters of correct forms and conventional routines and traditional knowledge. Even its innovations have been bounded and often inspired by the strict double purpose of compensatory education—to teach adults the fundamentals of college literacy in a hurry. Thus while the rhetoric of standards has continued to flourish, skills teachers have been exploring the real nature of the standards they have contracted to teach, not only defining those standards more precisely but assessing both the resources and difficulties their students bring to the task of learning to write and read for college.

Let me illustrate this difference in response to standards by discussing at some length that most familiar of territories in the teaching of basic or remedial writing—the territory of error. And then let me briefly suggest what the implications of such an exploration are for the teachers and institutions who are genuinely committed to the maintenance of standards.

For the basic writing student, academic writing has always been a trap, not a way of saying something to someone. Next to the rich orchestration of speech, writing is but a line that moves haltingly across the page, exposing as it goes all that the writer doesn't know, then passing into the hands of a stranger who reads it with a lawyer's eyes, searching for flaws.

By the time he reaches college, the basic writing student both resents and resists his vulnerability as a writer. He is aware that he leaves a trail of errors behind him when he writes. He can usually think of little else while he is writing. But he doesn't know what to do about it. Writing puts him on a line, and he doesn't want to be there. For every three hundred words he writes, he is likely to use from ten to thirty forms that the academic reader regards as serious errors. Some writers, inhibited by their fear of error, produce but a few lines an hour or keep trying to begin, crossing out one try after another until the sentence is hopelessly tangled.

So absolute is the importance of error in the minds of many writers that "good writing" to them means "correct writing," nothing more. Much about the "remedial" situation encourages this obsession with error. First, there is the reality of academia, the fact that most college teachers have little tolerance for the kinds of errors that basic writing students make, that they perceive certain types of errors as indicators of ineducability, and that they have the power of the F. Second, there is the urgency of the students to meet their teachers' criteria, even to request more of the prescriptive teaching they have had before in the hope that this time it might "take." Third, there is the awareness of the teacher and administrator that remedial programs are likely to be evaluated (and budgeted) according to the speed with which they produce correct writers, correctness being a highly quantifiable feature of good writing.

Teachers respond differently to these realities. Some rebel against the idea of error itself. All linguistic forms, they argue, are finally arbitrary. The spelling of a word, the inflectional systems that carry or reinforce certain kinds of information in sentences—these are merely conventions that differ from language to language and from dialect to dialect. And because the forms of language are arbitrary, the reasoning goes, they are not obligatory, not, at least, in those situations where variant forms can be understood by a reader or where the imposition of new forms undermines the writer's pride or confidence in his native language or vernacular.

Such a view excludes many forms from the province of "error." Certainly it leaves no room for those refinements of usage that have come to be associated with writing handbooks and English teachers. Beyond this, it would exclude variant grammatical forms and syntactical patterns that originate in English vernaculars that have long been spoken but only recently written, and then only in folk and imaginative literature. These forms would include such features as double negatives, variant patterns of inflection, or zero inflections in redundant situations, and a range of orthographic accommodations to vernacular forms.

When one considers the damage that has been done to students in the name of correct writing, this effort to redefine error so as to exclude most of the forms that give students trouble in school and to assert the legitimacy of other kinds of English is understandable. Doubtless it is part of a much vaster move within this society not only to reduce the penalties for being culturally different but to be enriched by that diversity.

Nonetheless, the teacher who faces a class of writers who have acquired but a rudimentary control of the skill discovers that the issue of error is much more complex and troubling than it seems in theory. He finds, for example, that errors his students make cannot be neatly traced to one particular source, namely, the habitual preference of a vernacular form over a standard form. Instead he finds evidence of a number of interacting linguistic influences: for example, the generally humiliating encounter with school language, which produces ambivalent feelings about mastery; the pleasures of peer and neighborhood talk, where language flows most naturally; the contagion of the media, those hours of TV and radio and movies and ads, where standard forms blend with all that is alluring in the society.

The writing that emerges from these experiences bears traces of the different pressures and codes and confusions that have gone to make up "English" for the basic writing student. Variant and standard forms mix, as if students had half-learned two inflectional systems; hypercorrections that belong to no system jut out in unexpected places; idiosyncratic schemes of punctuation and spelling substitute for systems that were never learned and possibly never taught; evasive circumlocutions, syntactical derailments, timid script, and near-guesses fog the meaning, if any remains after the student has thus spent himself on the sheer mechanics of getting something down on paper. One senses the struggle to fashion out of the fragments of past instruction a system that will relieve the writer of the task of deciding what to do in each instance where alternative forms or conventions stick in the mind.

Confusion, rather than conflict, seems to paralyze the writer at this level. Language learners at any level instinctively seek out the underlying patterns that govern the language they are learning. They are pressed by their language-learning faculties to increase the degree of predictability and efficiency in their use of language. This is less a choice they make than an urge they have to move across the territory of language as if they had a map and not as if they were being forced to make their way across a mine-field. What has been so damaging about the experience of basic writing students with written English is that it has been so confusing, and worse, that they have been resigned to this confusion, to not-knowing, to the substitution of protective tactics or private systems or makeshift strategies for genuine mastery of written English in *any* form. Most damaging of all, they have lost confidence in the very faculties that serve all language learners: their ability to draw analogies between what they knew of language when they began school and what they had to learn produced mistakes; their ability to distinguish between essential and redundant features of a language left them logical but wrong; and such was the quality of their instruction that no one saw the intelligence of their mistakes or thought to harness that intelligence in the service of learning.

There is no easy or quick way to undo this damage. The absence of errors, it is true, does not automatically guarantee good writing, yet the pile-up of errors that characterizes basic writing papers reflects more difficulty with written English than the term "error" is likely to imply. To try to persuade a student who makes these errors that the problems with his writing are all on the outside, or that he has no problems, may well be to perpetuate his confusion and deny him the ultimate freedom of deciding how and when and where he will use which language. For him, error is more than a mishap; it is a barrier that keeps him not only from writing something in formal English but from having something to write. In any event, students themselves are uneasy about encouragements to ignore the problem of error, often interpreting them as evasions of the hard work that lies before teachers and students if the craft of writing is ever to be mastered. Indeed, many students still insist, despite the miseries of their earlier encounters with school grammar and despite the reluctance of teachers who have lost confidence in the power of grammatical study to affect writing, that they need more prescriptive grammar. Perhaps, as some would say, the propaganda of a long line of grammar teachers "took." But it may also be that for some students grammar still seems to offer one last chance to understand what is going on with written language so that they can control it rather than be controlled by it.

There is another reason why the phenomenon of error cannot be ignored at this level. It has to do with the writer's relationship to his audience, with what might be called the economics of energy in the writing situation. Although speakers and listeners, writers and readers, are in one sense engaged in a cooperative effort to understand one another, they are also in conflict over the amount of effort each will expend on the other. That is, the speaker or writer wants to say what he has to say with as little energy as possible, and the listener or reader wants to understand with as little energy as possible. In a speech situation, the speaker has ways of encouraging or pressing for more energy than the listener might initially want to give. He can, for example, use attention-getting gestures or frowns or smiles or he can play upon the social responsiveness of his listener; the listener, in turn, can query or quiz or withhold his nods until he has received the "goods" he requires from the speaker.

Nothing like this open bargaining can go on in the writing situation, where the writer cannot keep an eye on his reader. Anything that facilitates the transfer of his meaning is important in this tight economy of energy. Great writers, it is true, have drawn deeply upon the energies of readers, holding them through pages of exasperating density or withholding them from conventional word order or vocabulary or punctuation in order to refresh the language or create new perceptions, but even here the reader expects his investment to pay off in intellectual or emotional enrichment. He is, after all, a buyer in a buyer's market.

Errors, however, are unintentional and unprofitable intrusions upon the consciousness of the reader. They introduce in accidental ways alternative forms in spots where usage has stabilized a particular form. They demand energy without giving any return in meaning; they shift the reader's attention from where he is going (meaning) to how he is getting there (code). In a better world, it is true, readers might be more generous with their energies, pausing to divine the meaning of a writer or mentally to edit the errors out of his text without expecting to be rewarded for their efforts, but it would be foolhardy to bank on that kind of persistence except perhaps in English teachers or good friends.

All codes become codes by doing some things regularly and not others, and it is not so much the ultimate logic of these regularities that makes them obligatory but rather the fact that, logical or not, they have become habitual to those who communicate within that code. The truth is that even slight departures from a code cost the writer something, in whatever system he happens to be communicating, and, given the hard bargain he must drive with his reader, he usually cannot afford many of them.

This is not to say, of course, that the boundaries of error do not shift nor to suggest that certain battles along those borderlines are not worth waging. English has been robustly inventing itself for centuries— stretching and reshaping and enriching itself with every language and dialect it has encountered. Ironically, some of the very irregularities that students struggle with today are there because at some point along the way the English language yielded to another way of saying something.

But when we move out of the centuries and into Monday morning, into the life of the young man or woman sitting in a basic writing class, our linguistic contemplations are likely to hover over a more immediate reality—namely, the fact that a person who does not control the dominant code of literacy in a society that generates more writing than any society in history is likely to be pitched against more obstacles than are apparent to those who have already mastered that code. From such a vantage point, one feels the conserving pull of language, the force that has preserved variant dialects of English as well as the general dialect of literacy, and one knows that errors matter, knows further, that a teacher who would work with basic writing students might well begin by trying to understand the logic of their mistakes in order to determine at what point or points along the developmental path error should or can become a subject for instruction.

I have returned, as you see, by a circuitous route to saying what has been said by many teachers before me—that the mastery of conventional forms is an important part of learning to write, and a crucial part of the training of the basic or remedial-level writer. But the route has taken us through new territory that suggests new responsibilities for the college or university that has decided not simply to *identify* those who can write competently but to *produce* competent writers. It suggests first the need for teachers who are psychologically and professionally prepared to work with adult students who happen to be beginning writers, teachers who understand enough about their students' resources as learners to grant them the power to learn what their readers have learned, but who are also precise enough about the gaps and distortions in their students' formal education to be able to decide what ought to come first and what follows what.

Our route through error also suggests the need for timetables and curricular plans that correspond to developmental realities. We must stop designing remedial fix-it stations that reflect what we *wish* would happen rather than what *can* happen. We must acknowledge that there are stages in the acquisition of writing skill, that there is, to be sure, a time for introducing the student, conceptually and through intensive practice, to the basic conventions of formal written English—a time that we have come to call remedial instruction; but that the fragile competence that results from this kind of instruction must be nourished in other courses across the curriculum and throughout the student's career in college or it will certainly disappear.

To think of testing without having these realities in mind is to think of testing as a managerial task, a matter of identifying and removing the under-skilled from our campuses but not from our society, and, in the process, perpetuating the various brands of class and race prejudice that have pervaded society since its creation.

But to speak responsibly of testing is to link an institution's educational *treatment* with its *testing,* which, I believe, the Task Force statement is attempting to do when it incorporates recommendations for curricular and staff development into its plan for testing. In this way it becomes possible for us to determine not simply who can write and who can't, but whether we as teachers and administrators are earning our keep and improving our students' prospects for the future. For our students have not been undone by testing but by irrelevant and irresponsible testing, not by the setting of standards but by the widespread acceptance in our society of *double* standards.

If we imagine a continuum, with at one end the exceptionally competent and at the other the barely competent, we could say that colleges have traditionally felt it their responsibility to identify students at the upper end of this scale and extend *their* education by four more years. The open admissions college, however, makes a commitment to involve itself in the education of young men and women all along the continuum on the assumption, first, that people are not consigned to their places on that continuum forever but are capable of remarkable growth and development when given the opportunity; second, that the social benefits of advancing as many as possible along that continuum are inestimable; and third, that this broadening of the base of higher education, if properly planned and supported, can further the education of *all* students on the continuum.

We are as yet far from reconciling the entitlements and capacities of the new students with our traditional ways of doing things in higher education. But as we move closer to this goal, we will surely be improving the quality of college education for all students and moving deeper into the realizations of a democracy. To speak of standards without remembering these larger goals, is *not* to speak but to *doublespeak* of standards, forgetting that if we are serious about standards, we must set them for ourselves as teachers and administrators as well as for our students.

In your own determination to move toward these larger goals through the creation of a responsible system of writing instruction and evaluation, you are taking up what seems to me one of the most important tasks in higher education today. I wish you Godspeed.

Appendix E

Statement on Criteria for Writing Proficiency

Although instruction in writing usually focuses systematically on specific sub-skills of writing such as grammatical inflections and paragraph design, writing competence is more than the sum of these discrete competencies. Rather, it is the successful integration of a number of linguistic skills which interact and combine in ways so difficult to delineate and measure that the holistic judgment of an experienced reader remains the most accurate form of assessment in writing.

When we examine and discuss such judgments, we can see, however, that they involve assessments in two distinct territories of competence. One territory we can call the territory of *choices,* which is concerned with the *quality* of decisions a writer makes in the selection of words and sentence patterns and rhetorical strategies. The other territory we can call the territory of *givens,* which is concerned with correct forms. In the first territory a writer can be judged to be persuasive or unconvincing, interesting or dull, precise or imprecise, organized or disorganized, etc. In the second territory he is right or wrong, according to the conventions of the written code; that is, his grammar, his spelling, his punctuation, or his word choices will simply be perceived as right or wrong by the general reader.

Very little exists in the way of longitudinal research on writing progress to guide us in determining the role that instruction plays in the maturation of a writer in each of these territories. Furthermore,

"Statement on Criteria for Writing Proficiency" was prepared in November 1976 as a working paper for the CUNY Task Force on Writing. It was published in the Fall/Winter 1980 issue of Journal of Basic Writing.

what little research has been done on the correlation between traditional criteria for writing competence and the criteria that actually figure in readers' judgments suggests a need to reexamine the entire subject of criteria.

The experience with unprepared freshman writers in open admissions classes nonetheless suggests several important features of their development which ought in turn to influence any assessment of their proficiency as writers.

1. In general, skill in the area of *choices* is the result of long exposure to written English. The cultivation of judgment in any skill, while it can be guided and stimulated by direct instruction, is largely a matter of making numerous and often unconscious attempts to approximate the models that are presented to the learner, with a gradual and even imperceptible closing of the gap between the apprentice performance and the model. Much of this growth among writers takes place as a result of students' work in other classes throughout college and cannot be said to have reached its end when they are about to move into their second or third years of college. Genuine growth in vocabulary, for example, is inextricably linked to the students' entire college experience and must therefore be assessed in highly relative terms.

2. The pace and patterns of growth among remedial-level students suggest that they are not likely to "catch up" to their more skilled peers within a semester or two of remedial instruction but that in absolute terms the measure of their improvement is so much greater than that of their non-remedial peers as they progress through college that they can reach comparable levels of performance by the time they are seniors. Thus while an early test of writing proficiency in this territory of *choices* might well reflect significant gaps between the prepared and unprepared populations, it would be a mistake to interpret these gaps as permanent and, on that basis, screen out students who are in fact capable of steady and in some instances dramatic improvement as they proceed through college.

3. Within the territory of *choices* there are certain key competencies that can and ought to be reached by the end of formal instruction in writing, and they can provide the foundation for the student's independent development as a writer from then on (provided, of course, he be required to put these competencies into practice in his regular college courses). These include:

a. The ability to sustain the development of a point or idea over the span of 300 to 500 words
b. The ability to select words that fall within the range of approximateness for formal writing (such a criterion would exclude from competence essays that reflect a heavy reliance upon slang, the cliches of daily life, and formalese)
c. An ability to signal the unfolding plan of a written passage by the use of organized paragraphs, transitional sentences, phrases, and words.

4. Unlike the territory of *choices,* the territory of the *givens* is much easier to describe, arising as it does out of three relatively autonomous linguistic subsystems (grammar, punctuation, and spelling) that have been reduced to principles and rules. To be sure, many of the conditions that govern these rules are themselves so complex as to defeat any attempt to teach them directly. Nonetheless, there remains a substantial body of information about the "givens" that is transferrable by direct instruction. Indeed, it is in this area that remedial teachers have so far shown their greatest ingenuity and effectiveness. But even here there are developmental realities which should influence any decisions about criteria. Primarily there is the fact that there is generally a gap between a student's understanding of his errors and his habitual control over them, and this gap between theoretical grasp and practical application is likely to be largest where students write under stressful conditions that allow little time for revision or proofreading. In addition, some features of these subsystems (particularly those involving certain grammatical inflections and sentence patterns) run counter to vernacular and mother-tongue patterns that lie deep in many students' linguistic intuitions. Such features can be brought to the surface of students' awareness and the errors caused by them reduced to the point that they appear residual rather than habitual, but it would be unrealistic to expect such difficulties to disappear entirely from a student's formal writing by the end of his remedial instruction. More often, they will be substantially reduced during that period and then they will be gradually worn away by further practice and exposure to books and lectures. At least one survey of CUNY faculty opinion suggests that professors are not, in any event, as distressed by occasional error of form as they are by the lack of development of order in student writing.

5. Within the boundaries dictated by the relative shortness of training time (in most colleges between one and two semesters of courses
with three to four hours of class time a week) and the nature of development in writing, it is possible to set criteria for correctness that indicate a readiness to manage college writing tasks without extra supervision (i.e. supervision beyond that which a professor is expected to
give when he assigns papers). These criteria would include:

   a. The ability to write sentences that reflect a command of syn-
       tax within the ordinary range of mature writing. This would
       exclude from competence writing that depends so exclusively
       upon the simple sentence patterns as to seem childish as well
       as writing that so tangles syntactic possibilities as to require
       several readings to comprehend.
   b. The ability to make conventional use of the capital and of the
       major marks of punctuation—the period, comma, semicolon,
       and quotation marks.
   c. The ability to spell the common words of the language with a
       high degree of accuracy and to manage the less common words
       of the college vocabulary with enough accuracy to sustain the
       reader's attention on the content rather than the spelling of
       words. Since the efficient use of the dictionary is itself a key
       academic skill and since the skill of spelling is in most writing
       situations a matter of knowing when to look up an uncertain
       spelling, we recommend that students be permitted to use dic-
       tionaries during writing examinations.
   d. The ability to use regularly, but not necessarily faultlessly, the
       grammatical inflections of formal written English and to ob-
       serve the rules of agreement that apply to subjects and verbs,
       pronouns and antecedents.

Such a list of criteria for both the territories of competence we
have described here raises questions about how the cutting points in
individual criteria are to be determined and how the various criteria
are to be weighted in relation to each other. To attempt to solve such
problems by developing detailed measures of scoring procedures (for
example, to set limits to the number of errors in particular categories
or to count the number of words in paragraphs or sentences) might
well increase the degree of agreement (reliability) among readers, par-

ticularly in the territory of correctness, but it will, in the judgment of this committee, reduce the *validity* of the judgment, for no scheme of quantification appears to be sensitive or flexible enough to gauge the point at which a piece of writing is perceived to be incompetent by a general reader. Such judgments arise out of an almost infinite number of possible combinations of strengths and weaknesses, with at one time a notable strength in one area lessening the importance of flaws in others, or at another time severe weaknesses in seemingly minor features outweighing other important accomplishments.

Much might ultimately be learned as data from examinations are accumulated about the correlations between readers' judgments and measurable features of students' essays, but lacking such data now and fearing that any attempt at quantification, no matter how conscientious, would also run the risk of shifting teaching priorities so as to encourage narrowly literal views of writing competence, the committee recommends that the criteria listed above be refined through the process of examining cases in reader-training sessions.

Appendix F
Some Needed Research on Writing

Among most of the arts and skills people attempt to acquire in this society, the sequences and goals of instruction are far more stable and specific than they seem to be for writing. Most students of piano, wherever they study, make their way through similar types of scales and exercises (many are still apprenticed to Czerny's exercises for finger dexterity, now over a hundred years old). Ballet students still practice their *plies* and *rond de jambes* in much the same order and according to similar developmental timetables, whether their studios are in Kansas City or New York. And athletes have familiar training rituals, known to coaches from big league to little. For such skills, teachers need not invent whole pedagogies as they go, nor return with debilitating regularity to fundamental questions about their purposes and procedures. They continue a vital tradition of instruction in which their roles are of unquestioned importance. It is assumed that to learn to play the piano or to dance or to play football, a person must generally become someone's student. And that someone, a teacher, understands what comes after what and what constitutes an acceptable level of performance at each step along the way.

Teachers of reading and writing, particularly those who teach ill-prepared freshmen, enjoy no such stability. In a culture that has been engaged in reading and writing for centuries, the pedagogies of literacy

"Some Needed Research on Writing" was delivered as an address at the Modern Language Association Convention in December 1976. It was published in College Composition and Communication *in December 1977.*

are in a puzzling state of discord, with theorists and practitioners and taxpayers all arguing about how people become literate or why they don't.

The reasons for this discord are clearly complex. It cannot be simply a matter of English teachers' having failed to do their homework. I have been the beneficiary, as both a writer and a teacher, of too many fine texts and theoretical works about rhetoric, grammar, style, and so on to be ready now to condemn the profession as roundly as it is being condemned for the state of literacy in America.

Still, I must admit that those pedagogies that served the profession for years seem no longer appropriate to large numbers of our students, and their inappropriateness lies largely in the fact that many of our students these days are exactly in the same relation to writing that beginning tennis students or piano students are to those skills: they are adult beginners and depend as students did not depend in the past upon the classroom and the teacher for the acquisition of the skill of writing.

Most of us learned to write through such a long, subtle process of socialization that we cannot remember how it happened. For some, freshman composition played an insignificant part of their maturation as writers, and for most, it was at best a helpful rather than an essential course. But the students we have now will be able to say—if they are fortunate in their teachers—that they learned to write in such a year, with such a teacher, and that their courses in writing were crucial to their advancement in college.

This is a tremendous responsibility for English teachers. But my own experience with unprepared—severely unprepared—students persuades me that it is a responsibility we can meet if we are willing to give our energies to the development of a pedagogy for writing that respects, in its goals and methods, the maturity of the adult, beginning writer and at the same time admits to the need to begin where the beginning is, even if that falls outside the traditional territory of college composition.

If we accept this responsibility, we are committed to research of a very ambitious sort—so ambitious that I have not been able to suggest its boundaries. What I will do instead is simply raise four questions that have concerned me lately and that might in turn generate specific research plans that would move us toward the pedagogy I speak of.

My first question is "WHAT ARE THE SIGNS OF GROWTH

IN WRITING AMONG ADULTS WHOSE DEVELOPMENT AS WRITERS HAS BEEN DELAYED BY INFERIOR PREPARATION BUT WHO ARE THEN EXPOSED TO INTENSIVE INSTRUCTION IN WRITING?" [Shaughnessy's capitalization] Just how, that is, at what pace and in what manner, do such students get to be better at the skills? From a managerial perspective, it would be convenient if the writing of such students were to advance regularly, on all fronts, preferably within one semester, in response to instruction, paralleling the developmental patterns that have been observed among younger learners over longer periods.

Yet experience with the unprepared adult writer suggests that the pattern of development is marked by puzzling plateaus and even retreats in some areas and remarkable leaps into competence in others, producing very different writing records from those we are accustomed to in better-prepared students, refusing throughout to bring the unprepared writers into parallel courses with their better-prepared peers. Thus, while the most dramatic difference between the prepared and unprepared writer is probably the incidence and quality of error in each group, errors, particularly the errors that are deeply rooted in linguistic habit and not simply the result of inattentiveness, may be more resistant to direct instruction than other seemingly more complex problems that are traditionally taken up after the slaying of the dragon error. I have in mind the skills of elucidation and validation and sequencing in expository writing or the management of complex sentence patterns (which are usually ripe for development among adult students even though their early writings produce many tangled and derailed sentences, a reality which complicates the use of measures of maturity such as the T-unit). I would guess that by the criteria for improvement now common in many remedial programs, the developing writer is likely to be penalized for his or her growth simply because the phenomenon of growth in writing for this population has not been looked at directly, through case studies, for example, over four- or five-year stretches.

My second question is "WHAT SUB-SKILLS OF WRITING, HERETOFORE ABSORBED BY STUDENTS OVER TIME IN A VARIETY OF SITUATIONS, CAN BE EFFECTIVELY DEVELOPED THROUGH DIRECT AND SYSTEMATIC INSTRUCTION AT THE FRESHMAN LEVEL?" Here I raise the question of whether some of the slow-growing skills, such as spelling, vocabulary, and syntax, which in ordinary development are acquired gradually and inductively, might not be approached through effective paradigms and conceptual keys appropriate for adult learners although inaccessible to young learners. Teachers' fatalistic views about many of their students' difficulties may well arise out of a failure so far to have found the most productive generalizations about those features of written language that give students the most difficulty, generalizations that may be already available to us in research literature or that lie around the corner, were English teachers inclined or encouraged to turn in that direction. It should not be difficult, for example, to link great improvements in the teaching of spelling at the elementary levels to the major work of Hanna and others in the analysis of phoneme-grapheme correspondences as clues to spelling improvement. There is much still to be drawn from that work, now a decade old, for the instruction of adult learners as well. Or, as another example, there is the recent work of Sandra Stotsky on vocabulary development, which not only gives special attention to the mastery of prefixes among young learners but suggests a systematic approach to vocabulary development that has applications for older students.

My third question is "WHAT SKILLS HAVE WE FAILED TO TAKE NOTE OF IN OUR ANALYSIS OF ACADEMIC TASKS?" "The aim of a skillful performance," Polanyi has written, "is achieved by the observance of a set of rules which are *not known as such* to the person following them." In my few attempts to work contrastively with experienced and inexperienced academic writers on the same assignments in order to discover hidden features of competency, I have been surprised by the emergence of certain skills and orientations I had not thought to isolate or emphasize as subjects of instruction. I have noted, for example, that the craft of writing has a larger measure of craftiness in it than our instruction seems to suggest. Experienced academic writers, for example, appear to spend little time deliberating over their main intent in answering a question or developing an essay; this conviction evidently reaches them through some subtle, swift process of assessment and association that has doubtless been highly cultivated after years of writing in academic situations. But after this recognition of intent, there follows a relatively long period of scheming and plotting during which the writer, often with great cunning, strives to present his or her intent in a way that will be seductive to an academic audience, which, while it aspires among other things to high standards of verification and sound reason, is nonetheless subject to other kinds of persuasion as well—to the deft manipulation of audience expectations and biases, to shrewd assessments of what constitutes "adequate proof" or enough examples in specific situations, to the stances of fairness, objectivity, and formal courtesy that smooth the surface of academic disputation. One has but to re-read such brilliant academic performances as Freud's introductory lectures on psychoanalysis to observe this craftiness at work.

Now, beginning adult writers are without protection in such situations. They do not know the rituals and ways of winning arguments in academia. Indeed, so open and vulnerable do they appear in their writing that teachers often turn sentimental in their response to it, urging them into the lion's den of academic disputation with no more than an honest face for protection. Furthermore, the traditional formulations of expository writing too easily lead to the conviction that only certain kinds of writing (poetry, for example, or fiction) are concerned with seduction, whereas the formal writing of academics and professionals is carried out at more spiritual (i.e. rational) levels of discourse where the neutral truth is thought to dwell.

This view not only inhibits students from joining in the academic contest but takes much of the fun and competition out of the sport. "The greatest minds," Leo Strauss has remarked, "do not all tell us the same things regarding the most important themes; the community of the greatest minds is rent by discord and even by various kinds of discord." College prepares students—or ought to prepare them—to survive intellectually in this atmosphere of discord. It teaches them, or should teach them, in the words of a Master of Eton in the 1860's, "to make mental efforts under criticism."

But the emphasis in writing instruction over the past years has not encouraged a close look at academic discourse nor favored such images as the contest or the dispute as acceptable metaphors for writing, with the result that too many students, especially at the remedial level, continue to write only or mainly in expressive and narrative modes, or to work with worn and inaccurate formulations of the academic mode.

As part of this exploration of academic discourse I am recommending, we need above all else to take a closer look at vocabulary, which is of course critical to the development of complex concepts, the maturation of syntax, and the acquisition of an appropriate tone or register.

This is probably the least cultivated field in all of the composition research, badly, barrenly treated in texts and not infrequently abandoned between the desks of reading teachers and writing teachers. We lack a precise taxonomy of the academic vocabulary that might enable us to identify those words and those features of words that would lend themselves to direct instruction or that might allow us to hypothesize realistic and multi-dimensioned timetables for vocabulary growth. We have done little to distinguish among the words in disciplines, except to isolate specialized terms in lists or glossaries, and we have done even less to describe the common stock of words teachers assume students know—proper names, words that have transcended their disciplines, words that initiate academic activities (*document, define,* etc.), words that articulate logical relationships, etc. In short, the territory of academic rhetoric—its vocabulary, its conventions, its purposes—is waiting for an Aristotle.

Finally, I must ask a fourth question, which is embarrassingly rudimentary: "WHAT GOES ON AND WHAT OUGHT TO GO ON IN THE COMPOSITION CLASSROOM?" The classroom, as I have said, has become a more important place than ever before. For some students, almost everything that is going to happen will happen there— or through work that is generated there. Yet we know surprisingly little about what goes on there. We know what teachers do by our own recollections of what our teachers did, by what teachers tell us they do (which opens up a vast territory of imaginative literature), and by the periodic observations of peers and students that are largely managerial in intent and that pose rather crude sorts of questions about teaching effectiveness.

But we have evolved no adequate scheme for observing precisely the classroom behavior of students and teachers nor for classifying the models of association between student and teacher that govern different styles of teaching. That is, we can perhaps locate metaphors that describe the orientations of teachers and students—the theater, the courtroom, the clinic, the editorial office, the couch—but we have not analyzed them nor related them to the teaching of discrete subskills in writing. Nor have we entertained or adequately tested any bold departures from the familiar classroom configurations and timetables, even though teaching the skill of writing may be more like coaching football than teaching literature or history or biology.

What I am suggesting through this question and others is that we have as yet no sociology nor psychology (not even an adequate history) of teaching the advanced skills of literacy to young adults who have not already acquired them. Yet many such students are now in college classrooms. We cannot hope to solve the problems that arise out of vast inequities in public education by arguing that when those problems were *not* being solved, or even thought about, higher education was in excellent shape.

Appendix G

The English Professor's Malady

It occurred to me not long ago, after having spent close to a decade seeking for ways to help ill prepared, so-called remedial, students learn to write, that I had perhaps been working on the wrong question. Instead of asking *how* to go about this task, I should probably, I realized, have been asking why so many English professors don't want to do it—and probably wouldn't even if our methods were to be measurably improved.

I have always liked English teachers, both as my teachers and, later, as my colleagues. They have seemed to me a particularly human group of professionals, with more self-irony and grace than the run of academicians, with even a kind of seasoned and pleasing worldliness that I have always supposed to be one of the results of spending so much time reading and talking and writing about great works of literature.

Still, I must admit that except for a few of the professional stars, the bulk of the work in basic writing has so far been taken up by the most marginal members of the profession—beginning teachers or graduate students, paraprofessionals, women, minorities, and of late, the underemployed but tenured members of other departments.

I have by now experienced this division of labor within the profession on a variety of campuses throughout the country. For me, the experience begins, generally, with an invitation to visit a campus as a consultant. Later I usually learn that the invitation has been hard-won

---

"The English Professor's Malady" was delivered as an address at the Association of Departments of English Conference in June 1977 in Albany, New York. It was published in the Spring 1994 issue of Journal of Basic Writing.

by a cluster of basic-writing teachers, with occasionally the support of a conscientious chairman, who have somehow managed to wrest some department funds for the occasion and are determined to make good use of it—of me, that is.

The invitation asks me to advise them on a number of specific matters—the creation of a more efficient writing lab, perhaps, or the design of a placement test. And each time, I set off with my wares in a canvas satchel, expecting to talk shop with a few practitioners. But almost invariably when I arrive I find that I have been called on quite another mission from the one specified in the invitation: I have been sent for, it turns out, to preach religion to the unconverted—at breakfast, or luncheons, cocktails and teas. I have been "planted" by the writing teachers in an effort to persuade English professors, and perhaps a dean or so for good measure, that it is both pedagogically possible and intellectually respectable to teach ill-prepared freshmen to write for college.

Now this sort of assignment would seem to me a perfectly honorable one to accept provided one's evangelism took hold and one could claim here and there a stable convert. But I have usually left each campus in its Laodicean calm, my satchel full of unused hand-outs and my spirits daunted by the engaging, impervious sufficiency of English professors.

It was after a number of such experiences, as I was saying, that I decided to take a closer look, not at the problems of basic writing students, but at the conditions that seem to govern the response of English professors to these students and to the subject of writing. And in my reasoning about the matter, I have come up with three conditions besides that of original sin, that figure in what I am calling the English Professor's Malady.

First, I would suggest that the subject of writing in most English departments is so flatly and narrowly perceived that it cannot be competitive with other subjects within the department. As a result it becomes the penalty courses in most teachers' programs, the course that full professors are often excused from teaching or that all teachers nobly accept as part of the price teachers pay for teaching their *real* subjects. It is the subject, too, which most English professors have never had to study formally and the subject, therefore, that generates each season a flurry of bright texts, only a few of which represent the best energies and motives of their authors. They are not books important enough to English professors to argue about. Many are never reviewed. They are academically unimportant occurrences in a vast ecumenical reserve called freshman or developmental or compensatory or remedial or basic English.

I do not at this point want to make the usual criticism of the profession for the emphasis it is said to have placed upon its custodial role in the teaching of writing, that is, upon the achievement of formal correctness and the mastery of the academic genres. To teach toward such competencies seems to me both realistic and respectable. My argument is that, for the most part, professors have perceived these tasks in pedagogically and linguistically unsophisticated ways and have as a result too often bored or defeated both themselves and their students.

This territory of the professors' general ill-preparedness can be divided into three parts. The first part concerns their unfamiliarity with the *psychology* of writing, that is, with the behavior of writing itself—how the ideas that lead to writing are generated, how they undergo stages of formulation and reformulation, how designs for the ordering and elaboration of ideas evolve, how certain tasks specific to writing (such as revising and proofreading) are contrary to our impulses as speakers are acquired, or how writing affects cognitive styles and development.

Already a substantial body of literature exists on the nature of the composing process, some of it going back to Aristotle, but except for the rhetoricians among us—and they tend either to have split off from English departments or to have taken them over the subject has inspired little research or pedagogical reform.

Then there is the historical part of writing—the record of what has gone on in the name of freshman composition over the past hundred years or so and the even more interesting record of how ordinary people learned to write and how they used writing in earlier eras of this country's history. From such records we begin to suspect (and studies of the history of literacy in America support this suspicion) that the ability to write was once distributed more widely across classes than it is today and that the uses of writing were more varied and personally gratifying than they are today. Restricted in our notions of what writing is for, we tend to present the skill either as a prestigious or exotic accomplishment (like being able to sketch or play the piano in Jane Austen's world) or as a bread-and-butter skill that guarantees mobility from jobs into professions. Such limited perceptions of this quite remarkable invention called writing encourage us to accept current ways of organizing and assessing writing instruction. They lock us into convictions about what is most important to learn, who should learn what, or who should teach whom at a point when the uses of literacy in this society need to be re-examined, when the possibilities for a much richer definition of literacy exist alongside the threat of a more and more exclusive cultivation of that power.

Third, there is what might be called the anthropological or cultural part of writing, by which I mean the study of the functions as well as the forms of academic writing, the attempt to construct the social realities that give rise to specific kinds of behavior (in this case to specific kinds of writing). Here I am suggesting that it is useful for teachers to think of college as a foreign land, a little world, if you will, with ways of perceiving and doing things that often seem peculiar or arbitrary to students. To someone from within that world, academic discourse is a way (to some *the* way) of using thought and language so as to make the largest general statements possible across a range of data and to do so for an audience that is expected to scrutinize the generalizations and the data.

From many students' perspective, however, academic writing is a formidable hurdle—an unfriendly register which pitches the writer against an anonymous and exacting reader who is apparently interested in arguments about issues that are either so grand as to be outside the possible control of either writer or reader or so refined as to seem foolish. At the same time, the writer's own impressions and convictions seem to become insubstantial unless they can in some way be neutralized by language and a special kind of analysis.

To approach such discourse in formulaic ways—simply identifying the recurrent and quantifiable features of the sentences, paragraphs, and parts of essays or research papers—is to assume already a kind of cultural consent and understanding among students, which in fact does not exist widely today. Somehow teachers must find ways of explaining the tasks of academia so that they make sense as human strategies, ways of solving the problems academicians pose for themselves. And it is difficult to imagine how they can do this without looking both more seriously into the sorts of discourse *they* generate and more widely at the various ways in which language is shaped to do the work of human communities.

It is hard, too, to imagine a pedagogy growing out of this perspective that would not be much more concerned than most pedagogies now are with the sequence and fit of lessons from one session to the next, as the student moves from the familiar strategies of conversation and the easier forms of writing into the denser forests of formal writing.

The English professor's malady, I am suggesting, then, is at least partly caused by provincialism—by too "local" a conception of the subject he teaches—its processes, its history, and its context. I would add to this a second, somewhat similar, condition that helps explain the malady—a tendency to underestimate the capabilities and the difficulties of students whose backgrounds and states of preparation are very different from his.

It is vital, of course, for a teacher to believe in the educability of his students. We tend finally to turn away from problems we can do nothing about. This is an intelligent response to futility. And the teacher who believes that his students are too limited or too far behind to learn what he has learned is almost certain to prove his point. Thus it becomes critically important that the teacher be right about such perceptions. And here he encounters difficulties, for he has generally had little experience with severely ill-prepared adult students and cannot, or at least ought not to, judge their capabilities until he has committed his best energies and imaginations to teaching them—a commitment he is not likely to make if he already believes them ineducable.

The only way out of this dilemma is for the teacher to *hypothesize* the educability of his students and to look at their behavior as writers from such a perspective, assuming, that is, that while what they write may be wrong or inappropriate or inadequate in relation to the models they must learn, their behavior is neither random nor illogical but ingeniously adaptive at one moment, linguistically conservative at another, or relentlessly—albeit wrongly—logical at still another.

Having by now examined thousands of student essays from such a perspective, I can commend the perspective as both pedagogically fertile and linguistically fascinating. Without ignoring the goal of correctness and cogency, the method liberates the teacher from a narrowly prescriptive response to student writing. It reveals in precise ways the intermixing of grammatical forms and logics from different grammatical systems, the intrusions of speaking strategies and habits into written English, the gaps and distortions from earlier instruction, and—above all—the persistent, ingenious urgings of intelligence, of the drive to do things for a reason, to create systems, to survive by wit.

To discover, however, that literateness is not to be confused with intelligence and that young adults who by all traditional measures don't belong in college do in fact have the capability of surviving and even flourishing there is to discover more truth than an English teacher may want to bear alone.

And this brings me to my final point in this etiology of the English professor's malady—namely, that as writing instruction is presently organized, the teacher who wishes to give his best energies to the instruction of ill-prepared freshmen must be ready to forgo many of the rewards and privileges of his profession. He must be resigned to being an altruistic teacher—and even though the study of literature may well have ripened the moral imaginations of English teachers to such an extent that the profession produces more than its share of generous (or as some would have it, bleeding) hearts, the fact remains that systems do not function efficiently on altruism, and the educational system must offer the same sorts of prizes and incentives that energize people in other systems—money, time, security, and working conditions that encourage excellence—if the teaching of writing is to advance beyond its present state.

To this, we must add another rude fact—that despite the opening of many educational doors since the late sixties, there is little evidence that much has changed behind those doors. If anything, the lines that divide the privileged from the unprivileged in this society have simply been extended into the terrain of higher education. And nowhere is the gap between the two groups far more sharply drawn than in the area of writing.

Of the two skills of literacy, reading has ever been judged the more important skill for ordinary citizens to acquire. Some people—English teachers among them—have even insisted that writing is a skill not everyone *can* acquire or needs to acquire, especially in an age when television and tapes have liberated speech from transiency and telephones have reduced the burden of ritual and routine correspondence.

To be sure, learning to write is hard work. And few, even among those who become highly skilled at it, ever seem to do it for fun, as they might watch television or read a book. Still, there is a special advantage to learning how to get one's thoughts down on a page, one that is related to the very functioning of a democracy. For one can imagine the advantages to *any* state of having a population of readers: reading remains the cheapest and most efficient technology for passing out directions and information and propaganda. But it is in the nature of writing to encourage individuals to discover and explore their *own* hunches, to ponder their *own* words, to respect their *own* thoughts enough to entrust them to the written page. Writing even teaches about reading. It is the other side of literacy, without which the reader too often reads uncritically.

Despite these benefits, or possibly because of them, the skill of writing in this society is essentially a class-distributed skill. Unless they are exceptionally talented, the children of the poor learn even less about writing than about reading. They learn handwriting, perhaps, in the early grades, but most of them leave school without having learned to compose and perfect their thoughts in the medium that allows for the greatest independence of mind and exacts the greatest effort at articulation. What is worse, they leave school persuaded that they were in some way natively unqualified to learn to write and must now find ways of evading the various writing tasks that are certain to be posed for them in their work and in their lives as parents and citizens.

The experience of open admissions both at City University and in other universities and colleges throughout the country has not only revealed the plight of such students but demonstrated that there are no pedagogical reasons why writing should be an exclusive skill rather than a common skill among our citizenry. It simply needs to be taught. And the fact that it is not taught well—and sometimes not taught at all—to the students who need it most constitutes a true crisis of literacy in this country, where being able to *initiate* messages should be as important as being able to receive them and where the most fruitful and necessary activity is arguing rather than agreeing.

Today, people are, for the most part, alarmed over the declining levels of literacy among the privileged, not over the traditional subliteracy of the poor, and it is in the prestigious colleges that a new seriousness about writing can now be found. But until the traditional illiteracy is as alarming to the American people as the declining literacy of the affluent, our schools will continue to cultivate advanced literacy as a privilege rather than an entitlement.

To prepare only some people to flourish in a democracy and then to argue that they are the only people with the native ability to do so is to consent to the existence, within the boundaries of what we call public education, of the most exclusive country club of all.

I am not certain what English department chairmen can do or what they might want to do about so large a problem. The responsibility for doing something has clearly fallen disproportionately upon English departments and some would argue that the English professor's very love of literature and his preparation to teach it have paradoxically robbed him of the patience and modesty needed to teach basic writing. If so, then of course the responsibility of a chairman might be simply to lead his department out of the wilderness of basic writing and into the promised land of literature. But should he decide instead to stay and try to bring some measure of order and meaning—and yes, even class—to the subject of basic writing, he will be struggling to meet the claims of both literature and literacy upon a department, and in doing this he will be helping his professors learn to *want* to do the work that waits to be done.

APPENDIX H
Basic Writing

I have been asked to speak about my research on student writing. But the word "research" prompts me to begin with a disclaimer. Most certainly "research" is a dignified and reassuring word these days, but one that suggests a mode of analysis that is quite far from the sort of study I have made of student writing, if by "research" one has in mind that formidable technology that has by now overtaken so much of language study—and that entails elaborate research designs, complete with computers and complex methods of quantification, which in turn lead generally to very cautious conclusions about strictly limited phenomena.

My own work, as I say, has been of a different sort—shaped by limitations I did not set for myself and directed less by a well-informed hypothesis about why certain students write the way they do than by the urgent need to make some sense out of the puzzling incompetencies of many hundreds of students who began to appear in our freshman classes at City University in the 60's and, in much greater numbers, in the early 70's under open admissions.

At City College, these new students made up about 1/4 of the freshman class, but they were the source of the moans, laments, and ultimatums of English professors. It was not that professors expected freshmen to be able to write well but rather that the new students introduced, into a fairly predictable universe of incompetency, stunningly new ways

"Basic Writing" was delivered as an address at the Modern Literature Conference at Michigan State University in October 1977. Mina Shaughnessy often revised her speeches up until the time she delivered them, making notations by hand directly on the typed manuscript. I have incorporated those changes into the text that appears here.

of being bad writers—ways that raised questions in the minds of teachers not merely about the preparation or sophistication of these students but about the prospects of their ever learning what they had to learn in order to survive in college.

It was not simply that their essays were shorter and more error-laden than the essays of typical freshmen. They differed in kind from the essays English teachers had come to expect of freshmen. There were errors in surprising places—at the familiar ends of words, where s's and -ed endings seemed to appear and disappear with baffling irregularity. There were syntactical tangles and derailments that defied analysis, that seemed to be new to Christendom. There were misspellings so dismayingly inventive as to turn the reading of an essay into an imaginative feat of decoding. There was a chaos of commas and periods, and no sign of an acquaintance with quotation marks, dashes, semicolons, parentheses, etc.

And beneath these surfaces of error and disjuncture one sensed squirming hapless writers, pinned to the page, to the merciless line, unprotected by craft or craftiness, bared to the world and doomed at last to the stroke of some teacher's restless red pencil.

So there they were—gathered into classrooms—those veteran watchers of teachers, waiting to see whether, for all the rhetoric that came with open admissions, things would be different this time around.

And there were their teachers—accustomed to learners who, like themselves, had over the years been slowly, silently acculturated to the ways of literacy in academia, reluctant in spirit to begin from scratch, and ill-equipped by education to determine where, in fact, scratch was.

Fortunately for them both, the composition class is a place where teachers and students must communicate with one another—at least some of the time. Students must put something down on paper every week or so and teachers must scribble something in the margins of those papers. Each party ponders the other's language and then occasionally teacher and student meet face to face to explain what each was trying to say to the other. Slowly, these strains of inquiry and response, these meditations upon imperfect texts, complicate the relationship of teacher and student, making it more and more difficult to turn away from the obligations of trying to understand one another.

Such at least was my experience with the new students. Stunned at first by their incompetencies as writers, I slowly began to acquire a respect for, and curiosity about, the sorts of difficulties they were having. I began to sense that little in their behavior as writers was random, that indeed, much of it was logical, even though it led to error, and that my chances of helping them depended largely upon my penetrating the various logics of their mistakes and misjudgments.

With this purpose in mind, therefore, I gathered some 4,000 placement essays written by ill-prepared freshman writers and began, first, to collect and classify all the things that went wrong with them, from punctuation to the organization of passages, and second, to try to tease out the possible reasons for these errors and misjudgments, drawing in part upon the explanations I was able to get directly from students, from the insights of fellow teachers, and from my own experience as a person who writes and therefore understands some of the pressures and peculiarities of that behavior.

I want to try, here, merely to mention some of the observations I made in the course of this rather laborious procedure, observations that seem now as I restate them both old and obvious to the profession. Still, they have yet to be translated, broadly, into the practice of teaching writing at the basic level. So allow me, for a while, to belabor my points.

My first point would seem at first glance to be utterly unnecessary to mention in an audience of English teachers. It is the point that errors matter, that they are, in fact, the distinguishing, even the individualizing feature of the writing of so-called remedial or, as I shall call them, "basic" writers, and that something has to be done about them.

I must belabor this point for two reasons: one, because of the many teachers who are convinced that although errors may matter, nothing can be done about them when they occur in such numbers and varieties as they do among basic writers of college age, and two, because other teachers have come to rebel against the idea of error itself. All linguistic forms, they contend, are finally arbitrary. The spelling of a word, the inflectional systems that carry or reinforce certain kinds of information in sentences—these are merely conventions that differ from language to language and dialect to dialect. And because the forms are arbitrary, they reason, they are not obligatory, not at least in those situations where variant forms can be understood by a reader or where the imposition of new forms undermines the writer's pride in his native language or vernacular.

To that first group of teachers who would consign basic writers to the ranks of the permanently semi-literate—and to the personal and social disadvantages of that condition—I can only say that the open admissions experiment, wherever it has been seriously undertaken, has yielded a few truths that I, and I suspect many other teachers, would walk the plank for—and one of them is that the young men and women we call remedial have the capacity (by now the proven capacity) to become competent writers and to do so, if everyone works very hard, even within the harsh time limits imposed by the college timetable.

To the second group of teachers who now insist that the arbitrariness of the formal written code relieves students of the need for mastering that code, I would first observe that the arbitrariness of conventions appears never to have been a reason among human beings for ignoring those conventions. But in any event, my study of the sentences and paragraphs of basic writers revealed that the conflict between standard and non-standard forms was but *one* of the causes of basic writers' problems. Furthermore, this conflict has generally narrowed to a few grammatical forms, by the time a student reaches college age, which are troublesome to a wide range of students from various language backgrounds but which by no means define the difficulties BW students have with written English. Many other pressures and codes and confusions have gone to make up English for the basic writing student, as even a glance at their writing will reveal. Variant and standard forms mix, as if students had half-learned two inflectional systems; hypercorrections that belong to no system jut out in unexpected places; idiosyncratic schemes of punctuation and spelling substitute for systems that were never learned or possibly taught; evasive circumlocutions, syntactic snarls, timid script, and near guesses fog the meaning if any remains after the student has spent himself on the sheer mechanics of getting something down on paper. One soon understands that the most important factor about BW students is a rather simple one: they have seldom written anything in any dialect; they are not so much poor writers as beginning writers. The pen, so indispensable to the academician who often needs it in *hand* just to start thinking—is for the basic writer a weapon used against himself.

Having said that errors matter, that they were, further, the distinguishing feature of the samples I studied, I quickly move to a second point, one that fewer teachers are likely to agree with—namely, that errors are interesting and that the flawed texts of students' passages not only reveal linguistic intelligence at work but illuminate the very nature of writing itself.

I am saying, in other words, that the errors and shortcomings we as teachers have become fleet at seeing and naming deserve a different quality of attention than we have customarily given them, something closer to the sort of careful and imaginative observations we have been trained to make of literary texts except that instead of focusing on how a successful text succeeds or what it means, our task is to note how and why unsuccessful texts fail and what it might have meant. And one of the paths to this sort of analysis is error.

Let me develop my first point—about the linguistic sophistication of basic writers—by discussing two general observations I made of their performances:

The first observation is that where a system of spelling or punctuation or grammar has not been adequately explained or learned, students tend to *invent* their own systems, reducing the number of units and options within the system but relating these units as much as possible to some sort of scheme or pattern that will increase predictability and reduce the energy required to decide in each instance what to do.

This is, of course, what logic (but not necessarily language customs) dictates and it results in idiosyncratic systems of spelling or punctuation or merged grammars that are clearly wrong but not necessarily totally inconsistent or illogical, once the premises of the student writer are known. Thus in punctuation, for example, a student may give the marks of punctuation different structural power than the conventional system allows—using commas, perhaps (as one student did) to separate the sentences of a thought cluster and periods to mark the end of a thought cluster or paragraph. Another student may have jumbled the meanings and the symbols, thinking, as one of my students did, that "comma" refers to the period mark, and the "period" to the comma mark, and what with the baffling and contrary signals from years of teachers, none of whom discovered this fundamental misunderstanding, finally concluded that it couldn't make much difference one way or the other and simply used the marks interchangeably. Still another student, taken with the accessibility of some marks and the austerity of others, generously scattered commas about his sentences "because," he explained, "they are so cheap."

More often than not, this urge I am speaking of to make sense out of the writing code leads students to apply, with the consistency of a good computer, the generalizations their teachers and textbooks give them, only to find that the reward for such literalism is frequently error—not because the student slipped up or forgot but because he was consistent and badly programmed. His teachers, following their own urge for predictability and simplicity, had imposed a deceptive order upon the mercurial language, passing on pedagogical schemes of analysis that worked in the past only because the students being taught already owned the language and accounted in their habits for what the formal explanations ignored.

So it is that a student's paper becomes a map not only of his own limited understanding of the formal written code, but of his teacher's limited understanding as well. It contains a history of pedagogical mishaps brought on usually by the best of impulses—the desire to simplify the task of learning to write, to provide simple and secure strategies to hold on to in the storm.

Put a comma before "and" said a teacher once, and the student learned to write "Hortense, and I."

Put a comma where you breathe, said another, with of course no guidelines on the breath-seconds required to produce semi-colons and colons. So the shortwinded produce a deluge of commas and the long-distance runners none.

When you start in the past tense, stay in it, said another, and some uncertain student, against all his intuitions, decided he should write "I watched the hands of the clock moved," or again "The school didn't required much writing."

> The first person is the person speaking.
> Second person the person spoken to.
> Third person the person spoken about.
> And it never got to be clear how elephants and skyscrapers and geo-physics got to become persons, further complicating the problem of putting -s on the third-person verb.

What such errors reveal is that students who have learned not to trust their intuitions tend to follow instructions literally, even where intuition or common sense might be more illuminating guides. School has taught them one perverse lesson—that when they think something is right—that is, it sounds right and feels comfortable—it's probably wrong. Teachers who have such students must be far more sensitive than they have had to be in the past to the ways in which grammatical information goes awry, lest their students be in almost as much danger by heeding their instruction as by ignoring it.

My second observation on the capabilities of BW students is an extension of the first—that students for whom the grammatical features of formal English are not habitual have their greatest difficulties at the points where formal English itself appears least logical or predictable.

Throughout the world at this moment, wherever standard English is being taught as a second language—there are students struggling to master the anomalous, redundant, and utterly exasperating S-inflection on the third-person singular verb—that "simple" form that quickly becomes very complicated when you must teach it to someone who doesn't already know it. Other students are grappling with the oldest of English verbs whose regularities have been rubbed off by the centuries. [At this point in the text, Shaughnessy made a note to herself to say "more on the verb to be."]

The crucial difference between those students in other lands and the students in our classrooms with their twelve years of schooling in this country is in the quality of attention that has been given to their difficulties with English. For the most part, the native-born students, while facing many of the same confusions as second-language students in their encounters with formal written English have been made to feel embarrassed and dumb about those difficulties. Rather than reveal their confusions, they have learned to settle for not knowing, for being just "naturally" bad at English. Tentativeness, discomfort, caution—these are the attitudes that shape their sentences and select their words and lead, ironically, into deeper thickets of error than their actual competencies dictate.

But because the trail into those thickets has often been made by logic (by overgeneralizations or analogical thinking) the way out of the thicket can also be logic, the exploration of *reasons* for doing what is done and the substitution of other reasons or more complex reasons for producing the wanted forms of written English.

In short, the papers of BW students, it is true, are laden with errors, but the close observation of those errors reveals that while what students write may be wrong or inappropriate in relation to the models they must learn, their behavior is neither random nor illogical but ingeniously adaptive at one moment, linguistically conservative at another, or relentlessly albeit wrongly logical at still another. Without ignoring the goals of correctness, the teacher who studies his students' writing with such expectations is certain to discover much—the precise ways, for example, in which the grammatical forms and logics of different language systems mix, the gaps and distortions created by earlier instruction—and above all the persistent urgings of intelligence, of the drive to do things for a reason, to create systems, to survive by wit.

I said earlier that the flawed texts of student writings reveal not only the nature of their difficulties with writing but something of the nature of writing itself, particularly of that form of writing we call expository or analytical prose, the bread-and-butter writing, you might say, of the academic and occupational world.

It is especially easy, of course, to find malignant examples of such prose written by so-called educated people, and it is important to expose the ways in which it has been used to sharpen class divisions or camouflage mediocrity of thought. Still this language is the most important part of the college student's inheritance, a language that has been developed over several centuries by men and women who were discovering and exploiting the analytical powers of written English. And learning to use it—to be comfortable with its syntax, resourceful with its lexicon, and capable of exploiting its strategies for inventing and organizing—is learning not simply how to translate from one mode of language to another but how to think in new ways.

What my look at BW samples revealed, however, was how deeply unprepared such students are for analytical writing and superficially equipped we are as teachers for teaching analytical writing to students who have not already absorbed it through their immersion in literacy over the years.

Let me speak first of the syntax of their sentences. Here, of course, I found many samples of simple sentence chains joined by ands and buts—the loose coordinators of talk:

> You are told "wait we'll get in touch with you" but by the tone of voice you know you'll never hear from them but after the first time you don't lose hope but when it has happened quite a few times you do. So you say to yourself maybe I should have gone to college but then not many colleges train you for such posts but some do I have found one.

More interesting, I found much evidence of a gap between the impulse to write complex sentences and the ability to do so. Unlike the children writers with whom basic writers are frequently compared, these adult writers seemed to be struggling for a syntax that will be commensurate in complexity with their meaning. Yet invariably they mismanage complexity when they attempt it. [At this point in the text, Shaughnessy noted, "Here I gave a much longer summary of the classifications—see my book, chapter on syntax."] If they began a sentence with a subordinate clause, they would often allow that clause to crowd out the real subject of the sentence. As in this example: "For those people who do not want an education, should go on to a training course." Often, they would compress to the point of incoherence: "In high school you learn a lot for example kindergarten which I took up in high school."

They would become entangled in formal structures of comparison (such as "not only but also") or derailed by sentences that begin with "It is my belief," or rattled by whiches—in whiches, to whiches, or just ordinary whiches.

Clearly then the experience of talk has not pressed basic writers into levels of complexity that writing seems to evoke nor has it equipped them to hold long sentences in their minds as they move across the page or turn back to see what they have wrought. They move always toward the open space—as talkers do—and the record of what has gone before closes after them, like a path in the jungle.

Still, they are much closer to competency with syntax than the confusion of their first papers would suggest.

Within only a semester of rigorous sentence combining, such students are generally able to increase their syntactic fluency dramatically, creating longer and more complex structures to order. Thus a student with little spanning power at the outset of a semester had no hesitation venturing into this sentence at the end when he was asked to add adverbial modifiers to the base of this simple sentence: "The problem will be solved." "The problem will be solved," he wrote,

> with the help of the Almighty, who except for an occasional thunderstorm, reigns unmolested, high in the heavens above, when all of us, regardless of race or religious differences, can come together and study this severe problem inside out, all day and night if necessary,

and are able to come to you on that great gettin' up morning and say, "Professor Shaughnessy, we do know our verbs and adverbs."

Such sentences, of course, are gymnastic feats. They do not take us into the heart of the problem. Like vocabulary study, they increase the writer's choices without necessarily giving him the judgment to make *good* choices. And it is here, on the matter of *good* choices—not simply of words and sentences but of lines of reasoning or styles and degrees of elaboration—that the basic writer is truly at sea. For he has never been able to imagine the reader of this peculiar and arbitrary prose he is trying to master. Certain facts about the reader have drifted his way from time to time (usually through those messengers called English teachers). But like the rumors that reach characters in Kafka, there is never enough information to guide, only enough to increase the uneasiness.

Of course, if the writer were himself an experienced reader of such prose, he could imagine himself as his reader and be guided in that way, but he is not and must therefore write in the dark, so to speak, straining for the language and the rhetorical strategies he thinks his reader is waiting for—or abandoning the effort altogether and simply writing to himself.

The signs of his isolation are everywhere—in, on the one hand, that sort of written anguish students produce when they attempt to approximate what they perceive to be the academic style: "The demand for jobs," writes such a student, has "prolifically declined." The college student that is "coercively taking courses is affluently wasting his mind." (I am reminded of the student who complained about her low mark on an essay, saying that she was certain it was good because she had read it to several of her friends and they hadn't understood it.)

Or the isolation may turn the writer in upon himself, luring him into those egocentricities of style that cut off everyone except perhaps relatives and friends—unmoored pronouns, vague nouns, foundling thoughts, abandoned in the midst of passages—in short all the features of bare thought before it has been wrought for a reader.

Above all one feels the absence of deliberate strategies for the development of analytical thought and observes the powerful influence of anecdote and reverie upon the organizing faculties of students. Saturated with stories—the stories of their childhoods and adult lives, of the movies and soap operas, of the news, and even of the few books they have had to read—they have difficulty deliberately re-ordering thoughts by other strategies, holding on to thoughts that are not secured by the grip of narrative, following out the implications of ideas and then remembering to go back where they left off—satisfying, in short, the taste of that exotic reader—the academic—for specificity and proof and synthesis.

But alas, we in academia are not ourselves well prepared to describe our habits to strangers. Like McLuhan's fish who are last to know they are swimming in water—we have tended not to see our ways of winning arguments, our routines for being nasty or nice, our vocabulary for making the world cohere. We have expected somehow that doing things our way was part of the developmental scheme of things— something people just grew into, with perhaps a little prodding.

And now—in colleges throughout the country—we have sitting in our classes students for whom the task of learning to write in college is essentially an alien task. They come to us at the last moment of their formal education, expecting, needing to encounter teachers who will finally make a difference.

And through their confusion and difficulties with the tasks we give them, we begin to limn the features of the culture we talk and write in and to discover more satisfactory ways of explaining the culture. To the extent that we succeed, we will be improving the world.

For the two skills of literacy, reading has ever been judged the more important skill for ordinary citizens to acquire. Some people—English teachers among them—have even insisted that writing is a skill not everyone *can* acquire or needs to acquire, especially in this age of telephones and tapes.

To be sure, learning to write is hard work. And few, even among those who become highly skilled at it, ever seem to do it for fun, as they might watch television or read a book. Still, there is a special advantage to learning how to get one's thoughts down on a page, one that is related to the very functioning of a democracy. For one can imagine the advantages to *any* state of having a population of readers: reading remains the cheapest and most efficient technology for passing out directions and information and propaganda.

But it is in the nature of writing to encourage individuals to discover and explore their own hunches, to ponder their own words, to respect their own thoughts enough to entrust them to the written page.

Despite these benefits, or perhaps because of them, the skill of writing is essentially today a class-distributed skill. Unless they are exceptionally talented, the children of the poor learn even less about writing than about reading. They learn handwriting, perhaps, in the early grades, but many of them leave school without having learned to compose and perfect their thoughts in the medium that allows for the greatest independence of mind and exacts the greatest effort at articulation. What is worse, they leave school believing that they were in some way natively unqualified to learn to write and must now find ways of evading the various writing tasks that are certain to be posed for them in their work and in their lives as parents and citizens.

The experience of open admissions both at City University and in other universities and colleges throughout the country has not only revealed the plights of such students but demonstrated that there are no pedagogical reasons why writing should be an exclusive skill rather than a common skill among our citizenry. It simply needs to be taught. And the fact that it is not taught to the students who need it most constitutes a true crisis of literacy in this country, where being able to initiate messages is as important as being able to receive them and where the most fruitful and necessary activity is arguing rather than agreeing.

To prepare only some people to flourish in a democracy and then to argue that they are the only people with the native ability to do so is to consent to the existence, within the boundaries of what we call public education, of the most exclusive country club of all.

Open admissions has been *one* way of exposing this inequity and of trying to do something about it. My examination of student writing has not only, I hope, documented the extent of the inequity in one American city but has suggested that the damage is not irreparable, that even the flaws and errors in the writing of ill-prepared students can lead us to more enlightened teaching that respects both the problems and the remarkable possibilities of basic writing students.

WORKS CITED

Ballard, Allen B. *The Education of Black Folk: The Afro-American Struggle for Knowledge in White America*. New York: Harper & Row, 1973.

Bartholomae, David. "Released into Language: Errors, Expectations, and the Legacy of Mina Shaughnessy." *The Territory of Language*. Ed. Donald A. McQuade. Carbondale: Southern Illinois UP, 1986.

Bernstein, Alison. Rev. of *Errors and Expectations,* by Mina P. Shaughnessy. *School Review* Feb. 1978: 292–94.

Bizzell, Patricia. *Academic Discourse and Critical Consciousness*. Pittsburgh: U of Pittsburgh P, 1992.

Bruffee, Kenneth A. "A New Intellectual Frontier." *The Chronicle of Higher Education* 27 Feb. 1978: 40.

Curtis, C. Michael. Rev. of *Errors and Expectations,* by Mina P. Shaughnessy. *The Atlantic Monthly* Sept. 1977: 75.

DeMott, Benjamin. *Close Imagining: An Introduction to Literature*. New York: St. Martin's P, 1988.

———. Foreword. *American Tongue and Cheek: A Populist Guide to Language.* By Jim Quinn. New York: Pantheon Books, 1980.

———. "Mina Shaughnessy: Meeting Challenges." *The Nation* 9 Dec. 1978: 645–48.

Emig, Janet. "Mina Pendo Shaughnessy." *College Composition and Communication* Feb. 1979: 37–38.

Fiske, Edward B. "City U. a Remedial Writing Leader." *The New York Times,* 4 Apr. 1977: 1.

Fosdick, Raymond B. *Adventure in Giving: The Story of the General Education Board*. New York: Harper & Row, 1962.

———. *John D. Rockefeller, Jr.: A Portrait*. New York: Harper, 1956.

Gross, Theodore L. "How to Kill a College: The Private Papers of a Campus Dean." *Saturday Review* 4 Feb. 1978: 12–20.

———. "Chairman's Report." City College *Department of English Newsletter* Jan. 1972: 1–4.

Heller, Louis G. *The Death of the American University.* New Rochelle: Arlington House, 1973.

Hirsch, E. D. Opening Remarks at an MLA Session in Memory of Mina Shaughnessy, San Francisco, Dec. 1979.

Howe, Irving. Eulogy to Mina P. Shaughnessy. New York, 8 Dec. 1978.

Hungiville, Maurice. Rev. of *Errors and Expectations,* by Mina P. Shaughnessy. *The Chronicle of Higher Education* 4 Apr. 1977: 18.

Kohl, Herbert. "Teaching the 'Unteachable': The Story of an Experiment in Children's Writing." *The New York Review of Books.* 17 Nov. 1966: 26.

Kriegel, Leonard. Eulogy to Mina P. Shaughnessy. New York, 8 Dec. 1978.

———. *Working Through: A Teacher's Journey in the Urban University.* New York: Saturday Review Press, 1972.

Letter to a Teacher by the Schoolboys of Barbiana. Trans. Nora Rossi and Tom Cole. New York: Vintage Books, 1971.

"Literacy." *The New Yorker* 6 Nov. 1978: 36–37.

Lyons, Robert. "Mina Shaughnessy." *Traditions of Inquiry.* Ed. John Brereton. New York: Oxford UP, 1985.

———. "Mina Shaughnessy and the Teaching of Writing." Conference of the CUNY Association of Writing Supervisors, 4 May 1979.

Marshak, Robert E. *Problems and Prospects of an Urban Public University.* New York: City College, 1973.

McQuade, Donald A., ed. *The Territory of Language.* Carbondale: Southern Illinois UP, 1986.

Neal, Patricia. *As I Am: An Autobiography.* New York: Simon & Shuster, 1988.

Pace, Eric. "Mina P. Shaughnessy, 54, Expert in Remedial Writing at City U." *The New York Times* 17 Nov. 1978, D1+.

Quinn, Edward. Eulogy to Mina P. Shaughnessy. New York, 8 Dec. 1978.

Rich, Adrienne. "Teaching Language in Open Admissions." *On Lies, Secrets, and Silence.* New York: W.W. Norton, 1979.

———. Eulogy to Mina P. Shaughnessy. New York, 8 Dec. 1978.

Shaughnessy, Mina P. "The English Professor's Malady." *Journal of Basic Writing* Spring 1994: 117–24.

———. "Teaching Basic Writing." *Journal of Basic Writing* Spring 1994: 103–16.

———. "Statement on Criteria for Writing Proficiency." *Journal of Basic Writing* Fall/Winter 1980: 115–19.

———. "Basic Writing." Modern Literature Conference, Michigan State University, Oct. 1977.

———. *Errors and Expectations: A Guide for the Teacher of Basic Writing.* New York: Oxford UP, 1977.

———. "Some Needed Research on Writing." *College Composition and Communication* Dec. 1977: 317–20.

———. "Diving In: An Introduction to Basic Writing." *College Composition and Communication* Oct. 1976: 234–39.

———. Introduction. *Journal of Basic Writing* Fall/Winter 1976: 1.

———. "The Miserable Truth." *The Congressional Record* 9 Sept. 1976: E4955–56.

———. "Speaking and Doublespeaking about Standards." California State University and Colleges Conference on Improvement of Student Writing Skills, Los Angeles, 3 June 1976.

———. "Basic Writing." *Teaching Composition: Ten Bibliographical Essays.* Ed. Gary Tate. Forth Worth: Texas Christian UP, 1975.

———. Introduction. *Journal of Basic Writing* Spring 1975: 3.

———. "Open Admissions and the Disadvantaged Teacher." *College Composition and Communication* Dec. 1973: 401–04.

———. "A Second Report: Open Admissions." City College *Department of English Newsletter* Jan. 1972: 5–8.

———. "Reason under the Ailanthus." *A Critical Edition of Henry James' Washington Square.* Ed. Gerald Willen. New York: Crowell, 1969.

———. "Milton." *Hofstra Review* Spring 1967: 3.

———. "Helene." *The Golden Magazine.* Sept. 1966, 3–9; Oct. 1966, 21–27; Nov. 1966, 63–67.

Staff. *Resource* (newsletter of the CUNY Instructional Resource Center) Apr. 1979: 1–2.

Stotsky, Sandra. Rev. of *Errors and Expectations,* by Mina P. Shaughnessy. *Harvard Educational Review* Dec. 1977: 594–97.

Traub, James. *City on A Hill: Testing the American Dream at City College.* Reading: Addison-Wesley, 1994.

Updike, John. "Still Afraid of Being Caught." *The New York Times Magazine* 8 Oct. 1995: 55.

Viscusi, Margo. Interview with Mina P. Shaughnessy (unpublished). New York, 29 Sept. and 17 Oct. 1977.

Wilkins, Lottie. Eulogy to Mina P. Shaughnessy. New York, 8 Dec. 1978.

INDEX

Abercrombie, H. L. M., 127
Academic discourse, 100, 287–289, 294
Academic Turmoil (Gross), 228
Accolades, for MPS
  by Andrew Young, 183–184
  at CAWS conference, 244
  by NCTE, 233–234
  by *New York Times, The*, 157–158
  by President Carter, 230–231
Acting, 18–19, 25–27, 30, 63–64
Addresses
  "As Yet We Lack . . . Notes on Open Admissions as 'A New York Tragedy'" (DeMott), 225–227
  "Basic Writing" (MPS), 209, 299–310
  "Dialect and Second Language Characteristics in Writing" (Reed), 176
  "Diving In: An Introduction to Basic Writing" (MPS), 162–166, 255–262
  "English Professor's Malady, The" (MPS), 291–298

"Examining Textbooks" (Weiner and Wright), 176
"Grammar in the Teaching of Writing" (D'Eloia), 176
"Mina Shaughnessy and the Teaching of Writing" (Lyons), 244
"Miserable Truth, The" (MPS), 180, 263–269
"Redefining the Literature of the Writing Course" (McQuade), 176
"Some Needed Research in Writing" (MPS), 193, 284–290
"Speaking and Doublespeaking of Standards" (MPS), 192, 270–278
"Teacher and Student in the Classroom" (Bruffee), 176
"Teacher and Student outside the Classroom" (Lyons and MPS), 176
"Teaching Forms of Non-Analytical Writing" (Ponsot), 176
"Writing as a Process: The Stages of Composition" (Emig), 176

Note: The abbreviation MPS is used in subentries to represent Mina P. Shaughnessy. Family relationships that appear parenthetically are relative to the biographee.

Advanced degrees, 94–95, 116–117,
134–137, 151, 174–175
*Adventure in Giving: The Story of the
General Education Board* (Fosdick),
77
Advisory positions, held by MPS
on Advisory Committee for
Alternatives to the Revolving
Door, 169
with FIPSE, 169–170, 203
with Modern Language Associa-
tion, 203
with National Institute of
Education, 158–159
with NCTE, 142, 144
African Americans
in City College (CUNY) adminis-
tration, 143
education in South, 77
in Open Admissions, 91–92
American Scholar, 131
Anatomy of Judgment, The
(Abercrombie), 127
Art, essentials of, 23
As I Am (Neal), 25–27
Association of Departments of
English, 205
Atlantic Monthly, The, 197, 198
*Attitudes and Motivation in Second-
Language Learning* (Gardner and
Lambert), 127

Ballard, Allen B., 143
Ballet lessons, 167
Bambara, Toni Cade, 107
Barnes, Douglas, 127
Bartholomae, David, 165, 190–191
Basic writing
crises of, 263–264
curriculum development for, 117
developmental scales for teachers,
162–163
frontier of, 159–161
introduction to, 255–262

MPS on, 159–161, 202–203,
245–246
MPS's stature in field, 141–142
potentials of, 108–109
program preparation for, 96
self-critiquing by students,
210–211
study of, 97, 120–122
and teacher motivation, 205–206,
209, 291–298
"Basic Writing" (MPS)
discussion of, 159–161, 209
text of, 299–310
Basic Writing Program (City
College)
financial cuts to, 172–173
MPS as director of, 126
stature of, 120
Bauer, Florence, 41–42, 54
Bay Area Writing Project Group,
203
Benedict, Ruth, 119
Berger, Leslie
hiring of MPS, 87–89
and Instructional Resource
Center, 152–153
at presidential recognition of MPS,
230
reflections on MPS, 95, 102–103
support of MPS, 101, 174
Bernstein, Alison, 169, 199
Berthoff, Ann, 171
Bible Presbyterian Church, 34–35
Bizzell, Patricia, 245–246
*Black Aesthetic, Freedom and Beyond,
The* (Gayle), 143
Black and Puerto Rican Student
Caucus, 114
Black Boy (Wright), 128
Blackburn, Paul, 107
Black Hills (South Dakota), 1–2,
15–16
Blacks, *See* African Americans
Bloom, Benjamin S., 127

Bloom, Harold, 185
Bonhoeffer, Dietrich, 107–108
Brandt, Alan, 46–48, 53, 220–221,
   235
Brandt, Mia, 60
Brandt, Priscilla
   dissatisfaction of, 61
   European sojourn of, 53
   health of, 173
   at MPS's death, 235
   during MPS's illness, 220–221,
      233
   at MPS's wedding, 46–48
Bread Loaf Conference (Vermont),
   246
Brereton, John, 203, 244
Britton, James, 118, 129
Brown, James I., 127
Bruffee, Kenneth, 119, 176, 180,
   198–199
Buckley, William, 200–201
Building Writing Skills (Casty), 127

Califano, Joseph A., 203
California State University, 206
Campbell, Jean, 114–115
Carnegie Foundation
   grant from, 122, 124–127
   interview with MPS, 214–218
Carter, Jimmy, 67, 230–231
Casty, Alan, 127
Catholicism, 209, 230
CAWS (CUNY Association of
   Writing Supervisors), 119, 137,
   180–183, 244
CCNY, *See* City College (of
   CUNY)
Change, 197, 199
Chavarria-Aguilar, Oscar, 128
Choice Magazine, 197
Christensen, Francis, 127
Christian Beacon, 34
Chronicle of Higher Education, The,
   197, 198–199, 225

Circumlocutions, 274
City College (of CUNY)
   creative writing program of,
      107
   English Department direction at,
      133–135
   financial problems of, 113–114,
      172
   MPS's reflections on, 212–213
   125th Anniversary Medallion of,
      120
   polarization over Open Admis-
      sions, 201
   politics of, 91–92, 148–152
   Pre-Baccalaureate Program of,
      87–90
City on a Hill (Traub), 172
City University of New York
   (CUNY)
   "Colloqium on the Teaching of
      Writing," 175
   financial problems of, 113–114,
      172, 178–179, 184, 194
   Graduate Center of, 174–175
   Gross article on, 227–228
   hierarchy of colleges, 87
   holistic grading at, 193
   Instructional Resource Center at,
      152–153, 168, 171–172, 176
   Office of Academic Development,
      117
   Open Admissions inauguration at,
      114
   polarization over Open Admis-
      sions, 201
   politics of, 91–92
   Task Force on Writing, 192
Close Imagining (DeMott), 245
Cobb, Jonathan, 119
Coles, Robert, 197
*College Composition and Communica-
tion*
   "Diving In: An Introduction to
      Basic Writing," 166–167

eulogy for MPS, 240–242
"Open Admissions and the
 Disadvantaged Teacher," 145
review of *Errors and Expectations*,
 197
"Some Needed Research in
 Writing," 193
College English, 197
"Colloqium on the Teaching of
 Writing" (graduate course), 175
Colum, Mary, 32
Colum, Padraic, 32
Columbia University, 32, 34, 36–37,
 51–52
Committee on Teaching and Its
 Evaluation in Composition, 203
Committee on the Teachers' Right
 to Teach (NCTE), 118
Communication, oral vs. written,
 72–73
Competence
 continuum of, 181–182, 192, 268,
 278
 and syntax command, 282
 territories of, 279–283
*Composing Processes of Twelfth Graders,
 The* (Emig), 119–120, 127, 129
Composition
 essays on, 159
 against literature, 102, 133–135
 MPS's stature in field, 175
 promotion of, 166
 research in, 289
Computer study, of error frequency,
 126–127
Conference of Writing Supervisors,
 180–183
Conference on College Composition and Communication, 142,
 144, 145, 203
Conference on Improvement of
 Student Writing Skills, 192
Confrontation, 96
Congressional Record, The, 183–184

Continuum of competence,
 181–182, 192, 268, 278
CONVERTING THE NATIVES,
 162, 257–258
Corbett, Edward, 166, 198, 203,
 208, 240
Correctness, criteria for, 282
Creative Behavior Guidebook
 (Parnes), 128
*Critical Edition of Henry James'
 Washington Square* (Willen), 82
Criticism, 111
Cross, K. Patricia, 169
Culture, 111, 205, 294
CUNY, *See* City University of New
 York (CUNY)
Curtis, C. Michael, 198
Curtis, Charlotte, 205

David H. Russell Award for
 Distinguished Research, 233–234
Davis, Allan, 88–89
Death of the American University, The
 (Heller), 94
DeBono, Edward, 127
Deighton, Lee C., 127
D'Eloia, Sarah, 98, 128, 144
Democracy, in education, 139
DeMott, Benjamin, 168, 197,
 225–227, 245
Department of Health, Education,
 and Welfare, 145, 203
Dialect interference, 189, 267
Dialects, 216–217, 259, 267
Disadvantaged students, study of,
 120–122
Dissatisfaction, as necessary prelude,
 62–65
Dissent (journal), 168
DIVING IN, 163, 262
"Diving In: An Introduction to
 Basic Writing" (MPS)
 discussion of, 162–166
 text of, 255–262

Doctoral degrees, *See* Advanced
   degrees
Double standards, 278, *See also*
   Standards
Downey, Marian J., 34
Dreams, 147–148
Duffey, Joseph, 230–232
Dunham, Alden, 125

Eagles Mere (Pennsylvania), 25–27
East End Avenue apartment, 200
Education
   for blacks in South, 77
   democracy in system of, 139
   failure of secondary schools, 137,
      178, 180–181, 263
   frontier of, 159–161
   MPS's stature in field, 158, 163
   vertical integration of system, 202
Education of Black Folk, The
   (Ballard), 143
Efficient Reading (Brown), 127
Elbow, Peter, 131, 185, 200
Elitism, 88, 135
Emig, Janet
   at CAWS conference, 180
   in *College Composition and
      Communication*, 171
   *Composing Processes of Twelfth
      Graders, The*, 119–120, 127
   as draft reader for *Errors and
      Expectations*, 129–130
   eulogy for MPS, 240–242
   friendship of, 120
   at National Institute of Education
      conference, 203
   "Writing as a Process: The Stages
      of Composition," 176
End of Education, The (Wagner), 94,
   199
English as a Second Language
   (ESL), 164
"English Professor's Malady, The"
   (MPS)

discussion of, 205–206
text of, 291–298
Epes, Mary, 129
Error frequency, computer study of,
   126–127
Errors
   codification of, 189
   concept of, 188
   correction potential of, 127
   exploration of, 259–260
   exposure of, 132–133
   as *Journal of Basic Writing* topic,
      132
   of linguistic habit, 286
   MPS's isolation of, 245
   revelations of, 302–305
   student understanding of, 281
   territory of, 272–277
Errors and Expectations
   (Shaughnessy)
   acknowledgments in, 190
   bibliographic citations in, 127–128
   and Carnegie Foundation grant,
      126
   chapbook for, 130–133
   colleague citations in, 128–129
   dedication of, 194
   drafts of, 129–130, 158
   evolution of, 115, 117, 118–119
   manuscript submission of, 158
   marketing of, 193–194
   MPS's description of, 186–187
   praise of, 66, 197–200, 225–227
   prose of, 195–196
   publication of, 184–191, 196
   receipt of Russell Award,
      233–234
   reviews of, 197–200, 225
   sabbatical to complete, 144
   success of, 199, 246
   title alternatives for, 194
ESL (English as a Second Language), 164
Essays, by MPS

"Basic Writing," 159–161,
    299–310
on James's *Washington Square*, 36
"Open Admissions and the
    Disadvantaged Teacher," 131,
    145–146, 196, 249–254
"Other Side of Literacy, The,"
    203–204
"Reading Comprehension and the
    High School Graduate," 159
"Reason under the Ailanthus," 82
"Some Needed Research in
    Writing," 193, 284–290
"Some New Approaches toward
    Teaching," 117–118
"Statement on Criteria for Writing
    Proficiency," 192–193, 279–283
submissions of, 66, 78–79
"Tactual Response," 23–24
"Teaching Basic Writing,"
    117–118
Essential boldness, 62, 64

Failure, 109–110, 121
Farrell, Tom, 137, 175–176
Feminist movement, 144
Finley Student Center, destruction
    by fire, 114
Firing Line, 200–201
Fiske, Edward B., 198
Flower, Linda, 203
Fosdick, Betty, 39, 54, 103, 147,
    148, 200
Fosdick, Harry Emerson, 38
Fosdick, Raymond B.
  background of, 38–39
  death of, 148
  friendship of, 54
  on General Education Board
    history, 76–77
  recommendation of MPS, 52
  on Rockefeller biography, 42, 54,
    67
4C's, *See* Conference on College

Composition and Communica-
    tion
Freire, Paolo, 110
French, Marilyn, 80–81, 104
Freud, Sigmund, 288
Fries, Charles, 127
Fund for the Improvement of Post-
    Secondary Education (FIPSE),
    169–170, 199

Gallagher, Buell, 114
Gardner, R. C., 127
Gayle, Addison, 143
Gender-neutral pronouns, 191–192
General Education Board, 77
Gibaldi, Joseph, 203
Golden, Stephanie, 191
Golden Magazine, The, 35, 83
Gould, Gerald, 128
Gracie Terrace apartment, 70
Grading, holistic, 192–193, 279
Grading alternatives, 178
Grammar
  conventional forms of, 277
  D'Eloia on, 176
  and dialect, 217
  inadequate explanation of, 303
  irrationalities of, 258
  in *Letter to a Teacher*, 110–111
  students' attitude toward, 275
  variant forms of, 272–274
  videotape series on, 144
Graves, Richard, 171
Gray, Barbara Quint, 98, 99–100,
    128, 144
Gray, Jim, 210
Gross, Ted
  Academic Turmoil, 228
  on City University of New York,
    227–228
  on composition vs. literature,
    133–135
  as English Department chair, 101
  on MPS's qualifications, 151

on MPS's value to City College
(CUNY), 140–142
and National Center for Literacy,
201–202
recommendation of MPS as dean,
148–152
at Rockefeller Foundation
conference, 225
*Growth and Structure of the English
Language* (Jesperson), 127
GUARDING THE TOWER, 162,
256
*Guide for Teachers of College English,
A*, 117
Gumperz, John, 203

Halsted, Bella, 172
Hammond, James, 219–220
*Handbook on Formative and
Summative Evaluation of Student
Learning* (Bloom, Hastings, and
Madau), 127
Hanna, Jean S., 127
Hanna, Paul R., 127
Hannah (South Dakota), 14
Harvard Educational Review, 197, 198
Hastings, J. Thomas, 127
Healy, Mary, 203
Healy, Timothy, 168, 202
Hearst, William Randolph, 2
Heath, Shirley Brice, 203
Heller, Louis, 94
Hellman, Lillian, 27
Hempstead (Long Island), 80
Heston, Charlton, 19
Hidden Injuries of Class, The (Sennett
and Cobb), 119
Hirsch, E. D., 163–164, 203, 207,
244
Hodges, Richard E., 127
Hofstra Review, 93
Hofstra University, 80–81
Holistic grading, 192–193, 279
Hollingsworth, Alan, 203

Homesickness, 35, 55–56
Howe, Irving
background of, 167–168
eulogy for MPS, 236–238,
239–240
at presidential recognition of MPS,
230, 232
"How to Kill a College" (Gross),
227–228
Hungiville, Maurice, 198
Hunter College, 76–78, 140–143,
179–180
Hypercorrections, 274, 302

Independence, 76
Instructional Resource Center
creation of, 152–153
financial cuts at, 176
MPS as director of, 168, 171–172
staff on MPS's death, 242–243
Intellectual arrogance, 110

James, Henry, 21, 36, 82, 131
Jensen, Georgia, 8, 10, 36
Jensen, Kathy, 36
Jesperson, Otto, 97, 127
Jobs, held by MPS, *See* Positions
John D. Rockefeller, Jr.: A Portrait
(Fosdick), 67
Johnson, Charles (uncle), 3
Johnson, Edith, 7, 15
Johnson, John (uncle), 11
Johnson, Mina (aunt), 3–4
Johnson, Peter (grandfather), 3, 4
Johnson, Ruby Alma, *See* Pendo,
Ruby Alma (mother)
Johnson, Susanna Jane (grand-
mother), 3
Jonathan Livingston Seagull (Bach),
131
Jordan, June, 107
Journal, of MPS, 11–12, 24
Journal of Basic Writing
and CUNY budget cuts, 184

editorial board of, 98
on errors, 188
on gender-neutral pronouns, 192
after MPS's death, 246
premiere issue of, 128, 132
"Some New Approaches toward
Teaching," 117
Joyce, James, 32, 131
Joyce, Nora, 32

Kauvar, Gerald, 100, 128
Koch, Kenneth, 127
Kohl, Herbert, 87
Kosinski, Jerzy, 131
Kozol, Jonathan, 197
Krause, Alvina
at Eagles Mere, 25–26
at Northwestern University, 19,
20, 22–23, 25
recommendation of MPS, 27–28
Kriegel, Leonard
eulogy for MPS, 236, 237, 239
during MPS's illness, 218, 224,
229
at presidential recognition of MPS,
230
reflections on MPS, 94–95, 96–97
support of MPS, 101, 122
Working Through, 96
Krishna, Valerie, 100, 128

Labov, William, 97, 127
Lambert, W. E., 127
Lane, Maggie, 221
Langer, Susanne, 128
Language
arbitrariness of forms, 272–274,
301, 302
dynamic nature of, 110, 276
and equality, 111
influences on, 273
spoken vs. written, 261, 267
Language, the Learner and the School
(Barnes), 127

Language and Public Policy (Rank),
128
Language in the Inner City (Labov),
127
Language (Sapir), 128
Laurence, Patricia, 98–99, 128, 137
Leachman, Cloris, 19
Lead (South Dakota), 1–5, 7,
18–19, 24
Letters and Papers from Prison
(Bonhoeffer), 107–108
*Letter to a Teacher by the Schoolboys of
Barbiani*, 110–111
Libo, Kenneth, 128
Lindsay, John V., 91
Linguistic diversity, 267
*Linguistic Guide to Language Learning,
A* (Moulton), 128
Linguistics, 175–176, 187
Literacy
crisis of, 210
dominant codes of, 276
MPS essay on, 203–205
national press on, 264
pedagogies of, 284–285
proposal for National Center for
Literacy, 201–202
reading vs. writing, 296–297,
309–310
Literary criticism, 215–216
Literature, against composition, 102,
133–135
Little Foxes, The, 27
Lives of the Cell (Thomas), 230
Lloyd-Jones, Richard, 203
Luce, Clare Boothe, 73–74, 76
Luce, Henry R., 73
Lunsford, Andrea, 167, 187
Lutheran Church, influence of, 12,
17
Lyons, Bob
at CAWS conference, 180
on errors, 188
on *Errors and Expectations*, 158

reflections on MPS, 127, 161–162, 244–245
"Teacher and Student outside the Classroom," 176
Lyons, Bridget, 158

McBurney, James, 27
Mcdonald, Dwight, 66–67
McGill, Dorothea, 106–107
McGraw Hill, 69, 70–71, 76
McQuade, Don, 176, 180, 245
Madau, George F., 127
Maiz, Marilyn
  friendship of, 105–106, 143
  Journal of Basic Writing oversight of, 246
  as MPS's administrative assistant, 173
  during MPS's illness, 218–219, 220–222, 224, 229
  at presidential recognition of MPS, 231
  reflections on MPS, 124–125
  tribute to MPS, 246–247
Macrorie, Ken, 131
Marshak, Robert, 148–152, 228
Martin, Nancy, 129, 131
Mellon, John C., 128
Michigan State University, 209
Miller, Susan, 187
Milton, John, 36
Mimmis, Jack H., 132–133
"Mina's Minions," 90, 140
Mind: An Essay on Human Feeling (Langer), 128
Mining industry, 2–4, 12–13, 14
Minority students
  at City College (CUNY), 77
  at CUNY, 91
  demands made by, 114
  learning needs of, 135
  in Open Admissions, 151–152
  in Project NOAH, 80
"Miserable Truth, The" (MPS)
  discussion of, 180
  text of, 263–269
Modern Language Association (MLA)
  Committee on Teaching and Related Professional Activities, 203
  Research in Writing Panel, 193
  San Francisco conference of, 162–166
  session in honor of MPS, 244
Modern Literature Conference, 209
Moffett, James, 128
Mother-tongue interference, 267
Motivation, 75–76, 111
Moulton, William G., 128
Munson, Thurman, 229–230, 238
Murray, Donald, 171
Music, 9, 12, 18

Naples (Italy), 56
Nation, The, 197, 225, 226
National Bible Institute, 34–35
National Center for Literacy, proposal for, 201–202
National Council of Teachers of English (NCTE)
  Committee on the Teachers' Right to Teach, 118
  Conference on College Composition and Communication, 142, 144, 145, 203
  David H. Russell Award of, 233–234
  Growth in Writing conference, 144
  MPS on Executive Committee, 142, 144
  publications of, 120
National Endowment for the Humanities, 230
National Humanities Faculty, 203
National Institute of Education, 145, 158, 203, 207–208

National Writing Project, 203, 210
Native Americans, 1–2
Native Son (Wright), 117
NCTE, *See* National Council of Teachers of English (NCTE)
Neal, Patricia, 19, 25–26, 61
New Think (DeBono), 127
New York City
  financial crisis of, 172
  polarization over Open Admissions, 201
  politics of, 91, 151
  relocation to, 29–30, 32
New Yorker, The, 232–233
New York Review of Books, The, 87
New York Times, The
  articles on MPS, 157–158, 163
  obituary of MPS, 235
  review of *Errors and Expectations*, 197, 198
  submissions to, 203–204
Nicknames, 76, 115
Nontraditional students, 77
Northwestern University, 19–24, 27–28
Notes Toward a New Rhetoric (Christensen), 127

Office space, 93, 173
O'Hare, Frank, 128
O'Hare, Kathleen
  on Catholicism, 209, 230
  at MPS's death, 235
  during MPS's illness, 233
  reflections on MPS, 220, 221
Oliver, Bill, 185
Olson, David, 203
O'Neill, Eugene, 27
Ong, Walter, 176
Open Admissions
  accomplishments of, 181–183, 266–268
  accountability debate over, 249–254

allies of, 107
beginnings of, 88, 114
black students in, 91–92
case study in, 251–252
conflicting goals of, 121
criticism of, 226
defense of, 177–178
effect on participants, 198–199
ethnic composition of population, 137–138, 151
field research in, 125
Firing Line debate on, 200–201
MPS's stature in field, 124–125, 130
national indifference to, 264
opponents of, 78, 94–95, 134, 152
people connected with, 98–100, 108–109
against political practicalities, 195
"Open Admissions and the Disadvantaged Teacher" (MPS)
  discussion of, 131, 145–146, 196
  text of, 249–254
"Opening the Door" (Farrell), 137
Overseas School (Rome, Italy), 57
Oxford University Press
  marketing of *Errors and Expectations*, 193–194
  popularity of *Errors and Expectations*, 198
  publication agreement with, 184–185, 187
  royalties from, 191–192
  submission of *Errors and Expectations*, 158

Pace, Eric, 235
Parental influence, and values, 12
Parnes, Sidney J., 128
Patterns of Culture (Benedict), 119
Pedagogical imagination, 218, 269
Pedagogy of the Oppressed (Freire), 110
Penale, Anthony, 89–90

Pendo, Albert (father)
  background of, 2–3
  with family, 9–11
  health of, 85–86, 122, 147,
    207–208
  humor of, 5, 35
  marriage of, 3–4, 122
  during MPS's illness, 233
  relationship with Don
    Shaughnessy, 49–50, 51, 72
  remarriage of, 158
  at Spearfish ranch, 24, 34–35,
    83–84, 87
Pendo, Elin (grandmother), 3
Pendo, Eliza (stepmother), 158, 207,
  233
Pendo, Esther (aunt), 8
Pendo, Florence (aunt), 7–8
Pendo, George (brother)
  birth of, 1, 5
  childhood of, 7, 9, 10, 12–13, 15
  in college, 19
  marriage of, 24–25
  during MPS's illness, 235
Pendo, Mina Jeanne (niece), 35, 61
Pendo, Norma (sister-in-law),
  24–25, 36
Pendo, Rado (grandfather), 3, 67
Pendo, Ralph (uncle), 3
Pendo, Ruby Alma (mother)
  background of, 3–4
  birth of MPS, 1
  death of, 156–158
  dedication of *Errors and Expecta-
    tions*, 194
  with family, 9–11
  health of, 147, 153–156
  journals of, 83
  marriage of, 3–4, 122
  memorabilia of, 5–6, 22
  at Spearfish ranch, 24, 34–35, 72,
    83–84
  teaching career of, 8, 35–36
Perl, Sondra, 180

Perman, Amelia, 7, 15
Perrit, Johnny, 16
Perry, William, 262
Personal Knowledge (Polanyi), 128
Peterson, Susanna Jane, *See* Johnson,
  Susanna Jane (grandmother)
Petrie, Ann, 98, 99
Peyron, Elin, *See* Pendo, Elin
  (grandmother)
Poetry, by MPS
  in childhood, 18
  "Evening schools are not for
    winnowing," 79–80
  "For Alice on her Fortieth
    Birthday," 228–229
  on her illness, 224–225
  on Milton, 36, 79, 93
  "On Re-reading a Sophomore
    Report on Shakespeare's *Hamlet*,"
    81
  on passion for literature, 95
  "The Invalid," 223
Polanyi, Michael, 128, 287
Politics, 91–92, 111, 112, 139,
  148–152
Ponsot, Marie, 129, 176
Positions, held by MPS
  as associate dean at CUNY, 153
  at City College, 87–90
  at City College (CUNY), 116, 143
  directorship of SEEK, 89–90
  on General Education Board
    history, 76–77
  at Hofstra University, 80–81,
    86–87
  at Hunter College, 76–78
  as Instructional Resource Center
    director, 152–153, 171–172
  at McGraw Hill, 69, 70–71, 76
  at National Bible Institute, 34–35
  on Riverside church project, 60,
    68
  on Rockefeller biography, 38–43,
    54, 67–68

at Shelton College, 36
as tutor at Hunter College,
    179–180
Practical Criticism (Richards),
    128
Pre-Baccalaureate Program (City
    College), 87–90, *See also* SEEK,
    (Search for Education, Elevation
    and Knowledge)
Prentice-Hall, 158, 185
Presentations, *See* Addresses
*Problems and Prospects of an Urban
    University* (Marshak), 149
Production functions, 131
Project NOAH, 80
Pronouns, and gender neutrality,
    191–192
Prose, by MPS
    in childhood, 18
    for children, 83
    "Helene" (*The Golden Magazine*),
        35
Protests, 100, 114
Publication, necessity of, 136
Public schools, failure of, 137, 178,
    180–181, 263
Punctuation
    in correctness criteria, 282
    idiosyncratic schemes of, 302
    inadequate explanation of, 303
    inventiveness in, 300
    student examples of, 304

Quinn, Ed
    eulogy for MPS, 236, 238
    on *Firing Line*, 200–201
    during MPS's illness, 222–223,
        224, 229
    in New York City financial crisis,
        172
    at presidential recognition of MPS,
        230
    reflections on MPS, 100, 101
    support of MPS, 122, 150

Racial discrimination, 106
Racism, 110, 217
Raimes, Ann, 164, 179
Rank, Hugh, 128
Reed, Carol, 176
"Released into Language: Errors,
    Expectations, and the Legacy of
    Mina Shaughnessy"
    (Bartholomae), 165
Religion
    in childhood, 12
    interest in Catholicism, 209, 230
    opinions on, 22, 41, 53
    reawakened interest in, 170
Remedial programs
    at college level, 78
    at CUNY, 88
    evaluation of, 272
    logistics of, 92–93
Research
    on composition, 289
    nature of, 213
    on Open Admissions, 125
    on writing, 193, 284–290, 299
Resource, 179, 242–243
Rhetoric, strategies of, 279
Rich, Adrienne
    at City College (CUNY), 107
    eulogy for MPS, 237, 239
    friendship of, 143
    reflections on MPS, 108–109, 118,
        171
    "Teaching Language in Open
        Admissions," 108
    tribute to MPS, 247
Richards, I. A., 128, 131
Riots, over minority demands, 114
Rizzo, Betty, 98, 128
Rockefeller, John D., Jr., 38–42, 54
Rockefeller Foundation conference,
    225–227
Roe, Kathy, 128
Rome (Italy), 55–60, 69
Rondinone, Peter, 201

Rosen, David, 131–132
Rosenthal, Marilyn, 187
Russell Award, 233–234

Salzburg (Austria), 66–67
Samuel Rubin Foundation, 80
Sapir, Edward, 128
Saturday Review, 227–228
Schlesinger, Alvin, 104, 113
Scholes, Robert, 203
School Review, 197, 199
Scott Foresman, 178, 185
Secondary schools, failure of, 137,
    178, 180–181, 263
SEEK (Search for Education,
    Elevation and Knowledge)
  black students in, 91–92
  budget strains on, 113–114
  expansion of, 104–105
  facilities for, 109
  growth in population, 114–115
  Kriegel on, 96–97
  logistics of, 92–93
  MPS's directorship of, 89
  MPS's interactions with staff,
    109–110
  opposition to, 93–95, 114
  politics of, 112
Self-confidence, 76
*Semantics: An Introduction to the
    Science of Meaning* (Ullmann),
    128
Sennett, Richard, 119
*Sentence Combining: A Composing
    Book* (Strong), 128
Sentence Combining and Sentencecraft
    (O'Hare), 128
Shaughnessy, Don (husband)
  at Columbia University, 70
  courtship of MPS, 43–46
  at MPS's death, 235
  during MPS's illness, 223, 233
  in New York City administration,
    91

relationship with Pendo family,
    49–50, 51, 72
remarriage of, 246
scholarship fund of, 246
separation from MPS, 75, 76, 104,
    123, 148, 170
in State Department, 104
wedding to MPS, 45
Shaughnessy, Mina Pendo
  beauty of, 9–10, 102–103, 164,
    167
  chair positions held by, 144–145
  childbearing inability of, 74–75
  childhood of, 1, 6–11, 12–16
  clothing passion of, 30–31, 33, 39,
    73–74, 80, 192
  courtship of, 43–46
  death of, 235
  eulogies for, 236–243
  family relationship of, 82–83,
    86
  health of, 74, 106, 200
  in high school, 10, 16–19
  humor of, 192, 222
  letters to friends, 41–42, 51–55,
    56–60, 62–66, 69, 104–105
  letters to parents, 33, 43–45,
    46–49, 52, 73–74, 116–117,
    122–123
  literature preferences of, 61, 95
  personal life of, 170–171
  postgraduate studies of, 32, 34,
    36–38, 51–52
  pro-Semitism of, 53
  separation from husband, 75, 76,
    104, 123, 148, 170
  terminal illness of, 200, 206–208,
    214, 218–225, 229–235
  undergraduate studies of, 19–24,
    27–28, 30–32, 32, 34
  wedding of, 45, 46–48
  work efficiency of, 124, 126, 129,
    149
Sheed, Wilfred, 148

Shelton College, 34, *See also* National Bible Institute
Shuy, Roger, 203
S-inflection, 259, 305
Skurnick, Blanche, 97–98, 122, 128, 137, 144
Smith, Virginia, 169
"Some Needed Research in Writing" (MPS)
  discussion of, 193
  text of, 284–290
SOUNDING THE DEPTHS, 163, 259–262
"Speaking and Doublespeaking about Standards" (MLS)
  discussion of, 192
  text of, 270–278
Spearfish ranch
  burial of MPS, 236
  deeded to MPS, 84
  descriptions of, 83–85
  purchase of, 24, 34–35
Speeches, *See* Addresses
Speech training, 21–22
Spelling
  as competence criterion, 282
  idiosyncratic schemes of, 302
  inadequate explanation of, 303
  inventiveness in, 300
  skill growth in, 286–287
Spelling: Structure and Strategies (Hanna, Hanna, and Hodges), 127
Standards, 121, 192, 271–278
"Statement on Criteria for Writing Proficiency" (MPS)
  discussion of, 192–193
  text of, 279–283
State of Literacy in America (proposed by MPS), 207
Sterling, Richard, 136, 180
Stotsky, Sandra, 198, 287
Strauss, Leo, 262, 288
Strong, William, 128

Structure of English, The (Fries), 127
Students
  analytical skills of, 216
  errors of, 188, 281
  grammar of, 275
  growth of, 251–252, 280, 285–286
  MPS's involvement with, 96–97, 100, 112–113
  nontraditional students, 77
  potentials of, 108, 206, 295–296
  punctuation of, 304
  relationship with teachers, 255–256, 300
  in "safe place," 215
  self-critiquing by, 210–211
  strikes by, 114
  success factors of, 178
  syntax of, 306–308
  underprepared students, 78, 88, 270, 285
  writing goals of, 117–118
Success, 107–108, 178
Swift, Jonathan, 131
Syntax
  command of, 282
  development of, 287, 288
  student examples of, 306–308
  syntactical derailments, 274
  syntactical tangles, 300

Tangiers (Morocco), 56
Tate, Gary, 159
Teachers
  as bridge to world, 215
  developmental scales for, 162–163
  goals of writing, 117–118
  motivation of, 205–206, 209, 291–298
  observations of, 252–253
  against outsiders, 162, 256
  and pedagogical imagination, 218, 269
  qualities of, 111, 133

relationship with students,
255–256, 300
remediation of, 160, 163, 262
workload in basic writing,
211–212
Teachers College Record, 197
Teaching
and error strategies, 132–133
evaluation of, 160
as opposed to presenting, 182, 268
of writing vs. literature, 266
*Teaching Composition: Ten Biblio-
graphical Essays* (Tate), 159
"Teaching Language in Open
Admissions" (Rich), 108
Teaching the Universe of Discourse
(Moffett), 128
"Teaching the 'Unteachable'"
(Kohl), 87
Tenure, 102, 116, 135
Terminal degrees, *See* Advanced
degrees
Territory of Language, The
(McQuade), 245
TESOL Newsletter, 197
Texas Christian University Press,
159
Theater, at Eagles Mere, 25–26
Thomas, Lewis, 230
Timid script, 274
Tousler, Saul, 140
Traditions of Inquiry (Brereton),
244–245
Transformational Sentence Combining
(Mellon), 128
Traub, James, 172
Trillin, Alice
children of, 105
citation in *Errors and Expectations*,
129
at City College (CUNY), 87–88
friendship of, 143
health of, 173–174
at Hofstra, 80

during MPS's illness, 222, 224,
229
MPS's poem to, 228
in New York City financial crisis,
173
at presidential recognition of MPS,
230
reflections on MPS, 214–215
on SEEK staff, 105
Trillin, Calvin, 80, 224
Trilling, Lionel, 185

Ullmann, Stephen, 128
Underprepared students, 78, 88,
270, 285

Vacations
in Greece, 103–104, 148, 149
with parents, 9, 11–12
at Spearfish ranch, 34–35, 51
Values, and parental influence, 12
Van Doren, Mark, 37
Vernacular, 273, 281, 301
Viscusi, Margo, 214–218
Vocabulary, 261, 286–287, 289
*Vocabulary Development in the
Classroom* (Deighton), 127
Volpe, Edmond L., 89–90, 92–93,
95, 101

Wagner, Geoffrey, 94, 199, 200–201
Walten, Maximilian, 37–38
Way of the New World, The (Gayle),
143
Wayward Child: A Personal Odyssey
(Gayle), 143
Weaver, Priscilla, *See also* Brandt,
Priscilla
in New York City, 29–30
at Northwestern University, 20–21
romance with Alan, 38
Weiner, Harvey, 176, 180
Wexler, Jacqueline, 140
Wheaton College, 30–32

White, Edward, 203

Wilkins, Lottie
  eulogy for MPS, 236–237,
    238–239
  at presidential recognition of MPS,
    230
  reflections on MPS, 111–113
  wedding of, 223

Willen, Gerald, 78, 89

Wilson, Woodrow, 38

Winterowd, Ross, 203

Winthrop Press, 158, 185

Wishes, Lies, and Dreams (Koch), 127

Women's Room, The (French), 80

Working Through (Kriegel), 96–97

World of Our Fathers (Howe), 168

Wright, John
  on Catholicism, 230
  as editor of *Errors and Expectations*,
    158, 185–187, 193–194
  "Examining Textbooks," 176
  on success of *Errors and Expecta-
    tions*, 198, 227

Wright, Richard, 117, 128

Writers
  audience relationship of, 275–276
  growth of, 280, 285–286

Writing
  for academic audiences, 287–289
  assessment of, 279
  goals of, 117–118
  history of, 205, 293–294
  measurement of, 160
  pedagogies of, 285
  psychology of, 205, 293
  research in, 193, 284–290, 299
  skills for, 70–71, 266–267
  student's perception of, 272
Writing Without Teachers (Elbow),
    200
"Written Anguish," 257, 308

Yiddish, 53

York Conference (England), 118

Young, Andrew, 183–184

Yugoslavia, 67

AUTHOR

Jane Maher teaches basic writing at Nassau Community College, Garden City, New York, where she is assistant professor in the Basic Education Program. She is a member of the editorial board of the *Journal of Basic Writing.* She has published two other biographies. *Biography of Broken Fortunes* is the story of Robertson and Garth Wilkinson James (the younger brothers of Henry and William), particularly their valiant service leading the 54th and 55th all-black regiments in the Civil War. *Seeing Language in Sign* is the story of William C. Stokoe's twenty-year struggle at Gallaudet University to reverse the reigning critical assessment of American Sign Language as little more than a crude system of communication. In addition, Jane Maher has written scores of biographical essays and is a senior writer for *Greenwich* magazine. She is currently completing *One Step More,* the biography of Father Joseph C. Martin, a nationally recognized leader in the field of alcoholism recovery. She resides in Greenwich, Connecticut.

*Text composed in Adobe's Bembo
with display lines in Castle System's Schneidler.
Cover display font Castle System's Schneidler.
Printed on Finch Opaque, 60 lb. paper.*